The Diversity Index

DISCARD

THE
DIVERSITY
INDEX

The Alarming Truth About Diversity
in Corporate America . . . and
What Can Be Done About It

Susan E. Reed

AMACOM

American Management Association

New York • Atlanta • Brussels • Chicago • Mexico City • San Francisco
Shanghai • Tokyo • Toronto • Washington, D.C.

This publication is designed to provide accurate and authoritative
information in regard to the subject matter covered. It is sold with the
understanding that the publisher is not engaged in rendering legal,
accounting, or other professional service. If legal advice or other expert
assistance is required, the services of a competent professional person
should be sought.

Sections of this book were previously published by the Alicia Patterson
Foundation.

Library of Congress Cataloging-in-Publication Data

Reed, Susan E.
   The diversity index : the alarming truth about diversity in corporate America and what
can be done about it / Susan E. Reed.
      p.   cm.
   Includes bibliographical references and index.
   ISBN-13: 978-0-8144-1649-5
   ISBN-10: 0-8144-1649-7
   1. Diversity in the workplace—United States.   2. Executives—United States.   I. Title.
HF5549.5.M5R44   2012
658.7008—dc23

                                                                    2011018635

About AMA
American Management Association (www.amanet.org) is a world
leader in talent development, advancing the skills of individuals to
drive business success. Our mission is to support the goals of
individuals and organizations through a complete range of products
and services, including classroom and virtual seminars, webcasts,
webinars, podcasts, conferences, corporate and government solutions,
business books and research. AMA's approach to improving performance
combines experiential learning—learning through doing—with opportunities
for ongoing professional growth at every step of one's career journey.

Printing number
10   9   8   7   6   5   4   3   2   1

For the strivers . . .

Contents

THE DIVERSITY INDEX

Introduction

THE PRESIDENT OF LOCKHEED AIRCRAFT CORPORATION and Vice President Lyndon Johnson agreed to end Lockheed's workforce segregation on May 25, 1961. Looking back, this contract, which was announced with great fanfare at the White House, signified far more than the public acknowledgment of systematic racial segregation in employment. It illustrated the leading role that prominent corporations were beginning to embrace by hiring and promoting the widest range of workers in this country. Businesses were accepting responsibility for actively shaping the full scope of the American workforce. If corporations wish to have the best educated, highest motivated and most diverse workforce in the world today, they should resume and expand the process of reaching out to students, teachers, communities, and employees started by this first Plan for Progress.

A diversity index measures the number of species in a natural environment. The more species there are, the healthier the environment is. My research showed that what is true in nature also applies to business. Developing and promoting a diverse workforce can lead to increased resilience in a corporation. Companies with high levels of diversity have been found to produce higher profit margins and greater returns on equity and assets.[1] Collective wisdom, the ideas contributed by diverse groups and individuals, exceeds the sum of its parts.[2]

We are just beginning to understand the full diversity dividend that was started by the Plan for Progress.

Yet, in the late 1990s, a rash of discrimination lawsuits spread across corporate America. Merrill Lynch paid more than $200 million to settle a class action filed by more than 900 of its current and former female brokers. In 2000, Coca-Cola agreed to pay $192.5 million in a racial discrimination case to African American workers who alleged they had been paid and promoted less than similarly situated white workers. In 2008, Walgreen pledged $24 million to resolve a federal lawsuit alleging widespread racial bias against 10,000 black workers.[3]

If workplaces were so accepting of diversity, why were so many workers suing their bosses? As I covered some of these lawsuits for *The New York Times* and other publications, I was struck—well, horrified really—by the toll the adversarial process takes on both the plaintiffs and the defendants. In discrimination lawsuits, the claims of the employee are pitted against the assertions of the employer. The allegations are frequently framed in reductive terms: The employee is incapable of performing the tasks, and the company is guilty of discrimination. The legal wrangling often saps years from employees' careers, undermines their mental and physical well-being, and jeopardizes their future employability. The suits cost the companies substantial amounts of intellectual and emotional energy that could have been spent on growing the business. Although the class action settlements often result in the companies' adopting new employee pay and promotion practices that promise to improve the workplace for everyone, the advances come at a high price. I wanted to find the companies that had the most diverse leadership and to find out how they did it so other companies could follow suit.

I conducted a study of race and gender of executive officers of the 2005 *Fortune 100*. An executive officer is defined as a president or vice president who is in charge of a principal business unit, division or function. Executive officers set policy for the corporation, and their names are usually contained in the annual report to shareholders. My researchers and I determined, from photographs and published profiles of the executive officers, their gender, race, and ethnicity according to categories used by the U.S. government. We also gathered data for the same companies for fiscal 1995 and 2009 to show change over 14 years. We then contacted the companies to verify the accuracy of our assessments and made adjustments to the data if the companies offered corrections that were consistent with the names listed in the 10-K, a document filed with the Securities and Exchange Commission (SEC). We operated on a fully transparent basis, notifying the companies of the information and statistics we had gathered and telling them that they would be published. We made every effort to get the facts right.[4]

I discovered that the companies with the highest diversity among their executive officers were using many of the same practices. Like most Americans, I had never before heard of the clunky-sounding Plans for Progress. I began reading *Inventing Equal Opportunity* (published in 2009) to understand how the companies had come to share the same diversity practices. Author Frank Dobbin described Plans for Progress. His footnote led me to a 1961 *New York Times* story quoting a spokesman for the National Association for the Advancement of Colored People (NAACP) criticizing the program's effectiveness.

As a journalist who has written and produced thousands of stories, a large portion while covering an ongoing issue or event, I knew that most news reports are simply snapshots in time and cannot be taken as the final evaluation of a program. When the article was published in 1961, the program had just begun, and it was too early to render a final judgment on its success. The NAACP's dismissal of the Plans for Progress as nothing but hype was premature. Today, the conclusion would be different.

Discovering Plans for Progress

Preserved in a simple manila folder at the John F. Kennedy Presidential Library and Museum in Boston, I found eight actual Plans for Progress contracts that had been signed by Vice President Johnson and the presidents of the largest defense companies. The contracts spelled out the steps that Boeing, Northrop, Lockheed, and other government contractors agreed to take in order to find, develop, and recruit minority employees. They reached out to students, teachers, and families to inform them of the skills, knowledge, and education they needed in their technologically advanced workforce. Then, like now, the country was not producing enough engineers or scientists of any race or gender to meet demand. If schools did not have the personnel who could teach specialized courses, the companies found the teachers who could, and paid their salaries. The Plans for Progress contracts illustrate how committed these companies were to developing a reliable and productive supply chain of qualified minority employees.

Deep in the library's archives, I came to know the architect of Plans for Progress, John Feild, and the advocate, Hobart Taylor, Jr. Many histories have referred to these government employees, but never in much detail. Yet what they created has lasted for five decades despite their initial struggles with corporations, politicians, and one another. Feild and Taylor came from different classes, had varied levels of education, used contrasting negotiating styles, and held divergent political beliefs. They were rivals, and their friction was a harbinger of similar struggles that newly integrated offices across the country would soon experience, as Hobart Taylor, Jr., a black man, ultimately became the boss of John Feild, a white man.

Feild and Taylor's achievement was contingent on their ability to persuade the white male leadership of government contractors in the 1960s to reform their hiring and promotion practices. The businessmen, who were mainly Republican, were called upon to include races that had often been disparaged as not educated enough and not as hardworking as white employees, or simply too different to fit into the same employment categories and job ladders. To succeed with integration, managers had to install conscious, deliberate programs in factories, offices, franchises, and corporate headquarters throughout the country. Finally, integration success depended on white employees and white customers lowering their resistance to working and interacting with people of color.

Newly released government documents containing information on the companies that participated in Plans for Progress illustrate that minorities were brought into nearly every job category by the late 1960s. Theoretically, minorities would have ascended to the rank of executive officer by 1995, more than 30 years after the program began. If the flow had continued, we would expect to see them throughout the corporations today—from top to bottom, from side to side, employed in jobs appropriate to their education and experience.

My research shows that the Plans for Progress companies on average achieved greater success in promoting minorities and women to executive officer positions than companies that had not joined or that were established after the program officially ended in 1969. These findings suggest that the Plans for Progress companies were more attuned to accepting and promoting people of all kinds than the companies that had not practiced the protocol. The study indicates that the protocol was effective and that the longer a company practices integration, the better it becomes at the process. (See Figure I.1.)

In every year except for 1995, the Plans for Progress companies employed more white female executive officers than the non–Plans for Progress companies. Interestingly, Plans for Progress began in 1961, before the Civil Rights Act of 1964 was passed, and was not aimed at women per se, but at minorities. Yet by 2005, the Plans for Progress companies had surpassed the companies that did not practice the protocol; 97 percent of Plans for Progress companies had white female executive officers whereas only 80 percent of non–Plans for Progress companies employed them. This finding indicates

Figure I.1 Comparison of Race, Ethnicity, and Gender Levels of Executive Officers of *Fortune 100* (%)

Executive Officers	1995	2005	2009
Plans for Progress companies with white females	36	97	90
Plans for Progress companies with minority males	39	48	53
Plans for Progress companies with minority females	3.6	19	33
Non–Plans for Progress companies with white females	54	80	83
Non–Plans for Progress companies with minority males	25	45	48
Non–Plans for Progress companies with minority females	1.8	10	15

that the Plans for Progress protocol was easily applied to include other groups.

By employing a series of repeatable, standardized, and scalable processes, these companies succeeded in integrating their workplaces and ultimately breaking the white male monopoly on the best jobs in America. Fifty years after it began, Plans for Progress can be described as an unquestionable success that resulted in the positive transformation of businesses and society. But the transformation has been far from complete. Only 53 percent of the Plans for Progress companies employed minority male executive officers in 2009. Just 33 percent of the Plans for Progress companies had promoted minority females to executive officers. The non-Plans for Progress companies have done far worse.

What Happened?

The Plans for Progress companies represent just one-third of the companies in my study. The majority of the firms either did not exist in the 1960s or had not signed on to the protocol. In addition, the Plans for Progress companies were not always perfect in their application of the protocol. For example, the aluminum producer Alcoa was a Plans for Progress company, but it had an all-white team of executive officers in every year of the study.

Also, Plans for Progress became known as affirmative action, which developed a bad reputation in the 1970s, often as a result of how it was applied. In a quest to improve racial representation, some corporations concentrated minorities in the lowest jobs, as laborers and service workers, which required the least skill and education. In 1969, IBM and Lockheed Aircraft employed more than 60 percent of minorities in the position of laborer. This was a nonmanagement job that usually required no training but demanded good physical condition to move materials in a warehouse or on a construction site. Overloading minorities into jobs that required the least skill potentially led them to be underemployed, while simultaneously creating excessive competition for these entry-level jobs among unskilled, uneducated whites.

Some Plans for Progress companies also concentrated minorities in white-collar jobs. By 1969, 12 percent of PepsiCo's white-collar workers were minorities, at a time when just 1 percent of minorities in the overall population were college educated. PepsiCo had more than its fair share of well-educated minorities. Integration was a new concept, and companies accomplished it in both clumsy and opportunistic ways.

The imbalances led to backlash. Allan Bakke, a white male, accused the University of California of reverse discrimination, preferring people of color to whites. He had been rejected twice by UC Davis Medical School while "special applicants" with lower test scores had been admitted. An important Supreme Court decision on the Bakke case in 1978 ruled that preferring members of a racial or ethnic group for no other reason than that they were group members was itself discrimination. In his decision, Justice Lewis F. Powell wrote that diversity "encompasses a far broader array of qualifications and characteristics, of which racial or ethnic origin is but a single, though important, element." In addition to race and gender, diversity included achievements, talent, social and economic background, and where a person grew up. Although the decision pertained to how universities accepted students, employers paid close attention to the Court. They realized they had to hire all kinds of people at all job levels. Diversity was the thing.[5]

Affirmative action became associated in the public's mind with quotas. But quotas had never been part of the Plans for Progress protocol. John Feild, the author of the Plans for Progress, had never advocated that companies give preference to people of color, nor had he recommended using quotas. In fact, the boilerplate contract of the Plans for Progress prohibited quotas. Feild let the companies decide how many people of color to hire and the jobs into which to hire them.

"When I was director, I fought rigidly against the establishment of quotas," said Feild, "but I did not feel we should abandon the notion of quantitative goals. We should keep it as a goal; we should be flexible about it; we should attempt to use it as a way of measuring performance."[6]

The misapplication of affirmative action by business resulted in ridicule by the public, the method seen as a process of hiring and promoting unqualified white women and minorities. Many people of color and women subsequently shunned affirmative action because they did not want their competence sullied by association with a tainted program. As it became scorned by both whites and minorities, even the phrase *affirmative action* fell out of common parlance. In the trade, the method is now known as *compliance* and *representation*. (Most government contractors, however, must still file an affirmative action plan with the Department of Labor's Office of Federal Contract Compliance Programs (OFCCP). An affirmative action plan expresses how the employer intends to reach out and find women or minorities with the required skills to hire into jobs where they are underutilized. It is an adaptation of the Plans for Progress protocol.)

Diversity became a popular concept after the late 1970s,

due to the backlash against affirmative action and a series of court decisions that reaffirmed the need to consider far more than race. Diversity meant companies should hire and promote everybody, but doing it was perplexing. Diversity experts were installed in nearly every *Fortune 100* company. Employees were then exposed to diversity training, where they were taught that everyone was the same, part of one great melting pot. Then they learned that everyone was different, like the ingredients of an immense salad bowl. The seeming contradictions required that diversity be conceived as a paradox. Employees were advised to be color and gender blind, but to recognize differences and to celebrate them. As the concept of diversity took hold, the fine points seemed to get lost, and white women advanced in more companies than minorities did.

Reasons for the White Ceiling

In the 50 years since businesses seriously began to apply a set of deliberate, company-wide practices that would produce a more thoroughly mixed workforce, much success has been achieved, but a white ceiling persists. Ninety percent of the *Fortune 100* employed white women as executive officers in 2009. Caucasian women should not be penalized for their notable accomplishments, and there is an average of only 1.66 women per executive team. Yet their broad success has contributed to a troubling pattern. One-third of the *Fortune 100* companies had all-white male and female executive officers in each of the three years under study, 1995, 2005, and 2009. Despite ongoing diversity initiatives and efforts to break the glass ceiling these companies had gender diversity but not racial diversity in the highest ranks. Unless this pattern is broken, discrimination lawsuits are going to continue to rage through corporate America.

Understanding Affinity Groups

Companies with the most diverse leadership had not only adopted the basic procedures from Plans for Progress, but they added new programs, such as affinity groups, as they sought to develop their workforce and overcome the glass ceiling. Affinity groups are employees such as women, African Americans, Hispanics, Asians, Native Americans, gay, lesbian, bisexual or transgendered people, veterans or the disabled, who meet to discuss issues in the company. I found that the number of groups doubled between 1995 and 2005. My study revealed a positive correlation between the employee groups and high officer diversity; 90 percent of the companies with the most integrated leadership have the groups. In some companies, the groups have become powerful resources as employees networked, learned leadership skills, and developed new products and ideas for the businesses. Many companies, in fact, call them employee resource groups or employee networks. Affinity groups, when backed by the CEO and led by the highest-ranking employees, create networks in which employees can positively influence the company's integration process. The most successful affinity groups act like a Plans for Progress program for employees.[7]

Interestingly, the white ceiling has resulted, in part, from the success of the women's affinity groups. Because of their numbers and their dominant race, they frequently wind up leading the affinity group. In some companies they have successfully challenged how women's performance is measured by the firm. The GE Women's Network is a fascinating example of how a group can advance after grappling with stereotypes in the workplace. Their success suggests that other affinity groups might benefit from a similar questioning of performance evaluations.

Diversity Requires Executive Support

A company, however, does not need to have affinity groups to have a highly diverse team of executive officers. Affinity groups alone cannot increase integration because they cannot hire, promote, or fire people; they constitute a strategy for developing employees. For example, Merck had the highest level of integration among its executive officers in the *Fortune 100* in 1995, 2005, and 2009, but its nascent affinity groups were not the reason. Merck's chief executives put white women, as well as female and male minorities, on their executive teams because they thought that doing so was important for the business, not because they waited for the affinity groups to offer them a candidate. Merck's Roy Vagelos promoted individuals he thought could one day lead the company. He also believed in social justice. His successor, Raymond Gilmartin, elevated women and minorities because he trusted them to do the jobs. He also believed in creating a diverse meritocracy. Gilmartin's successor, Richard Clark, advanced men and women of color because he believed they were necessary for the global growth of the business. These men surrounded themselves with diverse executive officers because they sought the best talent, they believed in social justice, they wanted to create a meritocracy, they thought diversity was good for business, and they wanted to set an example for the rest of the corporation. They did it all because they could.

In contrast, the chief executives who waited for the affinity groups to offer them the strongest candidates were not fully exercising their leadership capacity in the organization. The challenge ahead is for corporations to bring domestic minorities to the highest levels of leadership. The public summaries of companies' Equal Employment Opportunity data (EEO-1) indicate that the majority of the largest corporations have minorities but that the minorities are stuck below the corporate suite in the ranks of middle and upper management.[8] How do companies raise them to the highest levels?

First, corporations must confront the brutal reality that, despite the popular assumption that diversity has been achieved, it has not. Although the top job tier at corporations certainly has become more integrated, neither affirmative action nor diversity has entirely helped their intended beneficiaries. Nearly 50 percent of the *Fortune 100* companies employed no African, Asian, Hispanic, or Native American men as executive officers in 2009. Nearly 80 percent of the *Fortune 100* failed to promote minority women in executive officer positions. When it comes to business, women of color were left out of Plans for Progress, the civil rights and the women's movements.

One problem that was not anticipated in 1961 was how globalization would affect promotions in this country. In 2009, more than half of the Hispanic and Asian executive officers in the *Fortune 100* were born outside of the United States. In the competition to gain dominance in global markets, companies are hiring workers who come from those markets. If, after hard work, they wind up on staff at the U.S. headquarters, the internationals are counted as U.S. minorities.

This is all perfectly legal. The immigrant story is an essential component of the American narrative. The Civil Rights Act prohibits discrimination against national origin, as did President John F. Kennedy's executive order on which Plans for Progress was based. But these foreign nationals tend to be elites who come from wealthy families who could afford college in their home countries and graduate school in the United States. Most have not participated in the American bootstrap experience. As a group they frequently lack socioeconomic diversity.

Domestic Asian and Hispanic corporate executives—those born or raised in the United States—are getting squeezed out like never before. First, they lost out as affirmative action fell away in favor of diversity. Now they compete for the few slots on the executive floor with other nationalities. At the Coca-Cola Company, 57 percent of executive officers, including 100 percent of its "minorities," were born outside the United States in fiscal 2009. PepsiCo followed the same trend toward multinational diversity as Coca-Cola did; 45 percent of PepsiCo's executive officers were born beyond U.S. borders. Companies' expansion into worldwide markets has put all homegrown workers—even the most educated—in the midst of a full-blown, worldwide competition for talent.

Even white men are under intense competition from abroad; on average, 9 percent of Caucasian male executive officers of the *Fortune 100* were born outside of the United States. The aluminum producer Alcoa employed no minorities or women as executive officers in 2009, but 38 percent of its white males were born overseas. They came from Germany, Norway, and Austria.

Five decades after serious integration began, there are striking imbalances in the executive suite. Gender and multinational diversity are important assets to have among key decision makers, but alone they do not create a well-rounded team. Even though our economy has rapidly changed, we have made too much progress in the past five decades to abandon deeply held beliefs in equal opportunity now.

When Plans for Progress began in 1961, the country was emerging from a recession. Like now, there were too many unskilled workers, and not enough highly educated workers to produce the highly technical products—such as Mylar, computers, and advanced aircraft—that companies needed. And frequently, managers did not recognize, develop, or reward the employees that they had. As companies rebuild their workforces they can reassess their current and future needs. They have the opportunity to advance the employees who have been toiling in the trenches, reach out to the unemployed, and cultivate students from a younger age. If the United States is going to triumph in the global marketplace, where work flows to the places that produce either the best designed and best performing products or products that are most efficiently produced, corporations need to become deeply involved in developing the full range of the current and future workforce from elementary school onward.

As a journalist who has reported on businesses for 25 years for CBS News, and several publications, I have met many managers who welcome information that will help them improve their performance. During a Nieman Fellowship for journalists at Harvard in 1999, I studied corporate management at the business school, the history of discrimination at the law school, organizational sociology, and leadership. As I saw the business world embrace efficient, modern solutions to complex problems, I began to seek out programs that would improve the workplaces where we spend so many years of our lives. I hope that my analysis of the promotion patterns that have formed in the *Fortune 100* will enable corporations to chart a new course that will help them to meet the goals set years ago, while profiting in new and unanticipated ways from the diversity dividend. Plans for Progress is a useful program that can be revived and expanded to all races, genders, and classes so that the United States can have the best educated, most creative, and most determined workers in the world. It sets a powerful example for corporate leadership.

1 The Diversity Buffet

IVERSITY HAS BECOME A SMORGASBORD FROM WHICH companies are taking what they desire and leaving the rest. The partial use of the diversity concept has resulted in the formation of a persistent racial ceiling in corporate America. The difference between today and 50 years ago is that white women are now part of the problem.

In 2009, more than 40 percent of the *Fortune 100* had no minorities among their executive officers. These white-ceiling companies often display a rainbow of employees on the leadership pages of their Web sites. They advertise their employee networks and expound on their commitment to diversity with inspirational statements. But the executive officers who are entrusted with setting policy in the corporation—the names listed in the annual report—are Caucasian.

This book seeks to cut through the heavy layer of advertising and public relations in which corporations routinely cocoon themselves. It offers a frank discussion about who is getting some of the best jobs in America, and what a lack of diversity means for the future of the companies and for this country. To be sure, corporations are not the only ones who like to think of themselves as open-minded, tolerant, and modern. In the giddy aftermath of the election of the first black president, signs everywhere read, "Yes we did." Citizens of the United States proved they could overcome a long and painful history of racial subjugation.

When Barack Obama was elected in 2008, he became the most diverse president in American history. He was the child of a black African father and a white American mother, he was born in Hawaii, educated in Indonesia, and graduated from two Ivy League universities. His ascension to the highest office in the country marked a milestone for America. His election seemed to be the apotheosis of the equal opportunity society.

The joyful celebration also became a turning point for those who specialized in diversity. Suddenly, four decades after the concept of diversity had taken root, perhaps diversity experts were no longer needed. In 2009, during an online discussion at The Conference Board's Web site, a diversity consultant complained that the chief executive officer (CEO) of her company did not know who she was or what she did. During the Great Recession of 2008–2009, diversity experts were laid off, and entire diversity departments were cut as corporations moved to quickly reduce costs.

Diversity is increasingly being viewed as yesterday's topic. The overwhelming majority of 2009 annual reports of the *Fortune 100* did not even mention it. The omission marked a profound change from their annual reports in 2005, when diversity was still the buzzword, and their pages were filled with pictures of customers and employees of nearly every race, ethnicity, and gender. But in 2009, just four years later, sustainability had become the concept *du jour*. The new goal was to create long-lasting communities by reducing greenhouse gases, toxic environmental waste, and using more recyclable packaging materials. What these companies have overlooked is that communities will not be sustainable without diverse employment strategies.

To be sure, diversity exists in the popular imagination. Television shows depicting the workplace in the last decade have been dominated by the multicultural casts of situation comedies such as *Ugly Betty,* which crowded out the predominantly white workplace shows such as *Boston Legal.* The awkward struggle to achieve harmony in such mixed groups was portrayed with humor in the NBC sitcom, *Community.* In one episode, the nerdy, bald, white Dean Pelton of Greendale Community College took pains to be sensitive to diversity. He changed the name of the college's football team from the Greendale Grizzlies to the Greendale Human Beings because a lot of the students had "been called animals their whole lives." As he tried to develop a mascot for the team, he spent days eliminating broad noses, Asian eye folds, and Irish chins from the face. As the first football game began, he emerged with a bald, silvery figure in the shape of a human with black eyes and a mustache, but no eyebrows or mouth. It looked like a creature from another planet that only its creator, Dean Pelton, could love. Yet the fact that network audiences would laugh at his awkward attempt to overcome racial and ethnic stereotypes showed how accepting Americans had become of the ongoing, if imperfect struggle to create some kind of equality.[1]

Without doubt, many men and women of color have achieved enormous business success and made tremendous strides into the very positions inside organizations from which they had previously been absent. Kenneth Chennault, an African American, has led American Express, a large financial services company, since 2001. Indra Nooyi, an Asian Indian immigrant, who had spent 12 years working her way up the corporate ladder, was selected in 2006 to lead Pepsi-Co, the ever expanding packaged goods company that sells everything from cola to oatmeal. When American International Group, an insurance giant, teetered on the brink of failure in 2008 and became a ward of the U.S. government, Richard Parsons, a black lawyer and the former head of the media group Time Warner, was brought in as the chairman to help AIG regain solvency. And racial diversity has been accomplished in the top job tier of most *Fortune 100* corporations: 60 percent had minority executive officers in 2009.

Yet the other side of the coin remains vexing, the 40 percent of companies without minority officers. A key point to remember is that the leadership selection process in corporations is far less ecumenical than it is in the political realm. President Obama was elected by a truly diverse group of voters: Hispanics, Asians, African Americans, Native Americans, Pacific Islanders, Caucasians, and many more. Executive officers, in contrast, are usually selected by the chief executive officers, who are still predominantly white and male, before they are approved by the corporation's board of directors. The role of executive officer—setting and administering policy for the corporation—requires a great deal of experience, brainpower, and leadership. Executive officers usually have an advanced graduate degree and have spent 20–25 years at the firm before being trusted with such a position of responsibility, power, prestige, and high compensation. They often assume the position after decades of winnowing, emerging from a series of new and ever more challenging assignments.

Fewer White Male Bastions

Before examining the underbelly of twenty-first century diversity, it is heartening to note the progress that companies, as well as the predominantly white males who have led them, have made over 14 years. In 2009, only 6 percent of the *Fortune 100* consisted of entirely white male teams; this number reflects a rapid decrease from 15 percent in 2005 and from 38 percent in 1995. (See Figure 1.1.)

Figure 1.1 The Zero Companies: Least Integrated
Executive Officer Teams in the *Fortune 100*

1995	2005	2009
Alcoa	AmerisourceBergen	Alcoa
Archer Daniels Midland	AT&T	Berkshire Hathaway
Bank of America	Bellsouth Corp.	Costco Wholesale
Bellsouth Corp.	Berkshire Hathaway	Exxon Mobil
Berkshire Hathaway	CVS	News Corp.
Boeing	ConocoPhillips	
Cardinal Health	Costco Wholesale	
Chevron Corp.	ExxonMobil	
Cisco Systems	JP Morgan Chase	
Costco Wholesale	Lehman Brothers	
Dow Chemical	News Corp.	
Duke Energy	Sunoco	
Electronic Data Systems	United Technologies	
General Motors	Valero Energy	
Goldman Sachs	Wal-Mart	
Hewlett Packard Company		
Home Depot		
IBM		
Johnson & Johnson		
Kroger Company		
Lehman Brothers		
Lowe's Company		
MCI		
Mass Mutual Life Insurance		
Merrill Lynch		
Motorola		
State Farm Insurance		
United Technologies		

(Continues)

Figure 1.1 (Continued)

Valero Energy
Wachovia
Walgreen
Wal-Mart
Walt Disney

Such rare and disappearing breeds occurred in all the sectors—industrial products, retailing, insurance, energy, and media. Alcoa, Berkshire Hathaway, Costco, Exxon Mobil, and News Corp. were the last holdouts. The industries did not form a pattern, as they had done in 2005, when energy companies represented 40 percent of the homogeneous teams.

The corporations whose executive officers included men of color but no women of any race also decreased in the same time period. In the 2009 *Fortune 100*, just four companies featured an integrated male team but no females, a decline of 50 percent from 1995. (See Figure 1.2.) Corporations have made tremendous progress in promoting women to the top jobs. Overall, the number of firms that have failed to include women in the highest ranks has decreased to 10 percent in 2009 from 48 percent in 1995. Ninety percent of the *Fortune 100* had at least one female on the team in 2009. Men have demonstrated that they were ready to promote women, and the women have shown they were ready to be promoted. However, it was mainly white women who were promoted. In 2009, only 21 percent of the *Fortune 100* firms employed minority female executive officers. While their representation has improved from just 2 percent in 1995, it is still alarmingly low.

The White Ceiling

White male and female teams have come to form a new problem: a white ceiling. (See Figure 1.3.) One-third of the *Fortune*

Figure 1.2 *Fortune 100* Companies with White and Minority Male
Executive Officers but No Females of Any Color

1995	2005	2009
Coca-Cola	Delphi	Citigroup
E.I. DuPont De Nemours	E.I. DuPont De Nemours	Intel
General Electric	Intel	Sprint
Intel		Sysco
Lockheed Martin		
Procter & Gamble		
Time Warner		
Weyerhaeuser		

100 firms employed white male and white female executive
officers, but no minorities, in each of the three years studied
over 14 years: fiscal 1995, 2005, and 2009. Most of the companies did not have all-white executive leadership in each year
of the study. Some, such as the pharmaceutical giant Bristol-
Meyer Squibb, the computer maker Dell, and the insurance
companies MetLife and New York Life, had all white executive officers in 1995 and integrated their teams in 2005 and
2009. They suddenly progressed.

The integration of executive officers at other companies was
more cautious. The consumer products company Procter &
Gamble, the aerospace manufacturer Lockheed Martin, and the
forest products company Weyerhaeuser had minority executive
officers in 1995, but no women. By 2005, the companies had
white female officers, but no minorities. By 2009, they had both
minority and white female officers. Over 14 years, these companies moved carefully toward a mixed team. This pattern of integration is common, adding a male minority or a white female
as an opening occurs.

Other firms drifted into and out of total white representation at the highest level. The system-controls maker Honey-

(Text continues on page 26)

Figure 1.3 *Fortune 100* Companies with All White Male
and Female Executive Officers

Fiscal 1995	Fiscal 2005	Fiscal 2009
	Albertson's	
	Alcoa, Inc.	
		Altria Group, Inc.
		American International Group (AIG)
	Archer-Daniels Midland, Co.	
Bristol-Meyers Squibb Co.		
	Cardinal Health, Inc.	Cardinal Health, Inc.
		Caterpillar, Inc.
	Caremark Rx, Inc.	CVS Caremark
	Cisco Systems	Cisco Systems
	Coca-Cola Co.	
Dell, Inc.		
	Dow Chemical Co.	
	Duke Energy	Duke Energy
		E.I. DuPont De Nemours
	Electronic Data Systems	
Fed Ex Corp	Fed Ex Corp	Fed Ex Corp
		General Electric Co.
	General Motors	
	Goldman Sachs Group	Goldman Sachs Group
HCA, Inc.	HCA, Inc.	HCA, Inc.
Honeywell, Inc.		Honeywell, Inc.
International Paper Co.		
J.C. Penney Co. Inc.	J.C. Penney Co. Inc.	J.C. Penney Co. Inc.
	J.P. Morgan Chase & Co.	J.P. Morgan Chase & Co.
		Johnson & Johnson
Johnson Controls, Inc.		
	Lockheed Martin Corp.	
	Lowe's Co.	Lowe's Co.
		Massachusetts Mutual Life Insurance Co.
	McKesson Corp.	

MetLife, Inc.		
Microsoft Corp.	Microsoft Corp.	
	Morgan Stanley	Morgan Stanley
Nationwide Mutual Insurance Co.	Nationwide Mutual Insurance Co.	
New York Life Insurance Co.		
Northrop Grumman Corp.	Northrop Grumman Corp.	
Pfizer Inc.	Pfizer Inc.	
		Plains All American Pipeline
	Procter & Gamble Co.	
Sears Roebuck and Co.		
	St. Paul Travelers Co., Inc.	Travelers
SBC Communications		
Sprint Corp		
Sunoco, Inc.		Sunoco, Inc.
Sysco Corp.		
TIAA-CREF		
	Target Corp.	Target Corp.
		Time Warner, Inc.
UnitedHealth Group, Inc.	UnitedHealth Group, Inc.	
Tyson Foods, Inc.		
		United Technologies Corp.
		Valero Energy Corp.
Verizon Inc.	Verizon Inc.	Verizon Inc.
Viacom Inc.		
	Wachovia Corp.	
	Walt Disney Co.	Walt Disney Co
		Wellpoint, Inc.
Wells Fargo & Co.	Wells Fargo & Co.	Wells Fargo & Co.
	Weyerhaeuser	

well, for instance, had all white male and female executive officers in 1995, employed at least one person of color in 2005, but returned to total white staff again in 2009. The aluminum products company Alcoa had a white male team in 1995, promoted a white female in 2005, but returned to having an all white male team in 2009. General Electric had minority executive officers in 1995 and 2005, but had none by 2009. These companies regressed.

The companies with persistent white representation—those with all white male and female executive officers in every year of the study in which they were a company—came from different sectors. There was the telecom giant Verizon, the healthcare company HCA, Inc., and the insurance company Travelers. But the retail and financial services industries had the highest number of companies with only white executive officers. The retail companies were Target and J.C. Penney, and the financial services companies were Goldman Sachs, J.P. Morgan Chase, Morgan Stanley, and Wells Fargo.

How Did We Get Here?

In the mid-1990s, much scholarly research showed that whites generally were treated more favorably in the workplace than blacks.[2] A study that examined the relationship of race and gender, as managers rated the promotion potential of 1,268 managerial and professional employees, revealed that blacks and Asians were rated lower than whites. The study controlled for age, education, tenure, salary grade, and satisfaction with career support. The results also concluded that managers rated female employees lower than male employees.[3]

The acceleration of white women's upward movement beyond that of minorities, from 1995 to 2009, illustrates how gender has outpaced race. In 2009, 90 percent of *Fortune 100* companies employed female executive officers, whereas just 60 percent employed minority executive officers. Since the mid-1990s, chief executives have found it easier to move beyond gender than beyond race. The fact that one-third of the *Fortune 100* firms struggled with this issue since 1995 reveals that race remains a key factor when considering promotions.

A study published in 2008, the same year President Obama was elected, indicated that race plays a critical role during leadership evaluations and that whites are perceived to be prototypical business leaders in the United States. The visual images surrounding business, political, and military leadership have been predominantly of white leaders, driving the expectation that future leaders will be white. The study concluded that a multiplier effect "may persist such that positive evaluations are given to White leaders, White leaders continue to be the prototype for effective leadership and correspondingly, racial minority leaders are continually disadvantaged."[4]

White Diversity

The promotion of white women in corporate headquarters has helped to keep the racial ceiling in place because of an incomplete application of diversity. Of the companies that do not employ minority executive officers, most include white women. In 2009, 30 percent of the executive officers at Target were female, the highest proportion of women of the persistently white group of companies. Simply having two genders is one measure of diversity, even if it is white diversity.

National origin is another measure of difference. Verizon's

chief information officer was born in Iran, as was Wells Fargo's head of technology. Three of the executive officers at the investment firm Morgan Stanley came from Lebanon, Ireland, and the United Kingdom. In 2009, nearly 8 percent of the white executive officers in the *Fortune 100* were not born in the United States. They were born in Canada, Europe, or the Middle East, and they brought with them to the United States the sound of foreign accents and the allure of international markets.[5]

These findings present a troubling pattern, suggesting that some companies are interpreting diversity not as a melting pot or as a salad bowl, but as a smorgasbord from which they can take whatever they want and leave the rest. Diversity now appears to have varying definitions at companies. Some treat diversity as a nutritious main course; they hire and promote everyone. Others treat diversity as a condiment; they spice up the corporate suite with a white woman here, an exotic accent there. Diversity as an employment concept certainly has not solved white job segregation at the top of the company.

Job segregation occurs when the members of one race or gender are concentrated in a job category. In the 1960s, blacks tended to be overrepresented in jobs as laborers. Women were overrepresented as secretaries. One of the goals of the civil rights and women's movements was to free workers from these confining categories so that they could rise to their true potential, achieve better career outcomes, and enable themselves and their companies to excel.

Segregated jobs are believed to reinforce stereotypes that one race or gender is qualified to do only the job in which they are concentrated. The 40 percent of companies with no minorities among their executive officers could be evidence that ascription was at work. In other words, white workers were considered more seriously for promotion to executive officer level than were people of color. Sociologist Donald Tomaskovic-Devey has explained racial job segregation as social closure, that is, the effort by whites to distance themselves from minorities. The distancing by job description enables whites to preserve a higher status in the workplace, to maintain their authority, and to exclude minorities from better jobs.[6] The danger is that this process, however unconscious, telegraphs the message that the job of executive officer is reserved for whites and prevents others who may be just as qualified—or more so—from getting opportunities for promotion. According to sociologist James Baron, the process of categorization is self-perpetuating, no matter how capricious.[7]

Importing the Top Executives

The partial application of diversity, accompanied by globalization, has enabled white job segregation at the top to continue because the expansion into Canada, Europe, and the Middle East has brought other Caucasian nationalities into the firms. These people were educated, spoke the necessary languages, knew how to excel in foreign markets, and were considered diverse. Companies understandably hired people who were native to the markets into which they expanded. Local knowledge, experience, and language ability are all enormous assets when trying to gain market superiority. Once inside the corporate structure, many of these employees have worked their way into the highest ranks of leadership, moving well beyond the role of country director. The aluminum producer Alcoa employed no minorities or women as executive officers in 2009, but 38 percent of its white males were born abroad.

They came from Germany, Norway, and Austria. United Technologies, which includes Otis Elevators, Pratt & Whitney engines, and Sikorsky helicopters, had one white female on its otherwise white male team, but one-third of the executive officers were born outside the United States Three came from France, two from Canada. On average, 9 percent of white male executive officers of the *Fortune 100* in 2009 were born outside of the United States. (See Figure 1.4.)

In 2009, more than half of the Hispanic/Latino executive officers of the *Fortune 100*, 53 percent, were born outside the United States. They came from eight different countries in Latin America. More than half, 52 percent, of the Asian executive officers came from overseas, mainly India.

Overall, one-third of "minority" executive officers in the *Fortune 100* in 2009 were born beyond the U.S. borders, suggesting that companies have found a way to use the global worker as a diversity asset here in the United States. The microchip maker Ingram Micro employed 7 out of 11 executive officers who were born outside the United States, including 100 percent of its minorities. One hundred percent of the Coca-Cola Company's minority executive officers were born

Figure 1.4 Race/Ethnicity, Gender, and National Origin of Executive Officers of *Fortune 100* Companies in 2009 (%)

Race	Men	Born Ex–United States	Women	Born Ex–United States
Caucasian	76	9	14	3
African American	3	3	1	0
Hispanic/Latino	2	61	0.5	20
Asian	2	56	0.4	25
Native American	0.3	0	0	0

in Liberia, Colombia, and Mexico; others came from Turkey, France, Ireland, and Australia.

In 2009, executive officers of the *Fortune 100* who were born outside the country were overrepresented. They comprised an average of 10 percent of executive officers when the foreign-born cohort of people who would be educated and experienced enough by 2009 to hold such a position comprised just 1.5 percent of the total U.S. population.[8] This illustrates how the *Fortune 100*—the biggest and richest corporations in the country—were favoring multinational diversity over national diversity. There is nothing wrong with hiring people with different national origins. They are protected by the Civil Rights Act, and immigration is an essential component of American history. But some companies, in their drive for global profits, have used multinational diversity to trump U.S. diversity at the highest level of the corporation. This pattern is especially impacting American-born or -raised minorities.

Little scholarly research explores multinational hiring and promotions. But one study that examined promotion practices at a multinational *Fortune 500* financial services firm found that Hispanics, some of whom were born outside the United States, were rated more highly as potential managers than native-born blacks and Asians.[9] In other words, employers may have assumed that someone born outside the United States has greater knowledge of how to excel in foreign markets. But that is not necessarily guaranteed. U.S.-born or -raised minorities and whites may have just as much experience, or more, in developing international markets.

Corporate leaders frequently cite the cost of sending an American expatriate overseas as one reason for promoting more foreign nationals. A married American ex-pat with children can cost the company four times her salary in school fees, housing, and living allowances. Understandably, corporations prefer to save these costs and promote workers in their native country. But only one-third of the jobs that foreign-born executive officers held in 2009 were geographically specific, such as president of Latin America or vice president of Asia Pacific. The high cost of an ex-pat does not explain why so many foreign-born workers are in the top jobs here in the United States. In 2009, 42 percent of the jobs held by foreign-born executive officers were typical corporate duties such as human resources, finance, or marketing. One-quarter of the positions held by foreign-born executive officers involved technical or scientific operations at the firms.

One explanation could be that these companies do more business outside the United States, but that correlation does not hold up under scrutiny. For instance, Exxon Mobil received 80 percent of its profits from outside the United States, but the firm had only one foreign-born officer on its white male executive officer team in 2009. IBM took more than half its profits from outside the United States in the same period, and none of its mixed team of female, minority, and white male executive officers were born abroad.

Fifty years after the grand experiment to diversify the workplace began, a tremendous amount of progress has been made, but the original goals have yet to be fully achieved. Part of the reason is that the globalization of the workforce has enabled other workers to leapfrog ahead of homegrown minorities in the pursuit of promotions. Certainly, the United States has long been a haven for immigrants—nearly all U.S. families came from elsewhere at some point in the past—and allegations of discrimination in the workplace due to national origin are very rare. But the time has come for corporations to have a conversation about appropriate levels for international leadership.

The executive officers who were born outside the United States tend to come from elite, high-status groups in their birth countries. Many foreign nationals, for example, have been hired by U.S.-based corporations after gaining an advanced degree (a master's degree or doctorate) at an American university. Foreign students often have to pay for graduate school themselves in the United States, and their ability to afford college in their home country of, say, India or Mexico usually means they come from families with resources. These employees are not the traditional homegrown minorities that affirmative action and diversity were originally intended to recognize. Yet, if they wind up working on the U.S. side of a global corporation, drawing local pay and benefits, they are counted as minority group members in the company's annual census of its workers.[10] The Office of Federal Contract Compliance Programs (OFCCP) in the Department of Labor, which oversees government contracts, allows companies to count immigrants as minorities depending on their race. For instance, a black immigrant from Nigeria is considered a minority, but a white Nigerian immigrant is not. National origin is not considered.[11]

Corporate executives could argue that real diversity means bringing international perspectives to the leadership team. The contention could be that knowing how to excel abroad is more important than continuing an old-fashioned idea of "representation," the politically correct term for affirmative action in the United States. Andres Tapia, a management consultant for Hewitt Associates, believes that the tolerance or sensitivity resulting from the civil rights movement "gets sniffed out as too American once it crosses the border" and that its historical nature loses its effectiveness in a global context.[12] Certainly, executive teams can be composed of entirely different nationalities. In fact, the U.S.-based companies led by foreign-born CEOs had nearly four times the level of foreign-born executive officers than the average *Fortune 100* company had in 2009. They demonstrated far less affinity for traditional U.S. ideas of diversity. Before this trend accelerates, companies have an opportunity to decide how far they wish to stray from their American talent base.

Where We Stand

The United States is in the middle of a full-blown, worldwide competition for talent. The drive toward globalizing the corporation has distracted many companies from long-held American ideals and goals. Fifty years after corporations began a concerted effort to break the monopoly of white men on the best jobs in America, we have a chance to look at what went right and what went awry and to make corrections as the country adjusts to the realities of a globalized economy. It is time to get U.S. workers ready for the international markets in which they will have to compete. Learning to operate in foreign cultures is simply an expansion of the diversity work that corporations have done in the United States. Those that have created a learning culture will have a head start on the rest.

Through consistent attention and careful selection, some global corporations have chosen the perfect mix of executive officers. Even though they earn more than 50 percent of revenues from outside the United States, these companies have continued to develop their team so that they have a rich mix of

Caucasian, Asian, African, Hispanic, and Native Americans, while employing some of the best talent from abroad. The right mix all comes down to who the chief executives want on their teams and to the processes that they put into place to hire, retain, and promote the workforce.

2 | Merck's Deliberate Strategy: Just Do It

FOR HALF OF THE NINE YEARS WHEN ROY VAGELOS WAS chief executive of Merck, the top management was a tightly knit group of Caucasian men who had begun their careers before the 1960s. Most had traditional marriages, including him, in which wives managed the house, the kids, and even their spouses for the most part. Sometimes, persuading his colleagues to give a big promotion to someone who was not like them was difficult. "A few were simply prejudiced against women, certain they couldn't deal with the pressures of the executive suite," Vagelos wrote in a memoir. Other colleagues were comfortable with the positions they had achieved and were "convinced that all of their decisions about promotion were unbiased even when all the best jobs went to men."[1]

But Vagelos was aware of the different opportunities that men and women were given simply because of gender. Vagelos, who is the son of a Greek immigrant, received an education when his sister did not. His sister was encouraged to marry, while Vagelos went to college and medical school. With every opportunity well handled, he received even bigger opportunities and steadily accumulated advantage over competitors. Acknowledging this series of advantages, he wanted to distribute more opportunities at Merck beyond one race and gender.

Vagelos was not the first to have such an idea; at the time, CEOs were being encouraged to flaunt tradition. In 1986, Kay Landen, a vice president of the Central Bank of Denver, coined the phrase "glass ceiling" to describe a barrier that slowed women's advancement. To grapple with the problem, in 1991, the Department of Labor formed a Glass Ceiling Commission. The Commission urged businesses to voluntarily take proactive steps to recognize and promote both women and minorities to executive ranks.[2]

In 1990, when Merck's chief financial officer retired, Vagelos wanted to promote Judy Lewent, a white woman who had spent most of her career at Merck working as a controller and in finance. Lewent had graduated from Goucher College and then earned an MBA from the Sloan School of Management at the Massachusetts Institute of Technology (MIT). Vagelos was particularly impressed with her strategic analytical ability. She had created a computer program that predicted the value of the company's drug development from laboratory to launch.

Merck is a research-based organization that develops drugs to prevent, treat, and cure illness in humans and animals. It pours billions of dollars into research every year to develop treatments, some of which may be approved as safe and effective but most of which will not. Drug development is very costly and high risk because of the potential side effects and harm that can come to patients. Scientists are always balancing risk and reward, trying to stay at the cutting edge in fighting disease while complying with extensive federal regulations. The computer program that Lewent had developed to project costs helped the company manage its resources.

Although Vagelos may have anticipated objections to Lewent because she was female, he did not hear any. The other executive officers thought she was tough enough to handle the corporate suite. Her immediate supervisor, who was a member of the executive management team at the time, vouched for her. He said Lewent would make an excellent "Marine officer"—and he gave her his total support.[3]

Two years later, when another executive officer position—general counsel—opened, Vagelos wanted to promote Mary McDonald, a white lawyer who had worked in the company's legal department since the mid-1970s. She had handled discrimination complaints and labor issues and had translated business negotiations into sound contracts. But some of the other executive team members felt "she might not be forceful enough for the top position."[4] When Vagelos heard this, he was not certain what they were suggesting. Was it that female executives in general were not as aggressive as male executives, or were they talking about McDonald specifically? He decided to ignore the assertions because he was convinced that she was the strongest contender for the spot. McDonald was quieter than some of the male executive officers, but that did not prevent her from serving seven successful years as general counsel.

Perception Changer

Vagelos's willingness to go against stereotype in selecting his top executives put the company on an exceptional path to setting new records for the level of integration among its executive officers. The difference between Vagelos and other chief executives in the *Fortune 100* at the time is that he did not stop with one "diversity hire." He kept going. In 1993, he appointed Celia Colbert, an African American, to the position of corporate secretary and assistant general counsel. A graduate of Harvard University and Columbia Law School, she had started with Merck in 1986 after a few years of working with a law firm in New York City. In her appointed role, Colbert supported the board of directors and shareholder activities. In the 1990s, many firms included corporate secretaries among their executive officers.[5]

Vagelos did not stop after he had promoted three women. In January 1994, he appointed Caroline Dorsa, a white female, to the role of treasurer. Dorsa had earned her BA at Colgate and an MBA in finance and accounting at Columbia University's Graduate School of Business in 1987. Hired by Merck at the age of 28, she worked her way up through positions in financial evaluation, pricing, strategic planning, and customer marketing in the United States. As treasurer, she was responsible for treasury and tax functions and for providing financial support to several of Merck's divisions such as the research laboratories, manufacturing, and the Asia Pacific Division. After just seven years at Merck, by the age of 35, she was made an executive officer. She was moving fast.

It had taken Lewent and McDonald longer to break the glass ceiling. But once they demonstrated to skeptical males that women could perform the job of executive officer just as well as men could, younger women were able to make tracks.

In the 1990s, an already large pool of well-educated female university graduates and professionals were in the labor force. But to attract the best talent, Merck had to stand out as the best place to work. "Because women normally experience the tension between the demands of career and those of family and child rearing more acutely than men, it was important that we accommodate that situation," wrote Vagelos.[6]

The company provided child care facilities at all its major locations. And it allowed men and women to balance corporate and family responsibilities with flextime. Flextime was not always smiled upon by management who usually wanted work to be the employee's top priority. Still, family obligations were usually accommodated as long as the work got done.

As Vagelos defied conventional wisdom by hiring a critical mass of women, he sought out more information from a small group of African Americans at Merck to get their perspective on how they were advancing within the company. "I was surprised and saddened to learn that, in their opinion, an African American had to be 15 percent better than a White colleague to be promoted at Merck," he wrote. "I couldn't see this from my position at the top of the firm, but I believed them because they were intelligent, credible, sincere people."[7]

A lot of chief executives never engage in conversations about race or gender with their employees, but getting involved is one of the early processes that has to occur for a corporation to level the playing field. The studies for this book revealed that one of the most important qualities in a chief executive is soliciting feedback from employees about their perceptions of fairness in the company.

Timing is critical in promotions for both the employee and the company, but frequently reciprocal needs do not match up. Not having the right spot for the right candidate is often a problem on an executive team, and corporations can lose valuable people if they cannot promote candidates at the right time. "We lost some superb candidates for top jobs when other firms offered them opportunities we didn't have available," wrote Vagelos.[8]

One of the top people Merck lost was Cecil Pickett, an African American with a PhD from the University of California in Los Angeles (UCLA), whom Vagelos had recruited years earlier. In 1993, Pickett was appointed executive vice president of research at the Schering-Plough Research Institute where he was responsible for the planning and management of the company's new drug discovery programs.

As they lost talent, Merck recruited new executives. Kenneth Frazier, an African American lawyer, was hired in 1992 to serve as a vice president, general counsel, and secretary of Merck's venture with the Swedish firm Astra. Frazier had graduated from Pennsylvania State University and Harvard Law School, and he was a partner in Drinker, Biddle & Reath in Philadelphia, which had long provided counsel to Merck.

In April 1994, Vagelos promoted Frazier to the executive officer position of vice president of public affairs, in which he would be responsible for all of the corporation's communication with the public. Initially Frazier did not want to take it; he wanted to stay in law, but Vagelos pressured him. "I wanted to bring him into the central organization," said Vagelos. "His combination of technical and people skills, energy, and self-discipline put him on the corporate fast track. He's completely open and honest, which are qualities extremely important to me."[9]

Vagelos's deliberate strategy to diversify Merck's executive officer team made the company stand out from all others. By 1995, Merck was the only company in the study of the *Fortune 100* with a completely mixed team of white males and females and of minority males and females. In four years, Vagelos had promoted three Caucasian women, one African

American woman, and one African American man to the position of executive officer. All four women and Frazier had earned graduate degrees in law and business from the country's top schools. In 1995, the female and minority representation of Merck's executive officers was 28 percent, more than three times the *Fortune 100* average of 8 percent at the time.

"If you look at the white males I brought in, they had similar backgrounds. In other words, I was not different in my selection of minorities, women or men. I'm very, very demanding," said Vagelos.[10]

Some critics might argue that the four people Vagelos promoted did not have real power because they were not in operating roles, that they did not have profit-making responsibility at the corporation. Nonetheless, they were in necessary roles such as finance, general counsel, treasurer, and corporate communications, and they provided critical functions for the firm. Vagelos wanted to test them; if they did well in these roles, they could move on to other roles. "I thought one of these people could become CEO, but I didn't know which," he said.[11]

Vagelos began a process that would be continued by two of his successors and that would result in Merck's having the most diverse teams in 2005 and 2009, standing far above the other *Fortune 100* companies.

Systems Changer

In 1994, Vagelos did not feel ready to retire, but company policy forced him to do so by the age of 65. When Raymond Gilmartin arrived at the pharmaceutical giant in the summer to take over as CEO, he was an outsider. He was not a medical doctor or a scientist like Vagelos. He was an electrical engineer who had been chief executive and chairman of the medical equipment firm Becton-Dickinson, a much smaller company than Merck. But he was well aware of Merck's legendary efforts to foster a strong, ethical culture. Over the years, the firm had tried to follow the tenets of its founder George Merck to emphasize the role of the company as a maker of medicines to prevent, treat, and cure disease. His son, George W. Merck, built on that foundation and explained his father's vision this way: "We try to remember that medicine is for the patient. We try never to forget that medicine is for the people. It is not for the profits. The profits will follow and if we have remembered that, they have never failed to appear."[12] Gilmartin short-handed the message to telegraph to Merck's employees that he shared their values. Within minutes of beginning every internal speech, he said, "At Merck we never put profits ahead of patients."[13]

But as humane and ethical as Merck was thought to be, there were rumblings inside the company that it could do far better. Over the summer of 1994, Gilmartin spoke individually to about 40 people at different levels throughout the company to get their views of the organization before he officially took charge in the fall. He asked them, "What do you think are the important issues that we face? And if you were me where would you focus your potential?"

In addition to gaining a lot of insight as to how to shape the business, "in those interviews I picked up some concern about whether we really had an atmosphere that was promoting diversity," Gilmartin said.[14]

Many employees felt Merck still had not done enough, that more women and African Americans should be hired and promoted at the company. Mary McDonald, the general counsel at the time, told Gilmartin that she saw the deficit as an ethical inconsistency, given the kind of company it was supposed to be. "[Merck] is not as diverse at its senior level as it is deeper in the organization, but its goal is to become uniformly diverse at all levels," said McDonald.[15]

At the same time, Merck started getting similar feedback from outsiders. An African American preacher from Philadelphia, Robert Shine, stood up at the 1995 annual meeting and said Merck had not been fair to African American employees. Shine had worked at the West Point, Pennsylvania, facility that manufactures vaccines and knew about conditions there first-hand.

"It had a profound affect on me," said Gilmartin. Although Gilmartin is Caucasian, he understood on a class level what it was like to want to be appreciated and promoted for one's work. He wanted others to experience recognition also.

Gilmartin had grown up in a two-parent, working-class household on Long Island, New York, where the biggest accomplishment of his young adulthood was to be the first person in his family to go to college. He earned a degree in electrical engineering from Union College and went to work at Eastman Kodak. One day he learned that a friend was going to go to Harvard Business School. At the time, Gilmartin did not know that an advanced degree in business even existed. After he found out more about the program, he decided to apply. Gilmartin's parents thought he already had a great future ahead of him at Kodak, which, in the 1960s, was making the instamatic camera. They did not understand why he would want to go to business school, which they imagined would teach stenography and typing. Once Gilmartin enrolled, he learned a vision of leadership that was larger than business. It involved educating leaders to contribute to society in general.

Gilmartin found himself growing in directions that neither he nor his family had ever envisioned. He wanted to impart this larger leadership he had learned to the companies that he later would manage.

Years later, at Merck, the chorus of voices inside and outside the company, asserting that women and minorities were not being hired or promoted at Merck as much as they could be, told him that significant processes had to be put into place that would ensure greater integration. "We said we're going to create an atmosphere where everyone has the opportunity to fulfill their potential," Gilmartin said. "You have to have a certain amount of idealism and faith that we can do the right thing."[16]

The question for Gilmartin was what processes, systems, and training would enable Merck to transform itself?

"One person doesn't do this, the organization does it," he said.

As he described the processes, sitting in his Harvard Business School office, where he became a professor after retiring from Merck, he called them "dominant" and "emergent." At the top of the organization, a *dominant strategy* focuses on developing and promoting all different types of people in the company. At the entry or hiring level, the *emergent strategy* concentrates on hiring diverse employees. The CEO, officers, and managers of the corporation design these processes and put them into place. Gilmartin was looking for the alignment of the rest of the organization with his deliberate strategy of promoting all kinds of people. When parts of the business were too homogeneous, he sought to integrate them. "I remember we were concerned that our sales force wasn't diverse enough," he said.

His staff widened the pool of applicants to reach a more

diverse group of candidates. They applied objective hiring criteria against the pool, being very explicit about what they wanted, and wound up hiring a more diverse group of salespeople. Gilmartin also tied managers' compensation to their hiring and promotion of diverse individuals.

Trying to Walk the Talk

In 1996, the company was hit with a lawsuit by two women at the Merck Federal Credit Union. They filed a civil suit in Superior Court in Somerville, New Jersey, that accused the company of treating them differently from male colleagues. One of the women, a credit union manager, Shirley Galligan, alleged that she did not receive performance reviews or raises during her nearly 20 years of work. She asserted that she was unfairly treated by her male boss, who had claimed she was insubordinate when she asked for a raise and later terminated her.[17]

Merck settled with both of the women. But the suits were an example of the kinds of frustrations that—if allowed to fester—could grow into a protracted lawsuit. It showed that Merck had to refine its dominant processes to keep its stated values strong and operational throughout the company, every minute of every day. The suits had not resulted from employees who had been newly hired or those who were at the very top, but from long-term midlevel employees. And the suits involved long-term managers.

Sociologist Barbara Reskin, who has examined discrimination lawsuits and testified as an expert witness in discrimination cases, has concluded that discrimination problems are usually triggered by the behavior of managers. "Although individuals cannot banish the automatic unconscious distortions that limit women's careers, employers can minimize their discriminatory effects through personnel policies that reduce managers' discretion, such as formalizing hiring and promotion practices, holding managers accountable for fair decisions, encouraging employees to identify with groups in which membership is not associated with gender, and actively compensating for unconscious biases."[18]

Gilmartin saw that he had to have more tools in place to keep all employees on course. He kept asking his executive committee, what are the forcing mechanisms that will cause people to change more than what he and his human resources staff could accomplish at the top of the company and at the hiring level? "It has to be ingrained into the processes that have to do with how the company gets work done, how it functions," he said. "It's like getting into the DNA."[19]

He appointed Jacqueline Brevard, an African American lawyer, to be Merck's chief ethics officer. Under her leadership, Merck began to create a code of ethics to ensure that the company's policies were consistent with its values. The global initiative was translated into several languages. The firm ran ethics awareness training seminars worldwide to show its people how to recognize when they were in an ethical dilemma and how to resolve it. They turned a hotline that was used for whistle-blowing into an advice line that people could call to figure out how to deal with a situation. In addition, in each of the major units in the United States they had an ombudsman whom employees could contact if they saw something that was unethical or felt they had been treated unfairly. The employees could decide whether they wanted their complaint to be handled confidentially. An investigation was conducted, the facts were gathered, and lawyers or officers could become involved. The response was handled so that an executive would be aware that the issue was being looked into but not involved personally. Then the findings would come back to the person who made the complaint.

Gilmartin met with Brevard quarterly to discuss the patterns that were forming, and which issues might need to be included in management training. Nearly 90 percent of the complaints had to do with management-employee relationships and issues about fairness. Gilmartin remembered a specific case when a female sales representative complained that, whenever her boss traveled with her, he was very critical of her performance. She thought it was because she was female. Brevard looked into her complaint and spoke to the manager directly. It turned out that the manager felt that the woman was his best salesperson. His own leadership style—how he interacted with her—had caused the employee to feel that she was being treated badly because she was female.

If the ethics process had not been in place, the sales representative might have quit, sued the company, or done both. The company might have lost a very talented employee. She might have felt very discouraged or disillusioned about the company, and both parties might have become embroiled in an escalating lawsuit. Instead, the manager received feedback that he had to change his management style by being more appreciative and constructive in feedback to his workers. "This was a great forum where if you were a woman or a minority you could bring your concern very directly to be considered in a very serious way, but confidentially," said Gilmartin.[20]

Gilmartin focused on congruence. If he declared that diversity was important to the company, then he had to act accordingly. In 1999, when Mary McDonald retired, Gilmartin moved Ken Frazier from public affairs to general counsel. This was an important move because it signified that Merck did not have black jobs and white jobs or male jobs and female jobs in the executive suite, as many companies do (not explicitly but through tradition). Frequently in such companies, the first person of color who is hired into a spot in the executive group is replaced with another person of color.

Despite the efforts to make Merck more thoroughly integrated, some employees felt the company was not moving fast enough or trying hard enough. In 1999, 11 African American employees who worked at the West Point, Pennsylvania, facility filed a lawsuit alleging that the company had engaged in a pattern of racial discrimination and that it had created a work environment that was hostile to black employees.[21] The suit came after several Ku Klux Klan leaflets announcing a meeting to discuss "ethnic cleansing at Merck" were left on cars in a company parking lot, derogatory messages were sent by e-mail, and a noose was found swinging from a doorframe in a washroom.

After the complaint was filed, an activist Catholic nun, Sister Patricia Marshall, an 80-year-old member of the Sisters of the Blessed Sacrament in Philadelphia, took up the cause of the complainants. She asked Merck shareholders at the annual meeting to vote on a proposal that the company disclose its diversity programs and list its top 100 wage earners by race and gender. The company urged shareholders to vote against the proposal, saying it would duplicate information that already existed. At that time the company estimated that about one-fourth of its 69,300 employees were minorities. The measure did not pass, and Merck did not release the earnings information. But Sister Marshall brought publicity to Merck's race and gender problems. Her efforts demonstrated that the wider community was resisting Merck's claims of diversity.[22]

Although Gilmartin had already instigated several new changes to encourage a meritocracy, they still had not reached all the areas of the sprawling company, the 31 different plants across the country and in Canada. As a result, outsiders and insiders let them know that their lofty goals were not being met. Many executives at the headquarters in White House Station, New Jersey, felt embarrassed by the suits and wondered what the impact would be on the business.

"If you don't give people what they want and need to change," said Gilmartin, "they will force you to listen to them, constrain your interests and regulate you."

It is a challenge for most corporations to bring their distant sites into line with the new thinking at headquarters. But West Point, Pennsylvania, where several African American complainants worked, is less than 50 miles from Merck's headquarters in White House Station, New Jersey. If the company could not get all the employees and managers at such a nearby location to buy into the corporate strategy, it needed another mechanism to encourage managers and employees to respect one another regardless of race or gender.

Julius Webb is a college-educated African American who had worked in the maintenance department at Merck's West Point facility for 12 years. He had received strong reviews for his work and had repeatedly sought and been denied a promotion to supervisor. After the KKK leaflets were distributed, a noose was hung in a hallway, and a Caucasian manager referred to himself in an e-mail as a "zoo keeper," Webb filed an individual suit alleging a hostile and abusive work environment at the firm. Although the Caucasian manager apologized for his zoo keeper remarks, and the company concluded that the noose had been a bad joke, Webb felt he needed the law to help him. In early 2008, Webb settled with the company, which did promote him to supervisor.[23]

In 2002, the Federal Court in Philadelphia declined to certify the complaints by minority workers around the country against Merck into a class action with 5,000 potential members. The judge perceived no pattern and practice of discrimination from the complaints. Individuals, however, continued to pursue their own cases.[24]

Gilmartin's dominant change strategy was not reaching or sinking into locations and factories outside headquarters. In 2001, he hired Deborah Dagit to head Merck's diversity department. Dagit, a very well-respected diversity expert, is four feet tall and walks with a cane. She has osteogenesis imperfecta, a brittle bone disease, but her condition has not prevented her from talking and thinking about problems and their solutions in a fluid and wide-ranging manner. Dagit, who is Caucasian, believes that minorities in the company—be they women, African Americans, or any other group—offer a useful way of seeing the entire company. The issues they raise, such as whether compensation and evaluations for promotion are fair or not, tend to affect everyone, including white men. They tap into broader issues that apply to the whole company.[25]

She wanted Merck's employees to take responsibility for the integration process and began to build on the company's affinity groups to strengthen diversity awareness throughout the company. As Merck funded the groups, they brought in outside experts and learned more about their particular racial, ethnic, or gender group in relation to organizations.

- The Asia Pacific Network, which began in 2000, read *The Bamboo Ceiling* and invited its author to discuss why

Asians' stereotypical deference may put them at a disadvantage in the corporate world. In addition, they hired Leadership Education for Asian Pacifics (LEAP), a program specifically designed to develop leadership skills in Asian and Pacific Islanders.

• The Gay, Lesbian, Bisexual and Transgendered (GLBT) group, founded in 2002, asked Parents, Families and Friends of Lesbians and Gays (PFLAG) to offer seminars for Merck employees who have a family member who is GLBT on how to decrease their isolation through education. The group also invited Brian McNaught, a diversity consultant, to discuss how to include gay and lesbian employees in the workplace. The group informed employees of the Safe Space sign, a pink triangle inside a green circle, that indicates the company is a GLBT ally and does not tolerate bigotry.

• The Hispanic Network asked the publisher of *Diversity Inc.* to give a seminar on why companies are higher performing when they value and manage diversity.

• The Black Network invited a panel of senior African American executives to discuss their career paths and offer advice to employees.

Although there were several affinity groups, which Merck calls "employee resource groups," their membership was only about 2,500 out of 63,000 employees. Their meetings and groups were open to all employees to join or attend. If anyone questioned their activities (for example, "Why are we supporting the gay agenda?"), Dagit would invite the employee to come see her and express his or her objections. No one came.

In the Internet age, however, employees can express themselves in other ways. Public comments were posted on café pharma.com, an Internet chat room for medical and pharmaceutical salespeople. In 2004, an anonymous commenter began to rank the female sales reps around the nation and at headquarters for their sex appeal.

- "Here's your chance Merck! Vote for the Hottest Merck Representative and hottest HQ babe! I'll just sit back and drool . . . yum," wrote Anonymous.[26]

- "Metro has a couple winners on both sides," responded a contributor. "Check out the regional roster for the hunks and the babes. They're all in the Primary Care sales force. Specialty sales is filled with hags and old guys."[27]

The commenters named more than a dozen women and men and commented specifically on their physical attributes.[28]

- "So who do you want to do at HQ?" asked a commenter.[29]

- "[Female name], hotter than shit and a tight ass "the package."

- [Female name]-hot big hair and an accent to boot. Did I mention the hair?," answered another contributor.[30]

These kind of electronic comments can become a nightmare for companies because they can be considered to contribute to a hostile workplace if employees interpret them as such and claim that the comments impede their psychological well-being and work performance. Within Merck, there was considerable outrage over the comments, as well as debate about what to do about them. In the end, the company decided not to make overt efforts to end them out of fear it would only encourage the commenters.

Cafépharma.com offers a public view of the vast array of

clashing cultures within one company. The forum reveals tensions between men and women, impatience by the sales force with the research executives, and disapproval of the ongoing diversity efforts. Commenters complained that Merck had gone too far in its enthusiasm for diversity, implying that the company was hiring unqualified employees.

- "We are diverse and proud of it. Cannot perform but we are diverse!!!" wrote Anonymous.[31]

- "Merck's diversity numbers are still far below the national percentages, with the exception of Caucasian women. Yes, Caucasian women are considered a part of diversity in corporate America. And no I am not a diversity hire!" argued a contributor.[32]

- "The diversity agenda is a prime symptom of the disease. In and of itself it sounds noble and harmless in theory, but in practice it morphs into a cancer on any organization. No, I am not talking about hiring qualified candidates who happen to be people of color, but the inevitable mandating of QUOTAS etc. . . ." wrote Anonymous.[33]

Gilmartin denies that he ever used quotas.

Critical Mass

Despite resistance, he continued to develop a high-powered, mixed group of executive officers. Judy Lewent, the first female executive officer at Merck, developed Merck's business in Asia.

Gilmartin promoted Margaret McGlynn, a Caucasian female, to be president of one of Merck's drug divisions. Gilmartin raised the number of women to six, 40 percent of the team.

Women and minorities were no longer in support roles, they held profit-making positions. He tapped Brad Sheares, an African American research scientist turned marketer who had worked his way up through the company, to be head of the other drug division.

He promoted Richard Henriques, Jr., a Hispanic controller who had worked at the firm for several years after earning an MBA from the Wharton School of Finance in Philadelphia.

Gilmartin selected Peter Kim, a Korean American, to be president of the Merck Research Laboratories, an incredibly important job; this was the pipeline for Merck's products. In 2001, the company had persuaded Kim to leave his job as a professor of biology at the Massachusetts Institute of Technology (MIT), where he was also a member of the prestigious Whitehead Institute and an Investigator at the Howard Hughes Medical Institute, to lead research and development at Merck.

By 2005, as the result of Gilmartin's actions, 79 percent of Merck's executive officers were female and minority, the highest percentage that was ever reached by any of the *Fortune 100* companies in the 14-year study.

"Who you promote sends huge messages to the consistency of what you say," said Gilmartin.

Diversity is rarely the chief concern in a company; there would be no employees without the revenues produced by the firm's products and services. Cultural issues are usually secondary to the ongoing business narrative, the daily advances and setbacks that determine profitability. But what happened at Merck sheds new light on how diversity can contribute to the resilience of an organization as the people who were hired and developed wound up rescuing the company from a staggering business disaster. In 1999, the Food and Drug Administration (FDA) had approved Vioxx, a prescription arthritis painkiller that had become wildly successful, earning $2.4 billion in sales. In 2004, Merck would experience one of the biggest medical, financial, and legal crises of its entire history due to Vioxx.

On Friday, September 24, of that year, Gilmartin got a call from Peter Kim, head of research for Merck, who told him that the external board that was monitoring the safety of a Vioxx study recommended Merck stop the trial because of an increased risk of cardiovascular events. Gilmartin agreed with Kim to end the trial. The two discussed what to do about the painkiller itself. They agreed to withdraw Vioxx from the market. But the CEO wanted to involve other members of the management team so that everyone had a chance to participate in the decision. On Monday they got everyone on a conference call. There was no debate. They agreed to withdraw the drug. On Tuesday, they had a board meeting and informed the FDA of their decision. On Wednesday, they prepared for the announcement so that patients and doctors who had been relying on Vioxx would know what to do.

After the drug recall, the largest in U.S history, lawsuits alleging that Vioxx had been responsible for patients' deaths due to heart attacks or impairment from strokes or blood clots mounted. By the end of 2009, the company had been named as a defendant in more than 9,000 lawsuits alleging personal injury from the use of Vioxx. The firm set up a $4.5 billion settlement fund to resolve claims of myocardial infarction and ischemic stroke.[34] In 2010, the U.S. Supreme Court, in a unanimous vote, ruled that a shareholders' lawsuit against Merck for alleged misrepresentations regarding Vioxx was not time barred by the applicable statute of limitations and could go ahead.[35]

After 11 years as chief executive, president and chairman of the board Gilmartin resigned in 2005, at the age of 64, one year before mandatory retirement. The main question was why did the company fail to act sooner as questions about the drug, a sales blockbuster, emerged? Gilmartin said that the September 2004 study was the first "good evidence" they had and asserted that the company acted responsibly at all times.[36]

The executive officers who provided the most testimony in the Vioxx cases were already executive officers at Merck when the outsider Gilmartin came aboard. They had more experience with drug chemistry, drug testing, drug approval, and drug marketing than he did.

At the end of 2010, Merck had won more Vioxx cases than it had lost, although the litigation was still ongoing. Ken Frazier, the African American whom Gilmartin had promoted to general counsel, wound up crafting Merck's legal defense strategy in the Vioxx cases. Frazier received much praise and appreciation from Merck colleagues for his work in managing the damage to the company.

As Gilmartin reflected on the ramifications of promoting a diverse group of individuals, he concluded that it amplified the inherent strength of an organization by infusing it with resilience. "If you offer opportunity to everyone to fulfill their full potential," said Gilmartin, "you create an organization that would deal with adversity and be more resilient than others."

Frazier came from very humble circumstances. He had grown up in a rough North Philadelphia neighborhood. His mother died when he was 12 and his father, the son of a sharecropper, with the equivalent of a third-grade education, raised Frazier and his two siblings singlehandedly on a janitor's salary. "His view of what was possible was unconstrained by the circumstances we lived in," said Frazier. "We were raised to think we could do anything."[37]

Frazier was widely admired before the Vioxx suit for his honesty and integrity. He displayed intense determination to complete difficult assignments whether it was defending Merck or spending his free time working to get a man, whom he believed to be innocent, off death row. Frazier's success in defending the firm during the suit protected the company during a period of severe hardship and crisis.

Richard Clark, who is white, replaced Gilmartin as CEO. Clark had been a chief executive officer of Merck manufacturing and of Medco Health Solutions, a drug mail-order company that was a wholly owned Merck subsidiary. He had three decades of leadership experience, and he was going to need them in the wake of the Vioxx debacle. Merck's stock price plummeted after the Vioxx recall and by the end of 2010, still had not recovered.

After Frazier had crafted Merck's Vioxx defense, Clark put him in charge of restructuring Merck's worldwide marketing and sales of prescription drugs and vaccines. In 2007, as head of global human health, Frazier reduced the sales force by 30–35 percent and changed the way it did business. Instead of going in and hard selling a new brand such as Vioxx, the salespeople were encouraged to offer a range of products that were grouped into categories such as cardiovascular care or gynecological treatments, as a range of possible solutions for doctors to treat their diverse patients.[38]

Merck Continues to Promote Diversity

Richard Clark had very different ideas about diversity from those of his two predecessors. Clark believed that people from different backgrounds created better products, and he wanted to use diversity to grow the business internationally. In 2005, Merck operated in 140 countries. Clark theorized that a global company that produces drugs to prevent, treat, and cure disease should be deeply connected to the needs of very diverse patients because ailments often differ according to geographic region, race, gender, and ethnicity. For instance, river blindness does not occur in the United States, but it is very common in African countries because black fly bites spread microscopic worms that migrate to the eyes and cause blindness. Similarly, hepatitis B is a leading cause of death in many Asian and African countries, but it usually appears in the United States only among populations at risk for HIV.[39]

Responding to Clark's global diversity directive, Deb Dagit, the chief diversity officer, began to develop global constituency groups of middle and senior management people from around the world, including white males. The goal for those teams was to turn the affinity groups into feeder pools, and create a pipeline that developed personnel. The executive sponsors would report to CEO Clark and be held accountable for pulling these personnel through the pipeline. The groups were modeled on IBM's affinity groups. Ted Childs, who used to work at IBM, advised Merck on the project.

In 2008, 10 global constituency groups, with no more than 20 people each, were established worldwide across Merck's business units. One cochair on each team was from the United States and one cochair was from outside the United States. Each group had an executive sponsor from the executive management committee. The groups were divided into Black, Hispanic, Native American and Indigenous Peoples, Asian, Interfaith, Differently Abled, LGBT, Women, and Men.

They each focused on the same four questions.

1. What can we do internally to accelerate leadership development and inclusion from your group?

2. How can we enhance inclusion for your group externally?

3. How can we enhance our reputation with customers and your group externally?

4. Who are the key stakeholders outside the company that we should have a global partnership with?

The diversity team distilled the groups' answers into eight suggestions and acted on the easiest ones first. They created a global mentoring program to accelerate leadership development. They produced a calendar with the key international and religious holidays so that managers would know not to schedule meetings on those days. They established guidelines and designated a point person for establishing prayer rooms anywhere in the world. They implemented a global flexible work arrangement with a Web site that stated the rules and that offered tools to teach managers and employees about how the new policy should be used. They created same-sex, domestic-partner benefits in every country where it was legal to do so.

The global constituency groups grappled with the problem Merck had finding enough local workers in countries outside the United States. To better locate these potential workers, the groups recommended notifying foreign and domestic universities that they were seeking students who were planning to return to their country of origin after receiving their credentials.

The company also began a couple of pilot studies to understand the effect of pharmaceuticals on age, race, or gender in clinical trials. Scientists have long been criticized for focusing too much attention on the medical outcomes of white males. Merck and the pharmaceutical industry, in partnership with the FDA, planned to review data at the end of the trials to see whether the side effects or efficacy of the drugs differed in a diverse population. The groups also recommended focusing philanthropic efforts on healthcare literacy and access and improving the distribution of Merck's products in underserved communities.

Although the groups got off to a strong start, they did not influence the decisions made by Clark when he formed his executive team because they were created after he took charge.

Clark promoted Mirian Graddick-Weir, an African American, to be head of global human resources. She would be responsible for anticipating and securing the best talent for the company. She had arrived at Merck in 2006 after rising to become the first woman to head human resources at AT&T, where she began work in 1981 in a minority mentoring program. Graddick-Weir earned a BA in psychology from Hampton University and a PhD in organizational psychology from Pennsylvania State University.[40]

Clark hired Bridgette Heller, an African American, to be head of Consumer Health Care, the sales of products such as Afrin, Claritin, Coppertone, Dr. Scholl's, and MiraLax. Heller had come from Johnson & Johnson, where she had led the global baby care business, and she had worked previously at Kraft Foods. She earned an MBA at Northwestern University.

Peter Kim continued to lead Merck's Research Labs. Chris Scalet, a Native American, stayed on as Merck's chief information officer. Willie Deese, an African American, remained head of Merck's manufacturing. Bradley Sheares, an African American research scientist with a PhD in biochemistry from Purdue University, who had led a sales division, resigned from the executive board to take a job elsewhere. Gilmartin had recommended Sheares as a candidate for the job of CEO, but Merck's board of directors voted for Clark instead.

Clark had another reason for promoting diversity during his tenure. In 2009, he announced that Merck was buying the pharmaceutical company Schering-Plough for $49 billion, which would practically double the number of employees that Merck had. Careful integration of the two companies was critical to avoid wasting talent as the number of employees was reduced. Many mergers go awry when the merging firms do not wind up integrated enough. Most lose value. The process of integrating two companies, especially those of equal size, involves solving the cultural integration process among corporate cultures, national cultures, and professional cultures.

When Clark announced his retirement in 2010, the board of directors selected a successor who had devoted 18 years of service to improving the firm in many different roles. In 2011, Ken Frazier became chief executive officer of Merck, the second largest pharmaceutical maker in the United States. They flashed his smiling, serene, African American face across their Web site for months in a proud display of his achievement and theirs.

Diversity Helps Companies Succeed

As companies continue to explore diversity, they are realizing the many different benefits it can provide. Gilmartin believes that diversity increased Merck's resilience. Now, it could be argued that Frazier was simply the right person in the right place at the time. Yet Merck would not have benefited from Frazier's abilities without first giving him the opportunities to be in the right place. If employees feel that they have been fairly treated and rewarded by their companies, they tend to return the treatment.

In general, isolating diversity as the causal agent when trying to connect a metric to its effectiveness is difficult. There are many different variables involved in assessing the diversity dividend. One, is the type of corporation. Consumer products companies have had the most success making the direct monetary case. In 2005, for the first time, PepsiCo beat Coca-Cola in market capitalization because PepsiCo was able to reach more diverse markets with more diverse products than Coca-Cola was.[41] Several of PepsiCo's new products such as guacamole-flavored Doritos, wasabi-spiced snacks, and Mountain Dew Code Red were inspired by the company's affinity groups.

In other companies, the linkage is not as direct from affinity groups to potential customers. For instance, General Electric's Women's Network is unlikely to be successful in persuading individual women to buy a jet engine. The Hispanic Leadership Forum at United Technologies Corporation (UTC) will probably not sell many helicopters to individual Hispanics. Because of the diversity of products that companies produce and sell, there is not just one business case for diversity, but several.

Most companies approach diversity defensively—to ward off lawsuits by improving employee relations—instead of harnessing it for their business. But, used as a process within the business, diversity can help companies enhance their overall performance by securing the best talent, learning to grapple with larger employee issues such as fairness, and, in Merck's case, increasing resilience. A 2008 study that compared the financial performance of *Diversity Inc.*'s *Top 50 Companies for Diversity* to a matched sample showed that firms with a strong commitment to diversity outperformed their peers on average with higher profit margins and greater returns on equity and assets.[42]

A Diversity Model for Others

The curious fact about Merck's embrace of equal opportunity is that it started in earnest much later than hundreds of other companies, but it came out ahead. In 1966, Charles Spahr, who was president of Standard Oil of Ohio and who volunteered on the Plans for Progress Advisory Council, invited Merck to join the program, which had developed a protocol for recruiting minorities. But Merck's president, Henry Gadsden, declined. He explained that Merck already had a nondiscrimination policy. "It is our collective judgment that we wish to continue our present course without being affiliated in a formal manner with other programs," he wrote.[43]

A decade later, Merck learned that its own approach to equal opportunity was not working. In 1975, the company was hit with job discrimination complaints by female employees. Merck entered into a settlement agreement with the Labor Department to spend $3.2 million on "new and expanded affirmative action efforts" for the firm's 4,900 women and minority employees, including efforts to educate supervisors, managers, and local union officials about equal employment opportunity.[44] That's generally what Plans for Progress was intended to achieve.

Still, decades later, the firm wound up having the highest diversity among its executive officers of any firm in the *Fortune 100* in 1995, 2005, and 2009. (See Figure 2.1.) In addition, as the firm increased the numbers of homegrown executive officers, it reduced the percentage of foreign-born officers, even though it became a much more global company.

Figure 2.1 Diversity Among Merck's Executive Officers (%)

Executive Officers	1995	2005	2009
Caucasian Males	72.21	21.43	50
Caucasian Females	16.67	28.57	6.25
Minority Females	5.56	7.14	12.5
Minority Males	5.56	42.86	31.25
Total Born Ex-United States	27.78	14.29	12.5

Why was Merck so successful cultivating executive officer diversity when other companies have not been? Merck's chief executives were dedicated and persistent in their pursuit. Vagelos wanted to access the female and minority talent that had not been appreciated in the past. Gilmartin wished to create a meritocracy where everybody stood a chance. Clark believed diversity was good for the bottom line. Any argument for diversity—be it a righting of historical wrongs, a hearkening back to the American bootstrap story, or a business justification—can be used to justify change. Political scientist Carol Ogocs believes that a change message carried by an insider will be taken more seriously than one brought by someone who is an outsider or a member of an unfavored group.[45] (See Figure 2.2.)

The turnover of executive officers at Merck meant that po-

Figure 2.2 Conditions Needed to Diversify the Executive Officer Team

1. *Desire:* The chief executive officer must want to integrate the team.
2. *Vacancies:* There must be turnover to allow the promotion of new executive officers.
3. *Talent:* The company must have the diverse employees, male and female, waiting in the wings, or go out and get them.
4. *Improvisation:* If the exact spot does not match up with the exact needs, a close alignment of tasks with talents can also work.
5. *Persistence:* The chief executive has to keep promoting a diverse racial and gender mix, not stop at one, two, or three.

sitions for executive officers became available and allowed for change. Merck has a company policy that the chief executive officer must retire at 65 years of age. Making changes at the highest level requires vacancies. The number of Merck's executive officers has not fluctuated radically. From 18 in 1995, it declined to 14 in 2005 and increased to 16 in 2010.

Not one of Merck's chief executives stopped after promoting one white female or one minority and said, "One's enough." Among the white-ceiling companies identified in the research for this book, most had promoted one minority to executive officer in one of the three years of the study. But as that individual quit, retired, or was fired, he or she was often not replaced by another person of color, and no other minorities were promoted either. Having low numbers of minorities or women in the top jobs—"tokens"—never enables a company to achieve the critical mass, the momentum necessary to keep diversity going.[46] Research on tokens indicates that they experience greater pressure for performance and visibility, but also greater criticism if their exercise of authority threatens the majority members.[47] Increasing the number and authority of minorities at the top reduces the suspicion that they have received a "preferential promotion."

The fact that Merck made such enormous progress, coming from behind to lead the pack for 14 years, illustrates that other companies can do it too. By applying deliberate practices, both dominant and emergent, throughout the organization, in hiring and promotions—the very kinds of practices first established by Plans for Progress—managers can get into the DNA of their organizations and change the culture.

3 A Plan for Progress

ON MARCH 22, 1961, AT 6:35 A.M., FIVE BLACK EMPLOYEES AT Lockheed Aircraft's facility in Marietta, Georgia, tried to eat breakfast in the white cafeteria. The cafeteria workers closed down the line. The black employees entered another line. The food workers closed down that line also, as they had been instructed to do by Lockheed's management. The black employees retreated to the black cafeteria where they told everyone else in the cafeteria what had happened to them. The anger over segregated eating facilities resulted in "considerable unrest," according to Eugene Mattison, Lockheed's head of labor relations.[1]

Mattison and Lockheed's president, James Carmichael, met with the black employees in their lawyer's office. "Any incident of sufficient magnitude could cause the Government to switch the contract from Marietta to one of the California plants of our competitors," warned Carmichael.[2]

Just two months into his presidency, on March 6, 1961, President John F. Kennedy signed Executive Order 10925, which prohibited companies doing business with the U.S. government from discriminating against any employee or applicant for employment. It specified that contractors take "affirmative action to ensure that applicants are employed, and that employees are treated during employment, without regard to their race, creed, color, or national origin."[3] The order covered 35,000 companies and more than 15 million employees. It also included the nation's largest employer, the U.S. government.[4]

This was the first time that the phrase "affirmative action" was articulated in an executive order. The phrase would come to define the active effort to change an ingrained pattern of institutionalized segregation and discrimination in America. Yet, as President Kennedy uttered the phrase on that warm spring day, no one in the room had any idea of exactly how it would be implemented.

On March 3, just three days before the president issued the executive order, Lockheed had been given a government contract for $1 billion in jet-transfer planes. At the time, it was the largest contract the government had ever issued.[5] Lockheed desperately needed this contract. In 1960, the company lost nearly $43 million in net income. The firm was in the worst financial shape in 20 years after one of its Electra Turbo-prop commercial airliners, operated by Braniff, crashed in Texas when a propeller malfunctioned and a wing separated from the body of the plane in fight.[6]

Afraid of losing the contract, Carmichael wanted the black employees to pipe down. Instead, the group handed the two white executives a detailed and extensive list of complaints. They asserted that black workers had not been given equal opportunity for training or promotions in the previous ten years and that certain job categories had no blacks when many black employees were better educated than their white supervisors. They wanted segregated facilities to end.[7]

The white executives discussed the complaints with them and agreed that the "[c]ompany would continue to give consideration to the problems of the Negroes," according to Mattison.[8]

The black employees did not trust the company. They contacted the National Association for the Advancement of Colored People (NAACP). Just before Kennedy's executive order went into effect, 30 days after it was signed, the NAACP filed a report containing allegations from 494 black employees that Lockheed Aircraft Corporation's facility in Georgia engaged in discriminatory practices and segregated work conditions. Roy Wilkins, executive secretary of the NAACP, was testing the new President's Committee on Equal Employment Opportunity to see how it would react. Wilkins recommended that the contract with Lockheed be withheld.[9]

John Feild, executive director of the President's Committee, went to inspect the Marietta plant and found the facility that would be making the most advanced military cargo jet—a C-141 StarLifter was twice as large as the C-130 that preceded it—to be completely segregated. Blacks worked on separate assembly lines from whites. They used separate restrooms, lunchrooms, and water fountains. The few black supervisors managed only black employees. In addition, there were 20 whites to every one black, and union rules prescribed which employees would be called back to work to keep the ratio steady.

"There were a lot of blacks on layoff and a lot of whites on layoff," said Feild. "The blacks were concerned that the whites would use their seniority rights to move back in."

Although Lockheed-Georgia had signed a government contract agreeing not to discriminate according to race, religion, or national origin, in accordance with President Franklin D. Roosevelt's Fair Employment Practices Committee, it had never desegregated. In 1951, James Carmichael, who was then vice president of the Marietta facility, addressed the plant's 5,500 workers. "Lockheed will live the Southern tradition here," announced Carmichael. "We will employ colored people according to their ability, but they will not be mixed on the assembly line with whites."[10]

While pursuing the complaints against Lockheed-Georgia, John Feild discovered that several of the employees' complaints were nearly a decade old and that the Air Force had not resolved them. Although President Dwight Eisenhower had established the President's Committee on Government Contracts, which was empowered to cancel government contracts, the head of the Committee, Vice President Richard Nixon, never cancelled a contract.[11]

Feild met with Eugene Mattison and told him the production lines and training programs had to be integrated and qualified personnel had to be promoted without regard to color. "We recognize that this is in violation of the new executive order and we will change it," said Mattison. "The only question is, how much time do we have and how do we do it?"[12]

"You don't have any time. It's changed as of today, and we'll work out with you a written prescription as to how we're going to change it," replied Feild.[13] He integrated the company overnight. He took the signs off the drinking fountains, made one set of washrooms and lavatories, and combined the cafeterias, where everyone ate together.

"All those rednecks down there who were coping with that swallowed it," said Feild. "They didn't have any choice. The name of the game had changed."[14]

Under Kennedy's executive order, any contractor had to "permit access to his books, records, and accounts by the contracting agency and the Committee for purposes of investigation to ascertain compliance." Lockheed had to provide extensive employment data about its Georgia facility. The billion-dollar contract was put on hold until the company could answer the discrimination charges.

The company received a flurry of bad publicity, as well as intense pressure from the public, other businesses, and the government to resolve the matter. Vendors were waiting to deliver supplies. The Air Force was eager for work to start. Lockheed's headquarters in California wanted the problems resolved.

"Now, you can imagine my job," said Hugh Gordon, who was head of personnel at Lockheed-Georgia. "The calls kept coming from the West Coast," said Gordon. "'How are you coming on this?' I would say we are making progress, and are not in trouble. And then I'd get more calls. For good reason: Corporate kept close track of what was happening."[15]

It took two months for Gordon to answer the charges of discrimination. Eugene Mattison, Gordon's boss, asked the Aircraft Industry Association, to which all the aircraft manufacturers belonged, to produce aggregate employment data, which showed comparable employment statistics for blacks at all of the aircraft manufacturing centers. The data showed that the other aircraft manufacturers, such as Boeing, North American Aviation, and United Aircraft, also had blacks concentrated in unskilled or semiskilled positions. "That data was then shared with the federal investigators. Any notion they may have had to go elsewhere with the C-141 contract died right there," said Gordon.[16]

From his 20 years of experience with racial discrimination, Feild knew that the problem began far before it reached the workplace. With each new child raised in a segregated residential area, who attended second-rate schools and applied for work at an exclusionary employment agency or with a bigoted employer, the cycle repeated itself. Feild was executive director of the new Committee in a new administration that was about to confer the biggest defense contract in history. The position offered him the rare opportunity finally to create a blueprint that employers could use to stop discrimination at the door of the workplace. The tall, bespectacled Feild, who had a thick shock of reddish hair, sat down with Mattison and wrote out a protocol in long hand.

"I called it the Plan for Progress," said Feild.[17]

The First Plan for Progress

Lockheed's Plan for Progress was the first affirmative action plan imposed by the federal government and formed the basis of all future affirmative action plans for the next eight years, beginning well before and continuing well after the Civil Rights Act of 1964 was passed. In this plan, Feild articulated, in the form of a contract, the principles by which he felt that employers could both remedy and prevent discrimination and segregation based on race, creed, and national origin. (Gender was not covered by the Plan.) He set out to strengthen every link in the chain of the hiring process from high school to in-house promotions. With seven double-spaced pages, the contract launched what came to define the basic steps that companies would follow to take affirmative action to employ and promote more people of color.

• *Lockheed vowed to reach out to high schools to:*

Encourage the establishment of vocational training, help determine course content, furnish qualified instructors, and encourage minority group employee participation.

Encourage minority group participation in company-sponsored career development training, work study, and home study programs.

Ensure that qualified minority students are included in presupervisory and supervisory training courses on company time.

Hire minority teachers in the summer and to give minority teachers and students plant tours so that they will become aware of industry needs.

- *Lockheed pledged to contact colleges and employment agencies to:*

Advise colleges and state employment agencies of its nondiscrimination policy and ask them to refer minority group students who appear qualified.

Work through the President's Committee on Equal Employment Opportunity to seek assistance with employment from public and private agencies.

Aggressively seek out more qualified minority candidates to increase the number of employees in many job categories, including but not limited to design engineers, mathematicians, associate engineers, draftsmen, computer technicians, tabulating analysts, accountants and buyers, stenographers, typists, duplicating operators, machine operators, and assemblers.[18]

- *Corporate management agreed to:*

Distribute an up-to-date antidiscrimination policy signed by the president of the company and to assign responsibility for making progress. Require subsidiaries and divisions to issue plans to implement policies. Publicize the policies in company news publications.

Analyze all of its salaried job openings to see whether any current minority employees were eligible for promotion. Re-examine the records of minority employees to ensure that their skill and potential have been identified.

Include qualified minority group trainees in its apprenticeship programs.

Review transfer, layoff, and other termination practices to ensure they are nondiscriminatory.

Enforce nonsegregated facilities.

Make periodic checks to ensure that policy and objectives are being carried out.

Provide statistical data on the race and occupation of its personnel and answer questions on its employment policies and practices.

Report difficulties to the Committee in achieving its Plan for Progress.

- *The corporation agreed to review its plan with the Committee annually, knowing that it may need to amend it to reach equal employment opportunity faster.*

The contract stipulated, in the annual review of this plan, "it is not intended that specific numerical targets or goals be set. Nonetheless, it is intended that evaluation be made, in part, in terms of increases in the numbers of minority persons hired, promoted, involved in training, and occupying responsible positions within the Corporation."[19]

- *The President's Committee on Equal Employment Opportunity agreed to:*

Request the Department of Labor to assign personnel to work with the State Employment agencies to intensify efforts to refer applicants to Lockheed without regard to "race, creed, color, or national origin."

Solicit help from specialized community agencies to assist recruiting efforts under the Plan for Progress.

Request the Department of Labor's Bureau of Apprenticeship and Training to assist in the training of applicants without regard to race, creed, color, or national origin.

Request the Department of Health, Education and Welfare to assign personnel to encourage minority students to participate in its vocational programs. It would be asked to develop new programs to encourage cooperation between schools and employers. It would review, encourage, and strengthen guidance counseling in schools.

Work with the International Association of Machinists and other appropriate unions to review and support apprenticeship training, transfer procedures, and seniority rights.

Collaborate with the Department of the Air Force and other contracting agencies to assist Lockheed on its follow-through.

Lockheed's Plan for Progress formed the boilerplate for all future Plans for Progress contracts. It launched a new relationship between business and government in which the government inserts rules into companies' hiring, training, and promotion processes. It essentially changed the nature of how companies contracted with individuals. They could no longer contract with those whose skin color they preferred but were forced to open the process to other contenders.

As soon as the Plan went into effect, things at Lockheed-Georgia began to change. In the spring of 1961, managers began reviewing the files of 545 employees to study their educational backgrounds to see whether they might be eligible for other jobs at the plant. It went through its list of employees and began upgrading blacks who had the education or qualifications to do higher-ranked jobs. The company launched a nationwide search for black professionals. It hired a black engineer and offered to 12 other black candidates positions ranging from operations research analyst to aircraft field-service instructor. Lockheed reached out to all of Atlanta's black high schools and encouraged them to apply for entrance into its four-year apprenticeship for skilled mechanics and electronics experts. The company enlisted the help of black colleges and universities, professional organizations, and civic societies to find qualified employees.[20]

People in the community found it hard to believe Lockheed's newfound religion. Black high school students didn't exactly rush into the apprentice program because they found it too "fantastic" that the company would offer good jobs to blacks.[21]

The NAACP continued its pressure, saying it would not be satisfied with tokenism and wanted to see the total disappearance of racial barriers. Although the plant was trying to move blacks out of low-paying and low-skilled jobs, half of the blacks employed at the plant worked in the semiskilled job of assembler. Still, small changes created some hope for advancement. Willie J. Smith, who had only two years of high school, was working as a janitor at the plant, but he spent his own time learning how to operate the business machines in the tabulating department. When a clerk's position opened, he applied for the job and got it. Smith traded his mop for a machine when he became a data entry clerk.[22]

One Man's Story

In 1951, when Charles Ferguson, who is African American, applied for work at Lockheed in Marietta, just two jobs at the plant were reserved for blacks only: groundskeeper and janitor. Even though Ferguson had attended one year of college, he became a groundskeeper. As the company gradually opened up more jobs to blacks in the mid-1950s, he seized the opportunity to expand his career beyond a laborer's mind-numbing, menial tasks. Ferguson applied for training as a riveter, attended classes, passed the exam, and began refurbishing B-47s. Then he applied for and received an upgrade as a structural assembler.

He became one of the plant's first black supervisors, but he was allowed to supervise only other blacks. When segregation ended overnight in 1961, under its Plan for Progress, Lockheed-Georgia had to create a single job ladder that opened up training and opportunities to everyone.

Ferguson made a big play to advance. He applied to become an electrical installer, took a mathematics course with a professor from Georgia Tech, earned an A, and began to translate engineers' drawings of electrical systems into the complex wiring systems to fit inside aircraft.

Although Ferguson's career was suddenly on the move, integration wasn't always easy, especially at lunchtime. "If you would come in and sit down by a white person they would get up and move, go somewhere else," said Ferguson. "The image of the blacks that was planted was the hurtfulest [sic] thing. They would say you were no-good, a low person."[23]

After the water fountains were integrated, cups were placed at the drinking facilities to ward off any complaints of having to share. Pretty soon, 63,000 paper cups per day were being used, causing a headache and expense to replace and stock them.[24] "The blacks would go around and dump out the cups out of the container to make sure that [the whites] couldn't drink water," said Ferguson. "If they had no cup [they] had to drink from the fountain straight."[25]

Some white workers refused to share the bathrooms. "There were many white males that would not go into the integrated bathroom," he said. "I don't know how they did it, they would hold their water or something, but they wouldn't use the restroom."[26]

Advancing his career took persistence and vigilance. At one point, Ferguson had to go to the government office at the plant to make sure Lockheed followed the new rules. When he wanted to enroll in a class to become a development mechanic, an administrator claimed he could not find the entrance exam that Ferguson had taken to qualify. The administrator said the class, which had filled with 10 white students, had progressed too far for Ferguson to catch up. Ferguson went to the Equal Employment Opportunity office located at the plant and filed a complaint. Suddenly, his records were found, and he was allowed to enroll in the course.

On his second day of class, he ate his lunch at his desk, and none of the white students came back in the classroom to join him. He offered to leave so they could eat lunch together. Ferguson said they felt so ashamed of themselves for avoiding him that they asked him to join them in lunch the next day.

Once blacks and whites were learning together, working together, and eating together, the cold war began to thaw. "They found out that you weren't such a bad fellow after all," he said.[27]

As the result of Lockheed's Plan for Progress, Ferguson moved into complex electrical installations. He became one of the company's first black supervisors to manage both white and black employees, installing 30,000 wires of an all-weather landing system in one plane at a time. "I would keep up with the development of the airplane, the new systems of the airplane, and that made my job right easy," he said.[28]

Government Had Its Own Integration Problems

Lockheed was able to respond quickly to the government's demands because it knew how to integrate. In response to Roosevelt's Fair Employment Practices Committee (FEPC) in 1941, Lockheed-California had hired 350 skilled and semi-skilled black workers.[29] By 1953, the Burbank plant, which built the Neptune antisubmarine warplane, was fully integrated, and 8 percent of its engineers were black.[30]

That Lockheed would allow its Georgia facility to remain segregated seems strange, because the company was advanced in almost every other aspect of its business. By 1960, Lockheed had successfully launched the Polaris ballistic missile from a submarine and had put nine Agena space vehicles into orbit. It was already developing the Minuteman missile programs, an intercontinental ballistic missile that could be launched from underground silos. These programs were seen as critical to the nation's defense during the Cold

War. Lockheed designed and manufactured equipment that was essential to the country's arms and space race. The government should have used the power of the purse to insist that the company closely follow its rules, but before 1961, no government official had threatened to cancel a contract at Lockheed-Georgia. "The facility was completely owned by the federal government," said Feild, "and from its entire beginning had done nothing but make only government airplanes."[31]

In 1961, government and industry mirrored one another. Government agencies, like government contractors, frequently kept their black employees confined to menial, low-skilled jobs located in segregated offices. The Department of Labor had no black employees south of the Potomac and very few north of the Potomac.[32] No significant progress could be made on civil rights until the largest employer in the Western world—the U.S. government—got its own house in order. It had a federal workforce of two and a quarter million people.

Integration did not go any smoother for the government. When the Atlanta office of the Bureau of Labor Statistics (BLS) wanted to hire a young black woman to work as a statistical clerk, the head of the office had to get permission from the building owner for the black woman to enter. She received permission, and a torrent of other problems followed. The white women in the BLS refused to work with the new clerk. The office manager told them they could resign if they wished. The employees used the same restroom as the employees of an insurance company. On one occasion, a white insurance employee cursed at the black clerk for using the restroom. The office manager told the black employee to use the restroom on the main floor, but the room was frequently locked because the janitor was sleeping there. The BLS finally got the landlord to declare that the restroom on the seventh floor would be integrated.[33]

By the end of May, Lockheed Aircraft Corporation had done everything the Committee had requested. The company's president, Courtlandt Gross, was invited to the White House to publicize Lockheed's agreement to give Negroes, as they were called at the time, equal opportunity to gain employment and to be trained and promoted to higher-paying jobs across the company, which employed 60,000 people. It was a highly visible event that sought to act as a model for other companies to follow Lockheed's example and to counter the negative publicity raised by the NAACP.

"The president called it the best thing since sliced bread," said Feild.

The Reality of Change Must Accompany the Rhetoric of Change

4

C OMPANIES GET INTO TROUBLE WHEN THEY PROFESS ONE idea but act in a contradictory manner. Lockheed's black employees knew the company had signed an equal opportunity employment agreement with the U.S. government and did not like being denied equal opportunity. Merck's employees, shareholders, and members of the community rose up in the late 1990s to tell the firm that they did not believe the company, which professed to behaving ethically, had been fair to African American employees. Congruence—when leaders make their actions consistent with their words—is very important to the credibility and success of any program or organization.

Contradictory messages also threatened the very existence of Plans for Progress. In his public statements, President Kennedy had described Plans for Progress as voluntary in order to encourage other companies to take up the civil rights cause. It would be an easy, face-saving means for companies to appear that they were leading the way instead of being dragged along. He enlisted Robert Troutman, Jr., to join the President's Committee on Equal Employment Opportunity to help persuade Southern businesses that integration would be a positive step forward. Troutman was far from radical, or even progressive. And it may seem strange that he would even be on the President's Committee, except that President Kennedy wanted him there. He was a friend of the family.

Troutman, Jr., had grown up in Atlanta, the son of a lawyer who had worked as general counsel for Coca-Cola and other prominent businesses. When Troutman, Jr., attended Harvard Law School, he met Joseph P. Kennedy, Jr., who invited him to the family home on Cape Cod where Troutman reveled in the rambunctious sports and intellectual jousting of the Kennedy clan. After Joe was killed in a wartime plane explosion in 1944, Troutman was one of Joe's few friends who could attend the funeral because he could not fight in World War II due to the loss of a kidney when he was a teenager.[1] Troutman stayed in touch with John Kennedy, visiting him in Washington after Kennedy became a congressman and senator. When Kennedy ran for president, he relied on Troutman to use his political contacts with white Southerners to develop support for Kennedy in Georgia and across the South.

Troutman was also a friend and supporter of Herman Talmadge, a U.S. senator who had also served as Georgia's governor. Talmadge was an avowed racial segregationist who opposed civil rights, and Troutman shared many of Talmadge's beliefs. When Troutman learned that Kennedy wanted to speak to the followers of Martin Luther King, Jr., so that King would endorse him for president, Troutman told the candidate that he would no longer support him if he did that. "It was beneath his dignity," said Troutman.[2] Kennedy did not address King's followers on that occasion, explaining his absence as a scheduling conflict.

After Kennedy was elected president, Troutman visited him in Palm Beach, and Kennedy asked him to join the Committee on Equal Employment Opportunity because he wanted the perspective of a "middle-of-the-road Southerner." Troutman didn't want to move to Washington, and he thought affirmative action was too controversial. He asked his friend, Senator Talmadge, what he should do. Talmadge said it would be impossible for Troutman to satisfy either group. "The Negros will not appreciate what you do if you beat your brains out, and instead, the whites will feel that you are tainted for one reason or another for having gotten into it," said Talmadge.[3]

Vice President Lyndon Johnson also pressed him to serve on the Committee, but Troutman wanted to carve out a middle ground. He decided to volunteer for the Committee, putting up $35,000 of his own money for an office and expenses in Atlanta.[4]

Since the Supreme Court's 1954 decision, in *Brown v. the Board of Education,* which declared that segregated public schools were unconstitutional, the civil rights movement had expanded from its focus on integrating schools to integrating businesses. Atlanta, less than 20 miles from Lockheed's Marietta plant, was the home of Martin Luther King, Jr., and the epicenter of the nonviolent civil rights movement. In 1960, Atlanta had been getting nonstop national media coverage as students of all colors had been going through a series of sit-ins against white merchants who had failed to desegregate lunch counters, restrooms, changing rooms, and other store facilities.

Rich's department stores, the leading regional chain in the country, became a target of the protestors. The downtown store, an elegant, old, four-story building, was picketed by 20 college students carrying signs that denounced the segregation of its dressing rooms, its tea room, and its restrooms.[5] In addition, the family-owned business employed only whites. A group of young people claiming to represent 4,000 students from a local black college began to call for an economic boycott of the store, urging equal rights advocates to engage in a "selective buying" campaign.[6]

In response, a group of white Klansmen marched around the outside of Rich's in support of segregation. One of the signs they carried read, "We will not accept race-mixing in Atlanta."[7] Martin Luther King, Jr., head of the Southern Christian Leadership Conference (SCLC), was arrested during a sit-in when he refused to leave the Magnolia tearoom, which served only whites. Because King had already incurred a suspended sentence from a previous arrest, the judge denied him bail and sentenced him to four months of hard labor in a maximum security prison.[8]

While King served the harsh sentence, the sit-ins continued without him. Rich's department store tried to shoo away the protestors by boarding up the Magnolia tearoom and other cafes, replacing them with vending machines. But many regular customers also stayed away, either because they sympathized with the students or believed in racial segregation or because they were afraid of getting caught up in the potentially explosive atmosphere. As a result, the Christmas shopping season was ruined. Atlanta attracted nonstop media coverage as a segregationist tinderbox.

Robert Troutman, Sr., was the attorney for Rich's department store. A prominent black attorney, A. T. Walden, approached Troutman, Sr., about resolving the impasse. Together they contacted Ivan Allen, Jr., the new leader of Atlanta's Chamber of Commerce, who said the "national publicity was running us crazy" and jeopardizing the city's reputation. Allen met with white business leaders, who reached a consensus.

"Go ahead, work something out, get us off the hook, even if it means desegregating the stores," said Allen.[9] Black and white adult leaders agreed that the businesses would desegregate their facilities in September 1961, within 30 days of the schools being desegregated.

The student protestors initially rejected the agreement because it did not move quickly enough, but Martin Luther King, Jr., prevailed upon them to accept their leaders' agreement and stressed that the movement had to remain united. He characterized the agreement as "the first written contract" for desegregation to which Atlanta's white leadership had ever committed. "If this contract is broken, it will be a disaster and a disgrace," said King. "If anyone breaks this contract, let it be the white man."[10]

Trying to Expand the Plans for Progress

The Jim Crow South that had created a second-class group of citizens was rapidly coming to an end. No one recognized this more than Robert Troutman, Jr., the son of the attorney who had helped broker the deal on behalf of Rich's department store. Troutman, Jr., had accompanied John Feild on his expeditions to Lockheed and witnessed how the Plan for Progress had enabled the manufacturer to look better than the companies that were being picketed. "Why don't we go to all the rest of these aircraft manufacturers?" Troutman, Jr., asked Feild.[11]

Both men saw the opportunity to accelerate compliance with the executive order by approaching contractors and persuading them to sign a Plan for Progress instead of sitting back and waiting for complaints and bad publicity to roll in against them. Yet the men formed an odd couple. Feild, a

Northern liberal who had helped organize the black vote for Kennedy, paired up with Troutman, who had organized the white Southern vote for Kennedy.

After the Lockheed integration went smoothly, Troutman took up the Plans for Progress as an evangelical cause. He liked the concept because it made the changes sound like they were the companies' idea. He believed that desegregation had to be voluntary, not too radical, so that employees and communities could get used to integration. He also claimed, as a lawyer, he could see ways to get around the executive order if it were made compulsory.[12]

Most of the military contractors were based in the South and brought huge investment and increasingly sophisticated industry to the region. Troutman, Jr., wanted to demonstrate "that he was successful in defending the interests of Atlanta and Georgia, and of southern-based military contractors," said Feild. "He wanted to convert an apparent defeat into a blazing victory."[13]

By the summer of 1961, Troutman, Jr., and John Feild had persuaded eight more of the nation's largest contractors, employing more than 760,000 people, to sign Plans for Progress. The presidents of Boeing, Douglas Aircraft, General Electric, Martin, North American Aviation, Radio Corporation of America, United Aircraft, and Western Electric gathered at the White House in July 1961 for a big publicity event. President Kennedy touted it as an historic step forward to secure equal employment opportunity for every American.[14]

At the meeting, Vice President Johnson stressed that each company had developed its own plan voluntarily and independently with the Committee. Unfortunately, for some audiences, the word *voluntarily* carried with it the disappointment of decades of unfulfilled promises when previous executive orders were not well enforced. Although Johnson used the word to encourage other companies to plunge into affirmative action, it signaled a different meaning to civil rights groups that had labored for decades to end discrimination. To them it meant that companies would engage in a lot of hoopla, pretending to do something, while doing little or nothing at all. The NAACP remained suspicious of the plan. Herbert Hill, the organization's lawyer, told John Feild he thought Plans for Progress was nothing more than public relations.

By the fall of 1961, civil rights protestors had extended their sit-ins at restaurants to kneel-ins at churches, stand-ins at theaters, and protests of hotels that would not accept black customers. At the time, it was very difficult for black travelers to find decent places to stay in the South. Even Willie Mays, the outstanding black baseball player, had to stay in a different hotel than his white San Francisco Giant teammates when they played in the South.

In November 1961, Robert Troutman, Jr., sponsored a dinner at the whites-only Dinkler-Plaza Hotel in Atlanta to honor Senator Richard Russell and Representative Carl Vinson, who were both Democrats and chairmen of the powerful Senate and House Armed Services Committees, respectively. Secretary of Defense Robert McNamara, the featured speaker, addressed 1,300 members of the white Southern power elite, including Senator Herman Talmadge, the avowed segregationist.

Protestors picketed Secretary McNamara's arrival at the airport. His plane changed gates to avoid the picketers, and then he pretended not to see them when he entered the airport. Demonstrators gathered outside the Dinkler-Plaza to denounce the all-white event. When Troutman was asked by a reporter about the dinner, he replied in a very haughty tone:

"To me it is the height of rudeness and bad judgment for anyone, knowing that an occasion is social and private, to seek to force his presence without an invitation."[15] Outside the hotel, a tense standoff developed between protestors from the NAACP and three white separatist groups who called for President Kennedy's resignation.

Troutman failed to grasp the essential notion that hosting an all-white political dinner at an all-white hotel contradicted Kennedy's public stand on civil rights. His defense of the segregated evening was unseemly for a man who was supposed to be the face of affirmative action in Atlanta. Troutman's and McNamara's responses to criticism made them look like hypocrites on integration and sullied the hard work of the President's Committee on Equal Employment Opportunity.

Suspicion of Troutman continued, partly because his name was linked to the proposed desegregation of Atlanta's businesses that his father helped broker. Atlanta businesses were supposed to desegregate after the schools did, but many still had not done so when Troutman, Jr., received publicity for his all-white dinner at the whites-only hotel.

John Feild felt frustrated with Troutman. He had seen him negotiate seriously with the companies. But then Troutman would undercut the public's faith in the Committee with his political activities. "Troutman was very difficult to work with. He was a deeply Southern man who was not fully involved in speeding up the process," said Marilyn Feild, John's wife. "He was a headache to John."[16]

Yet President Kennedy had created this situation by recruiting Troutman for the President's Committee. Kennedy used the same poor recruiting practices as many companies did. In that era and well before then, many companies had relied on their executives' personal networks to find managers. They had sought recommendations from current workers about whom to hire, instead of engaging in an objective and comprehensive search. As a result, their labor forces often shared the same complexion and socioeconomic background. Managers had often been nepotistic, hiring family members into significant positions. Kennedy had recruited his own family members to work on his political campaigns. His mother and sisters sponsored tea parties for voters. He relied on his brother, Robert F. Kennedy, to direct his campaign and then made him U.S. attorney general. Kennedy made use of family contacts and the old boys' network. The president wanted Troutman to provide the perspective of a white Southerner on employment reform, but he did not conduct a wide search to find someone who was experienced in personnel practices.

Kennedy's use of Troutman on the President's Committee on Equal Employment Opportunity also reflected the president's mixed feelings about increased integration. President Kennedy was not deeply committed to civil rights when John Feild began to work on the campaign in 1959. "He did not feel this issue sharply; he did not have great pressures on him from his own constituency; he was very quick to say so," said Feild. Kennedy was generally sympathetic to the plight of black Americans but unprepared to make an extensive commitment.[17] Essentially, Kennedy was trying to keep white Southerners happy in order to get reelected, while learning on the job about the pent-up demand for full civil rights from blacks.

As Troutman raced around, signing up new companies for Plans for Progress, he developed the belief that the Committee no longer needed its million-dollar budget to enforce compliance. He felt the government could simply trust the companies to follow through on their agreements. Troutman made an impassioned speech before the Committee. "He was horrified about that million-dollar budget," said John Feild. "He didn't want that budget, didn't want to spend the taxpayers' money; and he didn't like all this business of regulation, and he didn't think anybody else in business liked it either; and that, therefore, what we ought to do is have this great Plan for Progress program, and let's not worry too much about all those regulations, all these forms and everything."[18]

Feild pushed back immediately and told Troutman it would be both: voluntary and compulsory. Feild had far more experience getting companies to comply with fair employment practices than Troutman had, and he knew that companies would simply carry on as usual without enforcement. Companies thought they knew how to integrate, Feild said, but really they had to be taught.

As Troutman's associations and beliefs became public, suspicion over Plans for Progress increased, even among members of the President's Committee. John Wheeler, a voluntary member of the Committee who was president of Mechanics Bank in Durham, North Carolina, the fourth largest African American bank in the country, raised concern that the Plans for Progress might be seen as voluntary, not compulsory.[19] He expressed fear that companies would be able to sign a Plan for Progress and then be inoculated against enforcement of the executive order. Wheeler, who was black, deepened the suspicion among Committee members that Robert Troutman, Jr., could not be trusted. He told the Committee that Troutman had a reputation for getting inside organizations and corrupting them from within. Apparently, Wheeler had confused the actions of Troutman, Jr., with those of Troutman, Sr., at Rich's department store and the delay of integration of

Atlanta's businesses. The NAACP's Herbert Hill had already criticized Troutman as a phony.

The Plans for Progress program came under intense scrutiny. Wheeler encouraged the Committee to commission a study on the efficacy of the program, which would take more than a year to complete.[20] "I was put under some suspicion because I had the appearance, the public appearance, of being Troutman's buddy-buddy," said Feild. "I mean, I was going everywhere with Troutman, I was visiting him in his home, I was going to his riding club down there in Atlanta with him for dinner parties, and I was going all over the country with the son of a bitch. So they wanted to check up, did I make any deals with any of these damned employers? Here I am the hard-line bastard!"[21]

John Feild: Dedicated to Advancing Race Relations

In fact, Feild was the most experienced person assigned full time to the President's Committee. He had led a life of congruent dedication to improving race relations. Feild's family had made the great migration North, away from the cotton plantation his great grandfather had owned, to the land of industry where jobs were plentiful. Feild was born in Little Rock, Arkansas, in 1923, and the next year his family moved to a working-class community in Detroit. His parents were not well educated. His mother was a hairdresser and homemaker. His father worked in the auto industry.[22]

On a break from college in the summer of 1942, Feild himself briefly joined the auto industry when he was hired at the immense River Rouge plant at Ford Motor Company. As a condition of employment, he had to join the United Auto Worker's union, Local 600, whose leadership wanted the company to increase its hiring of black workers. Feild quickly came to understand employment issues from their perspective. He had grown up listening to his father discussing the need for more worker safety protections. That summer, however, Feild did not work on the assembly line. Instead, he assisted the plant's head of production.[23]

By the time it was finished in 1928, the Rouge plant stretched for more than one and a half miles—the largest integrated factory in the world. As an assistant to the production supervisor, Feild would drive around the factory in a station wagon, spot-checking production sites to make sure they were on schedule and not holding up the elaborate production line. He was fascinated by the complex assembly process. His supervisor encouraged him to stay and forego college, arguing that working at the plant would provide a better future than getting an education.

Although Feild loved the character and kinetic energy of the plant and was tempted to stay, he chose a different path than his father had taken. He wanted to teach English at the college level. He returned to what was then Wayne University (later becoming Wayne State University), an urban research university located in the heart of Detroit that was partly funded by the auto barons who had helped convert Detroit into a thriving metropolis with smooth, wide roads and beautiful architecture. The school was the center of the city's cultural events and a hub of political ferment. It reveled in radical thought, like a Midwestern version of the City College of New York. There he met his wife, Marilyn Smith, who, like Feild, was an only child and had been raised Catholic.[24]

But the script he had imagined for his life of being a college professor was suddenly interrupted when Feild was called to active duty in World War II in April 1943. He spent the next two years abroad, mainly on an airbase in Kunming, China, getting a separate education on the power of the U.S. military. He served as a cryptographer for the Flying Tigers, the 14th Air Force, under the leadership of Brigadier General Claire Chennault, whose goal during the war was to destroy the Japanese military.

After the war, while Feild waited six weeks in India for a troop ship to return him to the States, he got his chance to become an English teacher. He volunteered at the University of Calcutta and received in return a broad cultural education about Hinduism and Islam from his students. Feild, whose family was Scots-English and Italian, came to see diversity at work in a country that was totally different from the United States. He saw the power of a people in seeking self-determination through widespread civil disobedience toward the government, long before the civil rights movement gained momentum in America.

In India, he watched a country of millions mourn peacefully the death of Kasturbai Gandhi, the wife of Mohandas Gandhi. The Gandhis had been imprisoned for their activities in the Indian independence movement. Mohandas, a proponent of nonviolent protest and civil disobedience, had led a campaign called "Quit India" that called for the British to leave India. Gandhi had refused to help defend Britain from attacks by Nazi Germany unless it granted India independence. For this, Gandhi and the entire Congress Working Committee were arrested. His wife, Kasturbai, died after being imprisoned for 18 months. Mohandas, who was also in jail at the time, was briefly released and allowed to speak at her funeral.[25]

Fearing a possible uprising if the Indians were denied public mourning, the British military erected a funeral pyre. They also connected 100 loudspeakers across a large plain outside Calcutta to a small speaker's stand near the pyre. Feild watched a large military presence surround the area while more than a million mourners quietly filled the space. Mohandas spoke briefly, but his followers spoke volumes, as their acclaim for him lasted for more than an hour. Then the prisoner and widower, Mohandas Gandhi, was returned to jail.[26]

In his two years abroad, Feild came to understand the human struggle against a broad canvas of different cultures, classes, and religions. He returned to Detroit with a more detailed vision of the world that expanded far beyond the city's frequent black-white polarization. Feild resumed his courses at Wayne University where he received a BA in English. Yet, after graduation, he did not pursue an advanced degree. Instead, he used the knowledge he had gained from his experience in private industry, the military, and his interactions abroad to get people with different backgrounds to accept one another. He felt very optimistic that, through persuasion, people would ultimately agree to work together. His positive outlook and his broad experience with different cultures gave him confidence in operating among different races and organizations.[27]

In 1947, at the age of 24, he became the director of the Mayor's Interracial Committee in Detroit where he investigated allegations of police brutality, helped resolve disputes as blacks moved into white neighborhoods, and worked to eliminate public segregation. After five years of helping to promote racial harmony in Detroit, Feild took a new job as the executive secretary for the Toledo Board of Community relations in Ohio. In 1952, public housing was still racially segregated in the Northern industrial city.

Feild mobilized a group of community leaders from many different sectors of society, including the publisher of *The Toledo Blade* newspaper, to pressure the city council to abolish segregation in the city's public housing projects. As the city council was scheduled to vote on desegregation, Feild got word that whites planned to protest against the ordinance on the day of the vote. To head off the protest, he persuaded the mayor to sponsor a lunch the day before the vote with Ralph Bunche as the keynote speaker. Bunche, who had been awarded the Nobel Peace Prize in 1950, spoke to the group about how racial prejudice had no scientific basis and how segregation was incompatible with democracy. At the time, blacks represented only 10 percent of the Toledo population. But on the day of the vote, more black protestors turned out than white protestors, and the city council voted to desegregate Toledo's public housing. Two years later, in 1955, Feild put together a fair employment practices ordinance, which passed unanimously.[28]

By the time he was 35, Feild had been made executive director of the Michigan Fair Employment Practices Commission (FEPC). Michigan was the tenth state to create a commission modeled on President Franklin Roosevelt's FEPC in 1941.[29] However, Michigan gave its commission more power than the others, including the power to remedy an unfair employment practice. It narrowly defined affirmative action as "hiring, restoring or upgrading employees with or without back pay."[30]

In this job, Feild investigated complaints of discrimination by job applicants and persuaded the affected companies to take affirmative action to remedy the complaint. He flew to

New York and asked the personnel director of American Airlines why he had refused to hire a black applicant to be a stewardess (now called a flight attendant) in Detroit. Feild warned the personnel director that, if the airline was found to have discriminatory practices, he would issue a corrective order. The personnel director relented, and the applicant became a ticket agent at the airline's downtown Detroit ticket office—a breakthrough. (The applicant was considered to be a flight attendant, but her medical exam revealed she had sickle cell anemia, which can cause blackouts at high altitudes. Instead, she was hired to sell plane tickets.)[31]

As part of his work for the commission, Feild also handled two complaints from other applicants who went on to become the first black flight attendants for Northwest and Trans World Airlines. As a result of Feild's intervention, a former Air Force pilot became the first black pilot to fly a corporate aircraft, after he was first refused but later hired by General Motors Executive Air Service.[32]

With the threat of issuing a corrective order, Feild was able to convince companies to hire minorities, and he felt increasingly successful doing it. Yet he was troubled by his ongoing interaction with General Motors, especially its headquarters—a huge building that occupied an entire block of downtown Detroit, where five thousand employees would come and go every day. "There were exactly two blacks in that whole building, one maid and one janitor. That was the real world out there," said Feild. "That was Detroit, Michigan, 1958."[33]

He wanted to work with employers such as General Motors on how to change their personnel practices, to eliminate exclusionary practices, and to unbar the door to people of color. "I was an advocate of a policy that would be affirmative—I invented the word affirmative action, by the way," he told an interviewer as part of an oral history project for the LBJ Library in 1984.[34]

Feild did not invent the phrase "affirmative action," which dates back to at least the nineteenth century and was used to describe positive action taken by a legislative body such as passing a bill. However, he did develop the contemporary definition of affirmative action as preventing discrimination. The Michigan FEPC act empowered the commission to *prevent* unfair employment practices through informal persuasion and conciliation. In this broad gray area, Feild later came to include as part of affirmative action that the government would require companies to actively prevent and eliminate discrimination in employment. In other words, companies had to do more than just hang Equal Employment Opportunity signs on their walls and then respond to complaints from employees or job applicants, as they had done in the past.

Breaking Down the Status Quo

For discrimination to be prevented, the casual hiring procedures of the status quo had to be changed. At the time, foremen commonly hired factory workers based on referrals from current workers. Information about job openings radiated out to the community through the employees, who passed it along to family members and friends. As a result, members of the same race, religion, and class tended to find out about the job openings and be hired. Thus, foremen hired from their own networks and their workers' networks.

If companies advertised for jobs, they specified the color and gender. Adverts titled "White Male Wanted" and "Negro Female Wanted" routinely appeared in prominent newspapers throughout the mid-1960s. Feild was focused on this crucial nexus—the hiring point, the entry to employment. He was growing aware that government needed to be able to advise companies on how to reform their practices in order to prevent and eliminate discrimination at the door.

Feild had spent years developing his expertise in this new and burgeoning area of equal opportunity. He had volunteered his time and expertise to the National Association of Intergroup Relations Officials (NAIRO). This organization was founded in 1947 by government officials, academicians, employment directors, journalists, and others who wanted to develop their knowledge and skill in working with different religious, ethnic, and racial groups. Members focused on very specific problems faced by a multifaceted society: the "problems of Negroes, Jews, Orientals, Puerto Ricans, Mexican Americans, and others facing discrimination or segregation; cultural problems faced by American Indians, Southern Mountain Whites." Other areas of interest were tensions arising out of church-state issues, the denial of civil rights to the foreign-born and migrant farm laborers, and the problems of the aged in employment discrimination.[35] Feild served as secretary for NAIRO for three years and as executive director for one year.

He also contributed several articles to the *Journal of Intergroup Relations*, which he and the other founders of NAIRO helped start. The journal enabled professionals to share their experiences, research, analysis, and opinions with one another to improve their understanding about working with different groups. The articles grappled with what would now be characterized as diversity issues: how Puerto Ricans were adjusting to living in New York City, how to handle bigotry, the observance of Christmas and Hanukkah in the public schools, how the nonwhite population was growing faster than the white population. The authors of the articles understood that many groups, not only blacks, struggled to find equal acceptance in American life. These so-called intergroup specialists were the first generation of professionals to invent the mechanics of equal opportunity through the lens of diversity. They wrote about *difference* 30 years before Justice Lewis Powell used *diversity* in his opinion in the *Bakke* case, and 40 years before R. Roosevelt Thomas popularized *diversity* as an employment strategy in his groundbreaking 1991 article in the *Harvard Business Review.*

Articles in the *Journal of Intergroup Relations* grappled with the issue of how to get companies to hire blacks and even explored the pros and cons of using quotas. In an article published in 1960, Dan W. Dodson, who was director of the Center for Human Relations and Community Studies at New York University, cautioned that it was difficult to get the proportionality of imposing quotas correct so that "one group does not constitute a threat to the other."[36] Dodson advocated following the "due regard for race or creed," but did not want it "to be used as an excuse to resort to the preferential treatment of people because of race, creed or color." The article is prescient in its anticipation of the controversies that would not emerge in mainstream America until nearly two decades later.[37]

In 1960, about 600 agencies throughout the nation employed about 1,500 intergroup relations officials. They worked in municipal offices, on redevelopment boards, in state FEP commissions, and on community relations boards. They were from the American Civil Liberties Union, the American Friends Service Committee, the Jewish Labor Committee, the Urban League, and the NAACP. Although the field was small, it was growing at a rate of 50 to 100 people each year. It was comprised of lawyers, social science researchers, journalists, community organizers, and adult educators.[38]

In an article written in 1960, Feild himself noted the incredible range of different specialists working in intergroup occupations. "We have reached that stage in this business where formal training and recognized standards of training and experience in dealing with problems of group relations is inevitable," he wrote. He called for the professionalization of the intergroup officials to advance "the attainment of individual freedom, on the one hand, and the acceptance of diverse group loyalties on the other."[39]

In another article, he scolded the intergroup specialists, expressing dissatisfaction that, after 10 years, the group still had not distilled a set of principles to be followed. "We have yet to evaluate whether one method is better than another, whether one program is better than another," he wrote. "We have very few standards of evaluating whether or not we are applying the knowledge that we have garnered about the kind of society that we are in such a way that it will affect that society."[40]

From his writings at the time and his later interviews, it is clear that Feild was searching for a protocol, a set of procedures that employers could follow to include nonwhites in the workplace. He begins to associate the prevention of exclusion with affirmative action. He starts to see himself and others in the field as specialists who could advance this change. In one article, he noted the emergence of an "intergroup professional," and he encouraged increased specialization of those who were working with different groups to become a professional group. He imagined that these groups could spread systemic change among employers far beyond the Michigan state border.

Brought to the Big Time

Feild needed to step onto the national stage in order to advance his vision. In 1958, while he was head of the Michigan FEPC, Feild campaigned for Phil Hart, a Democrat who was running for the U.S. Senate. After Hart was elected, he asked Feild to join him in Washington to serve as his administrative assistant. Shortly thereafter, in 1959, Hart loaned Feild to the John F. Kennedy presidential campaign where he advised the candidate on civil rights issues and was later tapped to help integrate businesses.[41]

As Feild, who was more experienced in changing employment practices than many of the other Committee members, kept trying to teach them the most successful process of integration, the tension on the President's Committee on Equal Opportunity became unbearable at times. Civil rights advocates expected widespread integration to happen overnight. President Kennedy and Vice President Johnson were eager to find out how the companies were progressing with affirmative action. They kept calling for the numbers. At the beginning of the program, they asked for new employee censuses to be taken in three months, then six months, then nine months, as if they expected immediate transformation. The fact was that the workforces of some of these companies were so large and so predominantly white that even the new hiring of hundreds of new nonwhite employees did not represent a significant percentage increase in overall minority representation.

At press conferences, however, Johnson would tout the statistical increase. The Committee engaged in a lot of statistical smoke and mirrors to make the effort appear successful. But in private they argued about how to make the companies comply. John Feild wanted the government to delay and to suspend

President Johnson, left, greets John Feild (tall and center with glasses) and other civil
rights advocates (ca. 1964).
(Courtesy Marilyn Feild.)

the contracts with the companies. Troutman trusted the companies to do the hiring without penalty. Feild frequently went
home at night with a headache.

The New York Times got word of their divisions and published a story on the front page just one year into the Plans for
Progress program. In the story, Troutman was quoted as saying that integrating restrooms and cafeterias in the workplace
was "not worth the fuss" as required by Feild's program but
rather that jobs were paramount. Troutman claimed that 2,000
"Negroes" had received jobs as the result of Plans for Progress. He suggested the program be turned over to a council of
business executives to run, instead of keeping it with the U.S.
government. In reference to the claims of racial discrimination
that were filed by employees against the companies, he called

them unfair harassment. Feild's office had received 850 discrimination complaints in just one year.[42]

Troutman's statements undermined the credibility and work of the President's Committee. The article exposed the Committee's lack of consistency toward the companies in expectation and raised suspicion about enforcement. Vice President Johnson encouraged the president to fire Troutman. "You're going to have all kinds of heat every day you wait," warned Johnson, who desperately wanted to revamp the Committee.[43]

President Kennedy agreed that Troutman seemed to stir up controversy with whatever he did. But he had been reluctant to reign in Troutman because he was a friend of the family. Troutman, a flamboyant, energetic man who rarely slept, was always turning up wherever the president or his brother Bobby went, on planes or trips. He ingratiated himself with the Kennedys.

Johnson wanted to get rid of Troutman. In his place and in charge of the Committee, Johnson wanted to put Hobart Taylor, Jr., a black lawyer who had been born in Texas but who had most recently lived in Michigan. Taylor, Jr., "was born in the South and he's the ablest man they got and he deals with them all satisfactorily," Johnson told the president.[44] Kennedy worried about the political ramifications of firing a white Southerner and promoting a black Northerner on the same day. He wanted an interval of time before Taylor was named. Johnson did not think Southerners would object to a black man succeeding a white man because the black man ostensibly was not Southern, but from Wayne County, Michigan. But Kennedy seemed to worry that it would not sit well with white voters to see a black man replacing a white man. He seemed to share the same concern that businesses faced when they promoted their black employees ahead of white employees. They feared rebellion.

Kennedy could not bring himself to ask for Troutman's resignation himself; so he asked his aide, Kenny O'Donnell, to do the dirty work. Kennedy met with Troutman the next day in the White House for ten minutes. In August 1962, Troutman submitted his resignation.[45] One month later, in September, Hobart Taylor, Jr., was named head of the Committee. *The New York Times* story announcing the news was buried deep in the first section of the paper, on page 20.[46]

John Feild knew the Committee could not have two bosses, and he did not approve of what he described as Hobart Taylor's management style. He said others in the office also shared his uneasiness about Taylor, who was said to invite employees to his home at night to catch up on work. "I almost brought charges against Hobart when I was executive director of the committee. I had two female employees come to me and give me very detailed descriptions of Hobart's actions with regard to them," said Feild. "And I put it to both of them, "If you want to press charges, I'll go with you. But it's up to you."[47]

Nobody on the Committee brought any charges against Taylor. The allegations occurred well before the Women's Movement gained momentum and sexual harassment laws were developed.

Vice President Johnson certainly backed Taylor. "The Vice President had lost faith in Feild's judgment. And I say, to be truthful about it, in his loyalty and integrity," said Taylor.[48]

After Taylor was promoted, John Feild—the executive director of the program who had developed a protocol for preventing employment discrimination, who was the architect of

Plans for Progress, and who had more experience in remedying workplace discrimination than Taylor—resigned. Being the good soldier, he agreed to stay for another six months with Taylor acting as his boss, while Labor Secretary Willard Wirtz settled into his new job.[49]

5 | The Cost of Exclusion

A T THE TIME, THE PLANS FOR PROGRESS CONTRACTS WERE kept confidential, and there was no way of verifying how far each company had agreed to go. A review of the contracts nearly 50 years after they were signed revealed that most of the contractors agreed to the boilerplate language, albeit with differing levels of enthusiasm. (See Figure 5.1.)

United Aircraft (now United Technologies Corporation) wrote a sincere, four-and-a-half-page, single-spaced contract that agreed to the basic points. The Boeing Company produced a very straightforward contract of five double-spaced pages that also hewed to the main points as Lockheed had. The agreements of Douglas Aircraft and Western Electric toed the line. These companies pledged to educate their employees as to the desirability and necessity of increased minority hiring and promotion. They promised to expand their outreach to minority high schools, colleges, and community organizations. They vowed to assign responsibility for the increased hiring to managers who would then hold supervisors accountable. They pledged to open up all training, jobs, and promotions to minorities. They agreed to work with unions to eliminate racial bias or limitations. They vowed to maintain nonsegregated facilities.

Other defense contractors were less enthusiastic. North American Aviation produced a contract with resistant, eye-rolling language: "North American Aviation intends to give

Figure 5.1 Comparison of Plans for Progress Contracts

Contractor	Expand minority recruitment.	Provide equal access to training and jobs.	Review current employees for promotion.	Disseminate policy.	Practice non-discrimination in layoffs, downgrades, termination.	Maintain nonsegregated restrooms, fountains, cafeterias.	Work with unions to eliminate bias.	Hold managers accountable
Boeing	X	X	X	X	X	X	X	X
Douglas Aircraft	X	X	X	X	X	X	X	X
General Electric								
Lockheed	X	X	X	X	X	X	X	X
Martin	X	X	X	X	X		X	X
Mobil	X	X	X	X			X	X
North American	X	X	X	X	X	X	X	X
Radio Corporation of America (RCA)	X	X	X	X				X
United Aircraft	X	X	X	X	X	X	X	X
Western Electric	X	X	X	X	X	X	X	

Source: Data is from Plans for Progress, 1961, Harris L. Wofford White House Staff Files, Series 1, Box 8, President's Committee on Equal Opportunity, 3/6/61–7/31/61, JFK Presidential Library, Boston.

its full support to the program of the President's Committee by giving increased emphasis to its efforts to attract qualified Negroes to positions for which they do not usually apply."[1] In other words, it was their fault, not ours, that blacks were not hired.

The Martin Company (now Lockheed Martin) failed to include a pledge to maintain desegregated facilities. Although the aerospace company had already made progress in hiring more people of color under Eisenhower, it continued to use segregated restrooms because managers said it was the hardest change for their employees to accept.[2]

Mobil Oil also failed to include the points on maintaining desegregated facilities, and it did not pledge to practice nondiscrimination in downgrades and terminations. In 1961, the oil company still contracted with segregated unions. When the NAACP accused the company of discrimination, Mobil's president, Fred Moore, denied it. Moore did not believe the company was perpetuating unequal employment conditions through its contracts with segregated unions.[3]

In its Plan for Progress contract, the Radio Corporation of America (later bought by GE) also failed to agree to maintain desegregated facilities and to practice nondiscrimination in downgrades and terminations. This is puzzling, as the electronics maker was ten years ahead of the other companies in race relations and had already reached out to black students and graduates in the early 1950s. In fact, RCA published its Plan for Progress contract in a brochure, which it distributed to employees. The pamphlet listed the 12 years of recruiting at "Negro colleges" and scholarships for Negro college and vocational students. RCA's president, John L. Burns, pledged to expand the company's previous efforts and programs and to provide "unstinting support" to the President's Committee.[4]

The only company that signed a wildly different contract was General Electric, which was then the nation's largest defense contractor, employing more than 200,000 people. In fact, General Electric's Plan for Progress could scarcely be called a plan at all. In fact, it did not even contain the words "Plan for Progress." Instead, it was a "statement."

In his statement, Ralph J. Cordiner, the president and chairman of GE, grandly pronounced that the company had been practicing its policy of equal opportunity since 1935. He acted as if he could learn little more from the Committee and promised only "constructive cooperation" and the assurance that "our corporate efforts to achieve equality of opportunity on the basis of merit will continue for all persons." GE did not agree to any of the new affirmative action measures to which the other companies did. Although the company was described by the White House as entering into a Plan for Progress, it in fact, did not.[5]

It is not clear whether Feild or Troutman negotiated the empty GE agreement, which was barely more than one double-spaced page in length. But Hobart Taylor, Jr., was not happy about it. As a lawyer and a man who believed in the power of contracts to change behavior, he wanted corporations' commitments spelled out. "Some of those contracts weren't worth the paper they were written on," said Taylor.[6] After the GE statement arrived, Vice President Johnson asked Taylor to approve all future Plans for Progress.

Hobart Taylor, Jr.: Segregation as an Economic Issue

Hobart Taylor, Jr., supported Lyndon Baines Johnson for president in 1960. He had listened to Kennedy's speeches, but, like many blacks, he did not sense much depth in Kennedy's commitment to civil rights. Johnson had led the 1957 Civil Rights Act through Congress. Senator Kennedy, however, had voted against the act, which primarily supported voting rights.

Like Feild, Taylor also claimed to have invented affirmative action. Although he did not coin the phrase, it appears that he was responsible for including the phrase in the executive order. In 1961, when Johnson saw Hobart Taylor, Jr., at an inaugural ball, the vice president asked Taylor to come see him in a few days. Johnson met with Taylor in February 1961 and showed him a draft of the executive order that would establish the Committee on Equal Employment Opportunity. As Johnson considered how his committee would be different from those that had gone before, he recommended that the nondiscrimination clause for government contractors in Eisenhower's executive order should "be revised to impose not merely the *negative obligation* of avoiding discrimination but the *affirmative duty* to employ applicants."[7]

Johnson gave him an hour to look it over in the office next door.[8]

"I would do a lot of things differently if I were doing this," said Taylor. "There are no teeth in this thing. And where there are teeth, they're too strong. You've got to cancel all of your relationships with somebody because they've done one thing wrong, and you're going to hesitate to use a power like that because the punishment is greater than the crime."

"Would you write it the way you want it?" asked Johnson.

"Well, yes, I could do that," Taylor said. "When will you need it?"

"How about tomorrow morning?" asked Johnson.[9]

Taylor agreed to the short deadline and checked into the Willard, a fine old hotel in Washington, where he stayed up all night rewriting the entire draft. He deliberated between writing "positive action" and "affirmative action." He wanted to convey the sense that employers would be expected to take positive steps. (Instead of the passive steps they had taken in the past under the old Fair Employment Practices Acts, such as simply posting equal opportunity signs.) Taylor also wanted a phrase that would develop significance as a legal concept over time, something that would protect people's economic rights. At this point, he had not envisioned exactly what positive steps the government would recommend to employers, he was thinking only in legal concepts. Ultimately, he decided to write "affirmative action," he said, because of the alliteration.[10]

Once the order was finalized, Johnson called and asked Taylor to join the Committee. Taylor almost declined the offer because he was reluctant to leave his law practice in Michigan. But after he accepted the opportunity and ultimately took charge of the Committee, it marked a profound turning point in America when the great grandson of a slave brought his knowledge of the law, his understanding of the power of contracts, and his unique experience as a member of a wealthy black family to transform future employment opportunities for other people of color.

Taylor himself was more conservative about civil rights than Feild was, and he was less involved in it on a daily basis in the sense that it was not his occupation. However, he was black, and so he experienced the frequent indignities of discrimination, which Feild, as a white man, rarely did.

Once, after a Detroit restaurant refused to serve Taylor and his wife, Lynette Dobbins, Taylor got an injunction against the restaurant owners and sued them for damages in a bench trial. With this new approach, he demonstrated to other people of color that, if they were refused service, they too could use this method of going before a judge instead of wasting time with criminal statutes and juries as they used to do. After Taylor won his case, he notified the Detroit restaurant association of his victory, and more restaurants began to open their doors to blacks.[11]

In mid-twentieth-century America, Taylor's background was just as unusual for a white person as it was for a black person. Unlike Feild's parents, Taylor's parents were both college educated, and they were wealthy. Taylor was born in Texarkana, Texas, and raised in Houston. His parents kept their only child strictly focused on education.[12] Taylor graduated from Prairie View State College with a BA in economics in 1937. He earned a master's degree in economics in 1939 from Howard University and then received a law degree from the University of Michigan in 1943. Taylor served as editor of the *Michigan Law Review* while he was a student and clerked for Raymond W. Starr, the chief justice of the Michigan Supreme Court between 1944 and 1945. He practiced law for four years, and, in 1949, he became a prosecuting attorney for Wayne County, Michigan, where he worked until 1950. He served as corporation counsel for Wayne County in 1950 and held that job until he and some partners opened their own firm in 1958.[13]

Taylor essentially viewed the civil rights struggle as the need for blacks to be able to freely contract in society, not to be confined by location or skin color. "What [a black man] needs is freedom to move in the society," he told an interviewer at the LBJ oral history project. "He ought to look at his Bill of Rights as a Bill of Rights to engage in business with everybody and not to restrict himself."[14]

To Taylor, the economic problem of segregation confined

blacks to contracting with other blacks, denying them the free-dom to expand their enterprises and ambitions beyond speci-fied customers and neighborhoods, thereby restricting their earnings and progress.

While Hobart Taylor, Jr.'s great grandfather had been a slave, he left slavery with money in his pocket and did not suffer the great privation of being sent out into the world as a freeman without learning how to contract first. Slaves had been legally prevented from entering into contracts to perform labor, to purchase land, or even to marry because courts had ruled that slaves were property. But John Sales, the man who had owned Taylor's great grandfather, put away 10 cents of every boot he sold and then gave his slaves this money when they were freed in 1865. As a result, Taylor's great grand-father, Mr. Shoemaker, left slavery with $600 in his pocket and went on to buy his own land, 600 acres in Kendleton, Texas.[15]

Taylor's great grandmother used to say: "Boys, let me tell you something. My master, old Colonel Sales, was one of the finest men in this world. But he knew the rattle of money. If you youngsters don't learn the rattle of money early, you're not going to get any."[16]

The great-grandparents passed along their knowledge of the power of money to their children. As a result, Taylor, Jr.'s grandfather was able to buy 700 acres in Wharton, Texas, and send all of his children to college.[17] Taylor's father, Hobart, Sr., received the kind of education that few blacks or whites could afford in the 1920s. After getting a degree in agriculture from the all-black Prairie View College in Prairie View, Texas, Hobart, Sr., attended the Wharton School of Finance in Philadelphia. He cofounded Watchtower Life Insurance Com-pany in Houston and became its director. He later opened a taxi franchise and gave rides to both black and white passengers, despite segregation, because he was determined to serve customers of all kinds; it was just good for business.[18] "All the white folks, so far as we're concerned, are our friends," said Hobart Taylor, Sr.[19]

Despite his education and his financial success, there were years when Hobart Taylor, Sr., his family, and his friends could not vote in Texas primaries because the Democratic Party allowed only whites to vote.[20] So he used much of his wealth to fund efforts to gain voting rights for blacks and to support candidates who believed in equal rights.[21]

When Lyndon Johnson campaigned for the U.S. Senate in Wharton County, Hobart, Sr., organized black voters to support Johnson but told them not to turn out at the rally. He did not want the white voters to think of Johnson as a black candidate, fearing it might hurt Johnson's chances of being elected. Instead, he met with Johnson privately to pledge his support.[22] "We had some of the wealthiest Negroes in this country, but they didn't publicize it. Nobody publicized it," said Taylor, Sr. "I've never been in jail, I've never been exposed to a lot of things that other people in my race are exposed to. I don't know anything about it. Hobart, Jr., doesn't know anything about it."[23]

Although having money may have cushioned the Taylors from many of the more extreme, violent forms of racism that other blacks had experienced, they still put great effort into eliminating discrimination by working within the establishment. Seeing discrimination from a legal and economic perspective, Taylor, Jr., sought to correct injustices with very specialized tools. He was the president of the first black mortgage company in Michigan. "We used the little money that we got together to break quite a bit of housing segregation. You see, a lot of housing segregation was caused," Taylor said, "simply because you can't get financing for people to buy outside of certain prescribed areas. And so obviously if you created a mechanism whereby people could get the financing, that's the end of the matter." [24]

Many housing developers used to write covenants into the property deeds that restricted homeownership to whites, and that form of segregation could not be overcome by money alone. So Taylor challenged the law. After World War II, white homeowners in one Detroit neighborhood insisted on enforcing the covenant against a black couple, the McGhees, after they had already bought the house and moved into the neighborhood. The Wayne County Circuit Court found that the McGhees were indeed "Negroes," barred them from living in their home, and ordered them to move out within 90 days. The case was appealed to the Michigan Supreme Court, and Taylor wrote a brief on behalf of the McGhees. When the Michigan Supreme Court affirmed the lower court's decision, the case was taken to the U.S. Supreme Court. Taylor wrote another brief on behalf of the McGhees, and the case was argued by a young NAACP attorney named Thurgood Marshall (who would later become the first black Supreme Court justice). In 1948, the Supreme Court upheld the McGhees' right to purchase and live in the house and ruled that states could not enforce racially restrictive covenants. [25]

By selecting Taylor to head the President's Committee, Kennedy and Johnson exhibited congruence between what they ordered companies to do and what they did themselves. They urged companies to promote minorities, and they led by example.

Taylor was highly educated and sophisticated, but Feild found his demeanor confusing. He, like Feild, was tall, about

6 foot 1 inch. Whereas Feild had a strong, confident, authoritative Northern voice, Taylor, Jr., spoke with a hesitant Southern drawl. Taylor, Jr., who had dark black skin, also had a rounded physique and a cherubic face. He had a disarming, mercurial style that Feild described as obsequious one moment and haughty the next. "He could be very flattering in one style, then you find out he's giving you a lot of bullshit the next day," said Feild.[26]

While Feild traveled the country signing up contractors for the new plans, handling discrimination complaints, and creating the government's compliance system, Taylor wrote the administrative rules as the Committee's special counsel. Taylor spent months hunkered down in the Washington office where he was inundated with letters from the legal departments of corporations complaining that they now would have to monitor their subcontractor's employment practices as well as their own. He received a five-page diatribe from The Boeing Company recommending that whole sections of the executive order be changed. Taylor responded with a polite letter containing two sentences that thanked them for their suggestions.

Taylor defined how the new executive order would be applied to contractors. Taylor copied his memos to Vice President Johnson, White House counsel Lee White, and everyone in the office. He made himself very visible. Feild seldom wrote a memo, and, when he did, it was usually brief and perfunctory. Feild's work, because it was in the field, was less visible. Taylor was the tailor of the system, making sure the new program would fit the government's best interests. So it was not a difficult decision to put Taylor in charge, and the decision showed that the President's Committee practiced what it preached.

Actually, Taylor had been selected to lead the Committee

years earlier. But then an article appeared in a local Texas newspaper that a black man from Michigan, presumed to be a liberal, was going to lead employment reform. Conservative Texans raised so much flack that Taylor was unselected and Feild got the job instead.[27]

Following Up on the Plans for Progress

Within a few months of signing their Plans for Progress, the companies had to submit a census of the color and occupation of their workers. All government contractors would have to do this, but the Plans for Progress companies had started a year before the others. As part of his overall concept for affirmative action, Feild wanted to augment the statistical reports that companies had been required to file for the government under the Eisenhower administration. Contractors had to complete an annual statistical self-analysis of the complexion of their workforce according to job category. Feild had a terrible time getting General Motors to conduct a census of its 650,000 workers at 220 locations. The first forms had only five categories for race: whites, Negroes, Indians, Orientals, and others. Essentially, the mainly white managers would decide on employees' race just by looking at them. (In the mid-1960s, the government added separate categories for Spanish-surnamed individuals and for male and female workers.) "We did insist upon the data, and therefore, we automatically elevated the preoccupation that everybody had with performance measured by numbers," said Feild.[28]

As Standard Form 40 evolved into the EEO-1, the reporting forms became more and more refined in measuring race, gender, and job category. The data enabled the Committee to ascertain whether the companies were complying with the executive order. Because the companies kept track of the color of employees and their jobs, the forms became the road maps to change that told the companies where they stood on race and where they needed to go. In addition, each contractor had to require its first level of subcontractors to submit compliance reports to the companies with which it contracted.

Of the largest contractors still existing under the same name in 2011 as they did 50 years earlier—Lockheed, Boeing, and General Electric—General Electric had the lowest percentage of minorities. (See Figure 5.2.) According to confidential reports filed with the President's Committee, in 1962, only 2.4 percent of GE's workforce was nonwhite. Boeing's was

Figure 5.2 Percentage of Nonwhite Employees in December 1962

Salaried Jobs	Boeing Company	General Electric	Lockheed
Officials & supervisors	0.5	0.4	0.9
Professionals and administrators	3.7	0.8	0.55
Sales	0	.1	0
Technicians	2.4	1.4	2
Office and clerical	2.4	1.2	1
Total	2.3	0.93	0.9
Hourly Jobs			
Craftsmen	3.2	2	2.7
Operatives	7	4.4	16
Service workers	15	8	14.8
Laborers	4.3	9	21.7
Total	5	3.8	8.7
Total jobs	3.2	2.4	3.7

Sources: Boeing (Summary of Progress Report, 1962, Box 79, Plans for Progress, National Archives, College Park, MD); GE (Box 79, Plans for Progress, National Archives, College Park, MD); Lockheed (Summary of Progress Report, Plans for Progress, 1962, Box 75, National Archives, College Park, MD).

somewhat larger at 3.2 percent. Lockheed, the company that had received the most intense scrutiny, had the highest non-white employment at 3.7 percent. GE, the company that had portrayed itself as a leader in equal employment and that avoided pledging to the same affirmative action commitment to which other defense companies had subscribed, was a laggard.[29]

Lockheed had problems that could be fixed fairly easily, like segregation. But GE had more complex challenges. As part of joining Plans for Progress, the companies had to complete a confidential self-analysis for the Committee. It was a detailed survey of 10 multipart questions about their employment practices, which was to remain confidential. The survey inquired about the firm's policies toward minorities in hiring, training, promotions, unionization, integration, and segregation. In these questionnaires, the companies began to divulge their experiments, struggles, and frustrations.

On its questionnaire in June 1961, GE said that its policy was "not to discriminate against any employee on account of race, color, sex, creed, marital status, or national origin." And it stated it had signed agreements with more than 100 unions to that end. In this way, GE was actually ahead of the President's Committee, which did not require companies to prohibit discrimination based on sex or marital status. That requirement would not come until Title VII of the Civil Rights Act was passed in 1964, three years later.

However, GE had experienced significant difficulty in enforcing its policies. At one of the company's southern plants, management announced its intention to hire some minority workers, and the local union threatened to call a plant-wide strike, even though its national union had signed an equal opportunity agreement with GE.[30]

"There was no question of the seriousness of this threat," explained the unnamed GE executive who responded to the survey. "While some unions apparently prefer white male members and do discriminate against minority groups as to union membership and seniority considerations, in general, the unions with whom we bargain have given us little trouble in obtaining compliance, with some exceptions."[31]

At a plant in Kentucky, GE's supervisors decided to hire several blacks to work with whites on an advanced mechanical assembly line. The supervisors announced their intentions to the plant workforce, "stating the desirability, fairness and other aspects of the proposal." They said they expected everyone to cooperate.[32] Most of the employees accepted it, but a few white employees vehemently resisted. Some union representatives threatened to strike if the blacks were hired. The company held steady and affirmed that the black employees would be hired, that the assembly line would operate as scheduled, and that any employees "not reporting for duty on schedule without a proper excuse would be immediately replaced. Fortunately, the plan was placed in operation without incident."[33]

GE said it could cite several examples of nonunion resistance and said experience had shown that planning, in tandem with the education and preparation of employees, had resulted in the greatest success.

However, GE's having such a low percentage of nonwhite workers indicated that the company had not tried very hard to hire and cultivate minorities. Judging from the census of its workers and the confidential reports it filed in 1961, its integration efforts were rare and experimental, and they had occurred mainly in the South. In fact, it still kept segregated restrooms in the South, "based upon social mores, custom, and state law."[34]

Above the Mason-Dixon line, the company faced a different problem. At least 14 GE locations in the Midwest alone had no minorities at all. They included a glass manufacturing plant in Logan, Ohio; a motor plant in Linton, Indiana; and an appliance controls facility in Morrison, Illinois. These were small towns with predominantly white populations. The company had either not tried or not succeeded in hiring or keeping minorities at these locations.[35]

Companies have extensive economic and social impact on the communities where they are located and on the people they employ. Although diversity experts in the late twentieth century focused on the effect of diversity on a company's bottom line, reformers in mid-century America measured the cost of discrimination in higher unemployment, increased poverty, and rising crime. Yet it is now clear that employment discrimination costs both companies and the communities where they operate. When companies consider how extensively they should engage in diversity, they rarely ask themselves how much it will cost them not to hire and promote a wide range of employees.

The High Cost of Resisting Integration

Tennessee Coal and Iron (TCI) is a powerful example of the cost of not practicing equal opportunity within the four walls of the business and the damage it causes in the larger community. The company had become wedded to one group of employees in a series of preferential contracts, promotions, and working conditions. As a result, it was unable to adapt to a series of dramatically changing market conditions in the steel industry.

In the early 1960s, TCI, a subsidiary of U.S. Steel, was the largest private employer in Birmingham, Alabama. The plant stretched for 10 miles along the edge of the city and had a workforce that ranged from 20,000 to 25,000 people, depending on how strong the demand for steel was. TCI was the state's largest bank depositor, and it was a powerful force in the city, helping to shape its values, economy, and culture.[36]

Birmingham, the largest city in the Deep South, was also one of the most deeply segregated. Even in the 1960s, blacks and whites rarely walked the same streets or breathed the same air because public transportation, neighborhoods, parks, and many schools were still segregated. Despite frequent efforts to obtain civil rights, black activism was greeted by 13 bombs that had exploded in black churches over ten years. As a result, the city had come to be called "Bombingham."

TCI had long favored white workers through its negotiations with the local unions, which had rules stipulating separate lines of employment and promotions for blacks and whites. The union leadership essentially formed a white labor cartel. When John Feild went to Birmingham in 1962 to get the company to join Plans for Progress, the company blamed its problems on the unions—13 of which were segregated. Feild managed to secure an agreement from TCI executives that they would end segregation and put black and white employees on equal standing for both promotions and layoffs. U.S. Attorney General Robert F. Kennedy publicized the agreement in July 1962, grandly announcing, "for the first time the colored employees are standing on the same footing in layoffs and promotions as their white fellow employees."[37]

Shortly after Robert Kennedy made his announcement, the President's Committee received seven complaints from TCI employees alleging discrimination in Steelworkers International by "virtue of separate lines of seniority and promotion for Negro and white employees resulting in the inability of Negro employees to gain transfer or promotion to higher rated positions."[38] TCI executives had not even proposed unifying the racially separate lines of employment and promotions to its 13 local steel workers unions. The one union that had amended its agreement had insisted on it, not the company.

TCI had a long history of treating blacks poorly. The mining and steelmaking company was the largest customer of black convict labor in Alabama. The Jim Crow period following Reconstruction was characterized by different laws for blacks and whites. Blacks were frequently arrested for trifling offenses such as vagrancy, a charge that amounted to failing to furnish proof of employment. After the arrestees were sentenced, employers would lease convicts from the state or county, pay their fines and monthly fees, and put them to work, usually in hard labor. As soon as U.S. Steel acquired TCI in 1907, the company signed a new lease for 400 prisoners from the state of Alabama. By 1908, nearly 60 convict laborers had died from disease, accidents, or homicide on just one mine slope at the edge of Birmingham.[39]

TCI finally ended its use of convict labor in 1928 and began to improve working conditions for blacks and whites, building more than 20 villages for its workers across Birmingham. But the neighborhoods were largely segregated, with whites living in one section and blacks in another. The company had more black workers—55 percent—and operated 14 African American schools and nine white schools.[40]

The company kept black workers one step below its white workers. In the 1930s, the United Mine Workers of America labor union had already experienced job losses brought by mechanization, and it responded by restricting the operation of equipment to white workers. Thus, blacks were confined to menial jobs and could not get training in how to use the equipment. Once they were laid off, they were also ineligible to apply for other jobs than those that they previously held.[41]

In 1962, TCI said that a new bargaining agreement with Steelworkers International would correct racially separate lines of employment and promotion by providing a broad-based labor pool below seniority level in each department from which employees could bid. The President's Committee rejected the plan, arguing that the proposal created dead-end lines of seniority for black employees from which they could not transfer. It also kept white employees in lines of promotion for highly paid jobs and perpetuated racially separate promotion lines for jobs above the pool.[42]

Feild warned Taylor in a memo that the company was intransigent. "Its president, Mr. [Arthur] Wieble, will resist necessary change because of fear of employee and civic reaction, and because of the company's general reluctance to permit Government interference with its internal policies and practices."[43]

In January 1963, Taylor met with the white officials of the firm. They agreed to study all the separate promotion lines at the company but warned it would take time because it was such a complex company. Taylor acknowledged the complexity but pushed them to commit to a timetable. Would it take one month, three months, six months? The officials agreed to complete the study by the end of the month and promised the amendments to the unions within three months. "I've always been kind of a sit-across-the-table fellow, and then we work it out, and if we don't work it out, then I find a way to put pressure on you 'til you come around and you see it my way, then I sit down with you again,"[44] said Taylor.

He asked what the men intended to do regarding the company's lack of black clerical and white-collar workers. The official said TCI was currently laying people off, not hiring. Business conditions, they said, would not allow new hiring.[45]

The company did not hire or promote more blacks partly because it was constrained by a complex set of business problems. In 1959, the United Steel Workers Union struck over its demand for a 15-cent increase in wage and benefits. The strike lasted six months, and it idled 85 percent of American steel production. Desperate American manufacturers turned to Korea and Japan for steel, which they found less expensive even with shipping costs.[46] With their international competitors crowding into the American market, U.S. Steel was cutting costs, trying to remain competitive. In 1960, TCI had to shut down the iron ore mines for weeks due to lack of demand. The number of workers declined as the company cut costs and tried to become more efficient. The company's move to computerized personnel records also resulted in layoffs. Business conditions resulted in not being able to hire more machinists. In addition, the U.S. government would frequently object if the company wanted to raise the price of steel.[47]

So the company was not enthusiastic when the government also asked them to improve race relations. A recent recession, competition from abroad, the loss of buyers due to work stoppages, and automation all led to declines in employment—layoffs—instead of hiring and promotions. At the same time, blacks in Birmingham were demanding a larger piece of the pie even as the pie was shrinking.

In April 1963, black college students resumed their sit-ins in the white sections of segregated lunch counters at Britt's, H.L. Green, and Woolworth's. They protested at department stores, such as Loveman's, that had refused to hire blacks.

Their so-called selective buying campaign went on for a month, but the protests diminished as the demonstrators were arrested. In early May, hundreds of black schoolchildren replaced the adult protestors who had been jailed. Children poured into the streets, sang songs, and marched for four hours. They too were arrested. The next day, on May 3, "Bull" Connor, Birmingham's white public safety commissioner, ordered firemen to take their positions on street corners and open their hoses against the demonstrators. Photographs and film went around the world showing people being sprayed with the powerful jets from the water cannon and lunged at by police dogs. Black bystanders then began hurling bottles and bricks at the police.[48]

Most Americans recoiled from the violence they saw on all sides: children being arrested, citizens being hosed down by firefighters, and rioters attacking the police.

A group of businessmen met over the next few days to grapple with their declining sales and their ruined reputations. They, like the businessmen of Atlanta, were ready to negotiate desegregation. But Arthur Wieble, the head of TCI, the area's largest employer, objected to settling with the black civil rights activists.[49]

The intransigence of the TCI leadership was starving the people of Birmingham. The lock that the unions had on TCI and that TCI, in turn, had on the city left it vulnerable to the wave of globalization that coursed through mining and manufacturing in the 1960s. Troubles at TCI triggered financial problems for the city. Birmingham began to run budget deficits in the late 1950s. In 1961, it was $800,000 in the red.[50] The city had failed to diversify its economy, and there were rumors that TCI–U.S. Steel had interfered with plans by General Motors and Ford Motors to locate plants near the city.[51]

TCI had discouraged the city from offering tax incentives to attract new businesses because they did not want to have to compete with other industries for workers in their wage scales.[52]

Birmingham was not the shiny new south like Dallas and Atlanta. Birmingham was in economic decline. It had lost more than 25,000 people from 1950 to 1960. Between 1950 and 1970, the region surrounding it lost 163,000 residents, mainly blacks who gave up and sought opportunities elsewhere.[53]

Eventually, white merchants agreed to gradually desegregate the downtown lunch counters, to remove signs designating "Colored" and "White," to hire black employees, and to release the remaining arrestees.

At the end of May, the President's Committee on Equal Employment Opportunity had a meeting in which Robert Kennedy began asking why blacks did not have more jobs in Birmingham. He had learned that whites had a lock on the jobs in federal government and that only 15 blacks were employed in a total federal workforce of 2,000. He drilled into Taylor, asking him why more blacks had not been hired into the defense industries in Birmingham. Kennedy wanted a detailed study to be done that looked at black employment in the city. Taylor, to his detriment, responded like a defensive bureaucrat, saying that they could do the study if they could get the proper form printed quickly.[54]

Taylor's response angered the attorney general. Kennedy concluded that Taylor was an ineffective and passive vice chairman. He described him as an "Uncle Tom," a racist, pejorative name that describes blacks who bow down to whites.[55]

Bobby Kennedy, far more than his brother, felt impassioned about civil rights. He wanted immediate action. Bobby had been immersed in the civil rights protests raging through the South and had worked assiduously to get businesses to desegregate and employ blacks. He met with large groups of hotel owners, restaurateurs, drugstore owners, and theater operators to spread the word that they had to serve and employ blacks. In June, he instructed the Justice Department to give him a daily report on the changes in racial practices in Southern businesses. The reports kept track of how many businesses had changed their practices. They tracked how many civil rights demonstrations were being held and why. The Justice Department even predicted where the next demonstrations would be held. Bobby Kennedy was racing to head off these demonstrations to prevent possible violence and loss of life. The situation was urgent, and he wanted action.

Sensing that urgency, the new labor secretary, Willard Wirtz, sprang to action. He compiled a list of government contractors in more than 200 metropolitan areas that had few white-collar black employees and no black employees at all. Wirtz had a copy of the list hand-delivered to Robert Kennedy, with a note that said it all: "These figures are obviously bad."[56]

Wirtz ordered Taylor to immediately compile a list of government contractors with more than 250 employees that were not complying with the government's order. It was called the "zero list," and it detailed 25,000 of the 35,000 contractors who still had not managed to hire a significant number of nonwhites.[57]

6 | Scaling Up: Creating a Minority Supply Chain

ALMOST EVERYBODY WANTED TO GET RID OF PLANS FOR Progress. President Kennedy, Vice President Johnson, and Labor Secretary Arthur Goldberg wanted to let it die and forget about it. When the new Labor Secretary Willard Wirtz discovered the so-called zero companies, with hardly any black employees, he wanted to override Taylor and directly inform the companies that they were not complying.[1]

Realizing the entire program was in jeopardy, including his own job, Taylor pitched Wirtz a new idea in July 1963 to hand the responsibility of spreading affirmative action to the companies themselves. Actually, the idea was not new. Troutman had proposed the plan the year he left the Committee.

Taylor persuaded the executives who were first involved in Plans for Progress to form an advisory council that would help spread integration practices based on the boilerplate contracts. In Taylor's mind, the Plans for Progress Advisory Council would become the businessman's version of the National Association of Intergroup Relations Officials (NAIRO), which Taylor had joined at Feild's invitation. Feild had helped place experts in intergroup relations into government contracting agencies during the Kennedy administration. Businesses needed the same kind of specialists.

In 1960, NAIRO surveyed all the federal agencies and found very few intergroup specialists employed by the government. Appalled by the lack of expertise and the low insistence on ending segregation demonstrated by the government, John Feild had arranged for President Kennedy to meet with NAIRO in the White House. In 1961, George Culberson, NAIRO's president, presented Kennedy with a report on how their specialists could help the federal government transform its relationship with different racial, ethnic, and religious groups.

"The purpose of that meeting was to strengthen in the president's mind," said Feild, "that to carry out these programs, required the assignment of specialists and the development of a professional specialty within the operating agencies to do this work."[2]

The president agreed. Harris Wofford, the head of Kennedy's civil rights office in the White House, kept the NAIRO survey in a file in his desk. He began acting on its recommendations to get the federal government to improve its own record of hiring and promotions and to provide it with specialists who would understand how to serve America's very diverse populations.[3]

Feild, a founder and past president of NAIRO, clearly influenced the group's analysis and recommendations to the president. After he discovered that the U.S. Air Force had tolerated segregation at Lockheed for years, Feild concluded that each government agency needed to place at least two people who were trained in affirmative action into its contract compliance offices. He urged for this to be done and suggested experts he knew who were part of NAIRO to take the jobs. The Air Force hired George Culberson, the president of NAIRO, to be its chief compliance officer. By 1963, the government had 6,000 employees who specialized in affirmative action compliance.[4] "We were beginning to get the caliber of people into our agencies who could perform," said Feild.

Through his association with NAIRO, Feild spread his vision of affirmative action throughout the government's compliance system. By starting the Plans for Progress Advisory Council, Taylor spread affirmative action to the corporations.

The Plans for Progress Advisory Council in Action

Starting in 1963, the Advisory Council for Plans for Progress was staffed by corporate personnel directors on loan. They were still fully paid by their corporations, but they spent as many as three years in Washington working with other personnel directors, trying to develop a scalable process for finding, hiring, and promoting people of color.[5] They worked in an office at 1800 G. Street, NW, separate from the President's Committee. Their goals were to spread Plans for Progress beyond the defense contractors, to the other 111 firms that had signed Plans for Progress and to attract more companies to the program. The Advisory Council, in essence, became a specialized consulting group that acted independently of the President's Committee on Equal Employment Opportunity. It was comprised of 19 members of Plans for Progress companies that divided into six groups.[6]

One of the whitest companies in America was International Business Machines (IBM), which made typewriters, office equipment, and mainframe computers. In December 1962, only 1.5 percent of its employees were minorities, even lower than GE's 2.7 percent. It was a zero company.[7]

The Plans for Progress Advisory Council meets in New York City with Hobart Taylor, Jr., at the head of the table (1964).
Source: Plans for Progress Advisory Council First Year Report, August 1964.

R. A. Whitehorne, a manager of personnel research with IBM, joined the Advisory Council and immediately confronted the issues. With news reports of sit-ins and protests at white-only or segregated establishments filling the newspapers and the airwaves, he tried to determine just who the agitators were and what they wanted. He prepared a summary of the civil rights groups and of their aims, methods, and "techniques" in the distinctively rounded letters of the Selectric Bookface type.

"There are five major civil and/or human rights agencies," according to his report. "Each has at its basic aim: equal treatment and opportunities for all citizens. Each agency is interracial in terms of leadership, administration, staff and supporters."[8]

1. The National Association for the Advancement of Colored

People (NAACP) uses legal methods and the courts to achieve its goals.

2. The Congress of Racial Equality (CORE) uses pickets and economic boycotts as its "major weapons. Most effective recent programs are the sponsorship of 'freedom rides' and selective buying campaigns."

3. The Southern Christian Leadership Conference (SCLC) "uses the philosophy of 'going to jail' and remaining there until appropriate community leaders agree 'to discuss' issues and make plans for alleviating the grievances outlined by Negro leaders."

4. The Student Non-Violent Coordinating Committee (SNCC) is a nationwide student group that organizes "sit-ins, walk-ins, wade-ins, and kneel-ins to focus attention on the problems faced by Negro citizens."

5. The Urban League plans conferences to inform community leaders from industry, labor, government, and education on issues facing urban Negroes and engages them in finding workable solutions.

IBM and other companies were just waking up to this other world outside their very homogeneous headquarters. The reductive list certainly does not convey a deep or compassionate understanding of the long history of the civil rights struggle, or of the deep commitment and, in some cases, life-risking efforts expended by civil rights activists. But it definitely illustrates the practicality with which the company approached the issue.

The task at hand was to hire more minority workers, and IBM was searching for an organization that could help the company do it with as little conflict as possible. Company officials did not want complaints lodged against them, as the NAACP had done, or protestors picketing in front of their headquarters. They wanted to solve the problem as quickly and as painlessly as possible. The men on the Advisory Council, who were predominantly white and Republican, were looking for a technical solution—a quick fix.[9] They sought out black organizations that could connect them with the people who could become productive employees without conflict or negative publicity.

In its cool, calculated search, the Advisory Council preferred the Urban League to any other group because it seemed to be the least radical. If the Urban League was not available, the NAACP was a distant second choice (because of its adversarial nature).

Even though all of the Plans for Progress companies had portrayed themselves publicly as perfect equal opportunity employers in their contracts, a different story emerged from the confidential questionnaires they were required to submit as part of the program. Companies complained about not being able to find enough qualified minorities. "It is our feeling that members of minority group applicants are not as well qualified as those coming from majority groups," the unnamed respondent from GE explained in the questionnaire. "Of course, there are individual exceptions. We have numbers of minority group employees whose performance is outstanding."[10]

The GE employee continued his analysis. "To the degree that minority applicants may be substantially less qualified, we believe this is so largely because of their lack of training, part of which has been due to their hesitancy to take advantage of available education and training; their lack of living within an industrial environment; and the lack of early direction and guidance during their formative years."[11]

In other words, it was their fault, not ours. The view that

minorities had not been prepared by their families, their environment, or their schools to work for a technologically sophisticated corporation was echoed throughout the companies' surveys. The word *qualified* appears repeatedly in the documents produced by the Plans for Progress companies. IBM used the word three times in a six-page statement, pledging to seek out minorities who were "qualified to staff higher level skill occupations."[12] North American Aviation pledged to attract "qualified Negroes" for employment, using the term four times in a five-page statement.[13]

The companies obviously were trying to protect themselves from being made to hire workers who could not do the jobs. No employer wants to do that. But looking back 50 years, one cannot help wondering whether emphasizing *qualified* would provide them with an excuse for not hiring any minority workers at all. Was it truly difficult for companies to find minority workers who were just as qualified as whites?

Unequal Educational Opportunities

The Jim Crow segregation laws had required blacks to attend separate schools in 17 Southern states plus the District of Columbia. Four other states—Kansas, Wyoming, New Mexico, and Arizona—permitted racial segregation, although Wyoming never engaged in it.[14] The unanimous 1954 Supreme Court decision, *Brown v. the Board of Education,* outlawed segregation, but by 1964, ten years later, only a few black Southern schoolchildren—1.2 percent—had won entry into an integrated school.[15]

When the Advisory Council began, many Southern states were still taking the first steps of integration in the face of considerable resistance. Although legislation had been enacted, people were slow to change their traditions and preferences. The public schools of Birmingham, Alabama, did not officially begin desegregating until September 1963, nine years after the Supreme Court decision in *Brown v. the Board of Education.*

The generation of black students who graduated from high school in the South in the early 1960s generally did not have the same educational opportunities as whites. Nor did the previous generation of black workers in the advanced industrial states of Pennsylvania, Illinois, Indiana, Ohio, and New Jersey have the same educational opportunities as whites because many school districts in those states had been segregated until the late 1940s.[16]

Although the majority of Northern states outlawed segregation in the 25 years following the Civil War, some school districts patently ignored their legislatures by keeping Native Americans, Asians, African Americans, and Hispanics separate from white students. Even when public schools were not segregated by law, they often wound up that way as the result of residential segregation. And there were profound disparities in financial support for minority schools. A 1954 study of the New York City schools found that white elementary schools received nearly eight times the expenditures per pupil for instructional equipment and furniture that black and Puerto Rican students received, as well as more than three times the total capital outlay.[17]

Graduation rates also differed. By 1962, more than one-third of whites had graduated from high school, compared with a little more than one fifth of nonwhites. Nearly 12 percent of whites had earned a college degree, whereas less than 5 percent of nonwhites had. (See Figure 6.1.)

Figure 6.1 1962 Education Rates

U.S. Workers	Percentage of Whites	Percentage of Nonwhites
1 to 3 years of high school	18.8	23.2
4 years of high school	33.5	21.0
1 to 3 years of college	11.3	5.7
4 years of college	11.8	4.8
Median years of schooling completed	12.2	9.6
Total percentage unemployed	4.9	11.0

Sources: From U.S. Bureau of the Census and Department of Labor Statistics, as cited by Ray Marshall in "Job problems of Negroes," in Herbert R. Northrup and Richard L. Rowan, eds., *The Negro and Employment Opportunity* (Ann Arbor: Bureau of Industrial Relations, Graduate School of Business Administration, The University of Michigan, 1965), 6 and 9.

Nonwhites, the majority of whom were black in 1962, generally were not as well educated as whites. A higher percentage of nonwhites dropped out of high school, and they had more than twice the unemployment rate of whites. At the same time, the economy was changing from its heavy reliance on unskilled labor to one that was increasingly powered by technology. Manufacturers needed more skilled labor. The United States had already entered the space race with the Soviet Union. Satellites and spacecraft had been launched into orbit, the nuclear industry was well developed, and the computer revolution was underway. The need for engineers, mathematicians, scientists, and business professionals was much greater than the need for unskilled labor.

As a prelude to his vision of the Great Society, Vice President Johnson painted an image of a fully utilized workforce. "The Council of Economic Advisers has estimated that our gross national product would be more than $20 billion greater than it is if the full potential of our Negro citizens were at work in our economy," he told new participants to Plans for Progress. He believed that affirmative action would enable the entire country, businesses and individuals, to grow wealthier.[18]

The sixties marked an era of innovation when science and technology produced new consumer products. IBM needed mathematicians to continue to develop algorithms for use in its Selectric typewriters and mainframe computers. DuPont relied on chemists to develop plastic-based products such as Teflon and Mylar. GE sought electrical engineers to perfect its X-rays and medical imaging.

But the educational system needed to supply a robust group of minority workers failed to prepare students for the technological economy. To fulfill the terms of their Plans for Progress and to help develop the minority employment market, the corporate personnel directors who staffed the Advisory Council set out to create a supply chain of minority workers, drawing on the interconnected groups in minority neighborhoods: families, schools, community organizations, vocational schools, and colleges. It sought to draw talent from the minority networks that were established outside the corporation but previously underappreciated and underdeveloped.

Eugene Mattison, director of industrial relations for Lockheed-Georgia, who was instrumental in the desegregation of the Marietta plant, became the head of the community relations committee for the Advisory Council. He experimented with other personnel directors in how to reach out to minorities and chronicled their successes and failures in a 31-page booklet, *Implementing Plans for Progress*. The publication is a fascinating artifact that indicates both how timid and inexperienced the companies were in dealing with blacks, yet how determined they were to find approaches and solutions that other companies could replicate and expand. Mattison, who knew how shameful it felt when one's company became the subject of public ridicule for shoddy race relations, concealed the names of the companies in the booklet.

Bold Initiatives for Improving Education

Companies boldly confronted the educational deficits of high school graduates. When one Southern company found very few minority applicants who could meet the basic job requirements, it began to inform school administrators of the "inadequacies and deficiencies" of applicants. The company invited school personnel into the plant for a workshop in which they explained the educational requirements for skilled, technical, and administrative occupations.[19]

Another company that needed employees with technical skills worked with the Urban League to host a Student Career Day. They gave plant tours to students and hosted a luncheon in which black employees and influential minority leaders were invited to speak and answer questions.

Executives from a firm in a large Southern community could not find any qualified blacks for its industrial training programs, but they felt uncomfortable informing the "various agencies and institutions [of] the inadequacies of current vocational education programs." Instead, the company partnered with the Urban League to develop an experimental community program to upgrade the skills of young people to meet entry-level requirements and submitted the improvement proposals to local, state and federal agencies for approval.[20]

The firms were trying to get the message across to schools and communities that children had to stay in school and that schools had to improve. But they wanted to send the message as smoothly as possible, without creating conflict and without appearing to be disapproving, judgmental, or racist.

One business circumvented this potential pitfall by asking its current black employees to contact the teachers and students from their schools and tell them exactly which training helped them get and keep their jobs. It was hoped that this message, coming from black employees in a white-dominated company, would carry more credence. Schools promised to change their curricula once they were informed of the precise job requirements.[21]

Companies made daring outreaches directly to families and students, encouraging them to consider preparing for work in their companies. One company that could not locate qualified minority applicants because of "inappropriate educational and preparation and motivation" produced a color-slide show. The presentation illustrated 30 black employees working in all major categories of employment but emphasized the positions in growth fields where the minimum of a high school degree was required. Then, working with the YMCA, two-person teams took the slide show into the homes of families with junior-high-school-aged students and showed the presentation to them and to the three or four other families who had been invited.[22]

The companies were trying to strengthen the links in the educational system to get families, teachers, counselors, and students to broaden their career visions and to prepare for those careers. When the Advisory Council realized that many secondary school counselors did not have updated knowledge of industry or the "proper sensitivities" to motivate minority youth, it sought to educate them by holding seminars throughout the country. As a result, 87 Vocational Guidance Institutes were held in 37 cities and were attended by 3,000 guidance counselors, teachers, and administrators. The meetings were paid for by donations solicited from companies.[23]

Yet minority youth were still not graduating. The Council then established the Youth Motivation Task Force to persuade students to stay in school. The Task Force was organized in 18 cities and reached 427,000 minority students in secondary school and 167,280 minority college students. Nearly 5,000 minority employees participated, giving testimonials to their experience.[24] The Advisory Council started a major, multimedia advertising campaign, "Things Are Changing," to encourage skilled and unskilled minorities to seek out jobs, participate in special training programs, and complete their formal educations.[25]

Companies came to realize that many minority colleges did not have the faculty or courses to prepare their graduates to compete with other schools on an equal basis for employment opportunities in industry. Companies therefore provided individual institutions with faculty from their industries. Forty-five companies organized to teach 100,000 students.[26]

The Advisory Council produced an annual 100-page directory of black colleges and universities. It listed the degrees they conferred, their areas of study, and how many males and females they had graduated. It told companies where to find black college graduates.

Expanding the Possibilities

As the corporations adapted to the new reality of integration, they shared the adaptive process with minorities who, in turn, had to change their views of the future and their places in it. One company in a "large West Coast community" reached out to the Urban League to find out why it wasn't getting minority job applicants. The Urban League did a study and reported that blacks simply did not conduct wide job searches because they feared discrimination. The study also concluded that teachers, guidance counselors, and employment agencies were unaware of, or did not appreciate, how serious the efforts were by local businesses and industry to create equal employment opportunities. As a result, 200 businesses put together a joint statement about their desire to have personnel agencies send them "qualified applicants." The Urban League planned to put together a book for job seekers, telling them how to broaden their job searches to include the companies that professed to practice equal opportunity.[27]

Hobart Taylor, Jr., also spread the word of the need for this adaptive work in black communities across the country. In his address to the National Association of Colored Women's clubs in 1963, he called on the black labor force to break a pattern developed in the previous 100 years in which blacks largely contracted with one another for services.

"A Negro can make a living off his fellow Negroes without ever touching white society at all," he told the group. He explained that this had occurred because the Emancipation Proclamation in 1863, while morally right, had come too quickly. It came without adequate preparation or planning for slaves to adjust from being chattel—property that was traded—to becoming traders and contractors themselves. And it had come without the agreement from the South where most of the slaves still were owned. As a result, he said, blacks had no "concept of wages or the labor-management relationship." So, they set out on the road to freedom but wound up contracting mainly with one another. Even educated Negroes who became lawyers, doctors, teachers, or preachers, he said, largely did business with other blacks.[28]

On the eve of the great exploration of space, the expansion of atomic energy, and the building of the electronics industry, Taylor described a labor shortage in the United States. There were not enough scientists and too many laborers. "Government administrators complain bitterly that young scientists on whom they lean heavily are snatched up by private industry that the government can never match," he said. "To find trained minds in the quantities we need we are going to have to go to the reservoir which now is scarcely touched—the 19 million Americans who are of Negro descent." He encouraged blacks to change their habit of assuming that doors to specialized jobs were closed to them and to make sure their educational institutions were capable of providing the proper training.

Taylor was a new kind of black leader. He was not a Martin Luther King, Jr., who appealed to people's moral courage and who lived his principles by exposing himself to physical risk—the danger of being arrested, attacked, and ultimately assassinated. "I wasn't like a lot of those church people," said Taylor. And he was not like the leaders of the more radical black movement that developed in the sixties. Taylor viewed the world through an economic and legal lens. Although he was a Democrat, he was conservative. He wanted to make deals and see them through.

Unlike Feild, Taylor, Jr., did not believe in threatening to withhold contracts. Taylor did not think that actually canceling a contract would do anyone any good: neither the government, which needed services, nor the companies that needed employees, nor the employees who needed jobs. "He was a good salesman," said Louis Martin, a black political advisor to Kennedy and Johnson. "He formed excellent relationships with a lot of the big business people."[29]

Hobart Taylor, Jr., center, surrounded by the Plans for Progress Advisory Council and guests after a tour of the Lockheed plant in Marietta, Georgia, April 28, 1964. G. William Miller, president of Textron and Chairman of the Advisory Council, is next to Taylor, on the right.
Source: Plans for Progress Advisory Council First Year Report, August 1964.

After selecting Taylor to head the committee, Johnson showcased his distinctive talents and capabilities, illustrating how corporations could trust blacks to manage significant operations. Vice President Johnson trusted Taylor so much that he moved him into the White House to serve as his own counsel. Once he arrived, Taylor called a designer to redecorate his office before being advised that that is not customary practice in the White House.

The most famous photograph of Hobart Taylor, Jr., appeared on the 1964 cover of *Ebony* magazine, which showed him standing over Johnson who was seated at a desk. It looks like Taylor was in charge of Johnson, who was president at the time. The image conveyed a startling reversal of traditional roles between the races. And it won points with companies, who felt pleased that Taylor, Jr., was their friend in the White House.[30]

Taylor developed a much higher media profile in Washington than John Feild had. In January 1965, Taylor helped organize five inaugural balls for President Johnson. His wife, Lynette Taylor, was featured in a cover story for *Jet* magazine as a "charming Washington socialite" and shown swathed in a Norwegian sada fox. The Taylors had a very modern marriage for the 1960s. Lynette Taylor, a Detroit school principal with a master's degree in education, commuted to Washington from Detroit, where she had started a program to put a dictionary and an atlas in every home and had organized school trips to visit various industries so that students would learn more about the world around them. The Taylors practiced what they preached and encouraged their two sons to study science.[31]

Calming the Community

Urging students to concentrate in math and science and getting them to stay in school was just one step in creating a reliable, productive supply chain of new workers. Northern companies also found they had to prepare the communities to accept the new hires.

One large company recruited a black college graduate to work in an overwhelmingly white Northern city where the level of minorities was a paltry 0.2 percent. Word spread through the community that the company planned to "bring in large numbers of negroes." The personnel director attended a civic meeting marked by considerable unrest and reassured people that this was not the company's intention. He told them that few people of any race could do such a specialized job. The controversy died down, but the company learned that they had to do far more preparatory work in speaking to community groups as well as employees to prepare them for the changes.

Minority employees often had difficulty finding housing. A black professional was hired to work at a precision-equip-ment-manufacturing company in a large Northeastern city. After eight days of being unable to find suitable housing, the man decided to take a job in a different city. The company intervened and helped him by arranging meetings with realtors and taking him to appointments. The company also contacted its other black employees and the Urban League for help.

In yet another city, black single professionals couldn't find places to live. Company managers were afraid to overtly pressure the community fearing a backlash. Instead, the firm quietly communicated its problems to city government, religious leaders, and trade organizations who formed a community relations group. They found owners of apartment buildings who were open to renting to minority single people; company managers invited the owners to lunch and solved the problem among themselves.

Sometimes the companies' avoidance of conflict may have resulted in slower integration. But other times, their speed of hiring, without carefully preparing the community and employees, caused resistance.

Standing Tall

To get white workers to accept new minority employees, the Advisory Council recommended first preparing employees and their communities for integration. Then the company could proceed with "pilot placements" where "carefully selected minority persons" were placed in a suitable job where they would be "accepted" and their performance would be noted by a large number of people.[32]

A utility company in a large Northeastern city with 30 percent minorities tried this approach. Managers of the employee relations department notified workers that the company would be hiring a minority for a "responsible position." Three white employees threatened to retire, and others vehemently refused to work with the new employee. But management remained steadfast and backed the new minority employee, who wound up being accepted by everyone.

A company in a medium-sized Southern city notified its employees that it would be hiring some black employees. It carefully selected two females for clerical and factory work, monitored their treatment in the workplace, and followed up with black leaders in the community to gauge reaction. Management was careful not to place the employees in jobs for which they would be overqualified, as many companies had done in the past. Everything went smoothly.

Although the Advisory Council ventured into affirmative action cautiously, even timidly, it scaled up very quickly. (See Figure 6.2.) The Council wrote 1,500 letters to companies asking them to join the voluntary organization.[33] Some companies such as Hughes-Bechtol responded enthusiastically; the mechanical and engineering contracting firm based in Toledo, Ohio, received 50 percent of its business from the U.S. government. Other firms, such as Black and Decker, wrote back that they would like to have more information sent to them but then failed to follow up. Merck flat out rejected the invitation as unnecessary for the firm. In six years, the Council increased

Figure 6.2 Members of the First Plans for Progress Advisory Council

G. William Miller, president of Textron, Inc., volunteered as chairman of the Advisory Council.

Arthur M. Doty, manager of personnel relations at Aluminum Company of America, became chairman of the Scholarship and Training Committee.

E. G. Mattison, director of industrial relations for Lockheed-Georgia, served as chairman of the Community Relations Committee.

Dr. C E. Scholl, director of labor relations, Defense and Space Groups, Burroughs Corporation.

H. W. Wittenborn, vice president of personnel and industrial relations, Cook Electric Company.

Edward Cudahy, Jr., president of The Cudahy Packing Company.

Paul S. Kempf, director of industrial relations, Hughes Aircraft Company.

Robert F. Crowel, manager of employee relations, International Harvester.

Harold Schroder, assistant vice president, American Telephone and Telegraph.

Dr. Frank Metzger, director of manpower administration, International Telephone and Telegraph Corporation.

G. Roy Fugal, consultant in personnel practices at General Electric.

W. D. Coursey, assistant vice president, Texas Instruments.

Edward Franks, manager of employment personnel, Chrysler.

Harold Mayfield, director of personnel at Owens-Illinois Glass.

R. A. Whitehorne, manager of personnel research and services, IBM Corporation.

P. B. Lewis, employee relations department, DuPont.

R. H. Berquist was in compensation administration and employee services at Colgate-Palmolive.

George A. Spater, general counsel, American Airlines.

A. H. Evans, manager of employment, Radio Corp. of America.

Source: Hobart Taylor, Jr., "Memorandum to Lee C. White, Assistant Counsel to the President, August 6, 1963, New Advisory Council on Plans for Progress," Lee C. White Civil Rights Files, White House 1963, 1/3/62–6/10/63, JFK Presidential Library.

membership nearly fourfold to 441 companies in 1969 from 111 companies in 1963.[34] Companies that did not join often attended one of the 46 major national and regional conferences that the Council hosted to exchange ideas and to share solutions and experiences to help industry improve its equal employment programs.[35] The Council especially sought out black professionals to speak at the gatherings so that white attendees would have proof before them that blacks could do the job, despite the shortage of "qualified" workers.

The protocol radiated through the business world, and independent consultants adopted the program and capitalized on it. Richard Clarke, an employment specialist, tried to attract clients by linking his name to Plans for Progress in newspaper advertisements. Lockheed's Eugene Mattison became irritated with Clarke and wrote him a letter ordering him to stop using the Plans for Progress name.[36]

Things Are Changing

In September 1965, Louis Martin, a political advisor to Presidents Kennedy and Johnson, got a phone call that marked the end of government work for Hobart Taylor, Jr., John Macy, chief headhunter at the White House, called him with an order from the president.[37]

"Look, the Chief wants Hobart out of the White House by Friday," said Macy.

"By Friday? Are you out of your mind?" asked Martin. Macy told Martin that what to do with Hobart was his problem.

Martin called a friend of Taylor's, the economist Eliot Janeway, and asked him what Taylor would want to do.

Janeway said Taylor, Jr., had always wanted to join the cabinet as head of an agency. Martin rolled his eyes and thought that ambition was typical of Taylor, Jr., who thought his own abilities were fantastic.

"Well, Jesus Christ, we can't do that. The man wants him out of here," said Martin, leveling with Janeway.

Martin made some calls and discovered that there was a vacancy in the Export-Import Bank, but he had difficulty getting Taylor to accept a position with no staff. So Martin enlisted Janeway's help.

"You've got to sell him," Martin told Janeway with desperation in his voice.

"We got to get him out by Friday," said Martin, hoping to avoid any newspaper headlines or public relations nightmares.[38]

Taylor's abrupt ouster came on the heels of a conflagration with Alfred Blumrosen, the new chief liaison with Federal and State Agencies at the Equal Employment Opportunity Commission (EEOC). The Commission was created to enforce the Title VII provisions of the Civil Rights Act of 1964, which prohibited employment discrimination on the basis of race, color, religion, sex, national origin, and age. The bill went into effect in July 1965 and replaced President Kennedy's Executive Order, on which Plans for Progress had been based. Blumrosen was a lawyer who had been a labor arbitrator in New Jersey before he was hired to help organize the new EEOC. He had walked into the President's Committee on Equal Employment Opportunity and found the 1963 zero list (companies with few or no minority workers). He was shocked to see that many of the firms were blue chip companies and that some were members of the much vaunted Plans for Progress.[39]

Blumrosen wanted to develop a crash training program for a group of investigators to deploy to the zero companies. Taylor nixed the idea. He did not want a different program other than Plans for Progress being foisted on the companies. Taylor had not authorized the EEOC to see the companies' data, which was to be private. Members of the office who worked on the President's Committee were angry that their data, history of work with companies, and territory were being usurped by the new EEOC.

Blumrosen was told to cancel his project. "A unique opportunity for administrative creativity had been bypassed," he wrote.[40]

When President Johnson realized that Taylor seemed to be standing in the way of progress, he let him go. The President's Committee on Equal Employment Opportunity was abolished two weeks later and replaced with the Office of Federal Contract Compliance Programs.

Significantly, the Plans for Progress Advisory Council operated for four years after Taylor left and the Committee was dissolved. The Council kept measuring its progress and making adjustments. An internal survey conducted in 1966 showed that Plans for Progress companies lagged behind other companies generally when it came to employing "negroes and Spanish-surnamed workers." (See Figure 6-3.) In 1968, the Advisory Council sponsored a Southwest Employers Conference in Albuquerque, New Mexico, to promote the employment of Hispanics, Latinos, and Native Americans, because the Council admitted it had responded inadequately to these groups."

In 1968, the Advisory Council issued a new blue 11-page pamphlet, "Affirmative Action Guidelines," for government contractors and subcontractors. It included the old Plans for Progress protocol, but added to it. The Council advised employers that the testing of applicants should be predictive or directly correlated to skills needed only for the specific job. It required companies to set measurable goals and achievable timetables for improving the hiring or job status of minorities in each division, department, location, and job description. For the first time, it introduced the idea of proportionality: "the rate of minority applicants recruited should approximate or

Figure 6.3 African American and Hispanic/Latino Employees Survey, 1966

Cities	Companies	Negro Employment Rates, 1966			Spanish-Surnamed Employment Rates, 1966		
		% All Employees	% White Collar	% Skilled Craftsmen	% All Employees	% White Collar	% Skilled Craftsmen
Atlanta	Total	15.2	2.3	6.4			
	PfP	9	1.7	3.2			
Chicago	Total	13.5	4.7	7.1			
	PfP	13.1	3.0	5.9			
Cleveland	Total	11.2	3.2	5.0			
	PfP	10.3	2.7	4.0			
Kansas City	Total	8.9	2.1	5.3			
	PfP	7.4	1.2	4.2			
Los Angeles	Total	6.9	2.8	4.1	9.7	4.0	9.9
	PfP	5.2	1.9	4.1	9.0	7.3	7.1
New Orleans	Total	20.1	3.0	10.2			
	PfP	11.2	1.9	3.3			
New York	Total	10.0	5.7	5.8	5.7	2.6	4.5
	PfP	6.7	5.4	3.6	2.6	1.6	1.4
San Francisco	Total	8.0	3.0	4.5	6.7	2.9	6.3
	PfP	6.8	2.7	3.3	6.5	3.1	5.3
Washington	Total	22.0	8.4	10.7			
	PfP	11.6	7.0	3.9			

Sources: Data from 1966 EEO-1s as produced in pages 1 and 2, January 9, 1968, Plans for Progress Advisory Report, Box 59, Plans for Progress, National Archives II, College Park, MD.

equal the ratio of minorities to the applicant population in each location." It suggested that companies create a career counseling system to ensure that minorities were not left out of the networks that transmitted information about strategies for advancing within the organization.[42]

The Council had managed to get grants from the Ford Foundation, as well as funding and staff assistance from the U.S. government. In 1969, the Advisory Council pitched the new Nixon administration to raise its funding to $1,265,000 from $216,000 and to increase the number of staffers paid by the Department of Labor to 29 from 12. But it did not boast how much more advanced the Plans for Progress companies were in hiring than the non–Plans for Progress companies. Instead, it boasted how much farther ahead the oldest members of Plans for Progress were compared to the newest members. The Council believed that it was trying to transform the whitest companies and, in this process, found that the longer a company actively participated in the program, the more integrated it became.

The new administration declined to fund the Advisory Council. Instead, President Richard Nixon wanted to develop "black capitalism" and decided to back programs that would support black entrepreneurs. After a six-year run, the Advisory Council office was shut down, personnel directors returned to their companies, and the best practices of affirmative action—how to go out and recruit more minorities—were seamlessly adopted by the OFCC as a set of repeatable, scalable employment practices.

Plans for Progress had acted as an incubator for social and economic change that influenced the management of companies employing a total of 10 million employees. The problem was that less than 1 percent, only 441 out of 35,000 government contractors, joined the vanguard.

7 No Room at the Top

AMERICANS WERE PUSHING BOUNDARIES ON ALL FRONTS in the 1960s. Plans for Progress gained momentum as businesses became swept up in the racial, social, and technological revolutions of the era. Yet the companies that adopted the protocol rarely understood its profound importance. Instead, they used it to solve pressing, short-term business concerns. Plans for Progress provided companies with a step-by-step solution that promised to allow them to keep their lucrative government contracts, to reverse bad publicity, and to be seen in the public's eye as modern and forward thinking. It offered companies a systematic method of coping with the turbulence, the protests, and the riots of the time.

Walgreen

Walgreen Drug Stores joined Plans for Progress to finally end a decade of demonstrations against its lunch counters, which featured separate dining rules for whites and blacks. In the 1950s and 1960s, the Congress of Racial Equality (CORE) protested at Walgreen stores for not allowing blacks to sit in the same restaurant as whites. While Charles Walgreen, Jr., would tell news reporters that the segregation had ended,

CORE members would always find another Walgreen in the South that was still segregated.

The drugstore chain was founded in 1901 by Charles Walgreen, Sr., the son of Swedish immigrants, who bought a drugstore on Chicago's South Side and began to expand. By 1916, he owned nine stores in the same area, each on a busy corner. By 1919, he owned 20 stores. By 1960 the chain had grown to 460 stores throughout the country.[1]

Walgreen was always experimenting with selling new products. He started with soaps and powders, and he added special purchases such as pots and pans whenever he got a chance. A soda fountain that served drinks grew into an ice cream parlor and later developed into counters and restaurants where people could sit down and get a quick meal.

In January 1962, Frances Sims, a 19-year-old freshman at Alabama A&M in Huntsville, launched her first sit-down. She and a friend went to a local Walgreen, which had a restaurant where you could get a hamburger and a soft drink, but you could sit down at the counter only if you were white. Blacks had to stand. Sims and Dwight Crawford, a 16-year-old high school student, who were both African American, had the gall to sit down and order a hamburger. Instead of being served a warm meal, the owner of the Walgreen called the police. The two were arrested and charged with trespassing.[2]

Over the next four months, Sims was arrested eight times for protesting at Walgreen. Every time she did it, she brought someone new with her. In April 1962, she arrived with one married woman who was six months pregnant and another married woman who carried a baby girl in her arms. As they sat down and ordered hamburgers, the staff ignored them. The three women and a girl illustrated the new generations of African Americans—college educated, newly married, newly

born, and yet to be born—who would no longer put up with
the exclusions of the past. They literally wanted a seat at the
table. Instead, they got a stern warning when the owner, William Hutchins, arrived.

"If you don't leave, I will have you arrested," he said.[3]

The women sat in silence for 20 minutes. The police arrived,
and all three of the women—and the baby—went to jail. The
married women were the wives of prominent African Americans. Martha Hereford, who was pregnant, was married to a
doctor, and Joan Cashin was married to a dentist. Their hus-
bands had frequently posted bail for demonstrators before. But
the women did not ask for an appeal bond. They wanted their
jailers to face their unusual captives. After some deliberation,
the police chief released them on their own recognizance.

The women later appeared for arraignment and again refused to post a bond. The judge ordered them to jail. They took
their place in a dirty county jail, across the corridor from some
white prostitutes. The mattresses had been removed from the
cell to make the women uncomfortable, but they piled up their
coats to provide a cushion for Martha Hereford. A day passed
and the mayor of Huntsville called John Cashin to ask him
when he was going to get his wife out of jail. "When she's
ready," replied Cashin. Papers from Huntsville to Baltimore
and New Jersey picked up the story.[4]

Sims helped radicalize the women by showing them how
to demonstrate. Soon Cashin and Hereford were deeply involved in demonstrations. Sims kept protesting at the Walgreen counters. She did not let up on them.

Walgreen was getting bad publicity all around the nation
as CORE sit-downers protested the public accommodation
laws and traditions across the South. Individual Walgreens
slowly responded. In 1962, the Walgreen in New Orleans de-

segregated. In February 1963, the Walgreen in Pinebluff, Arkansas, desegregated. In June 1963, the NAACP called for all stores and restaurants to end segregation immediately.

In that same year,1963, Walgreen Drug Stores joined Plans for Progress. Charles Walgreen, Jr., wanted to overcome the stigma of the demonstrations against his company. On page three of its contract, the company pledged it would "continue to establish store and plant facilities such as cafeterias and restrooms on a nonsegregated basis."[5] In its self-analysis, the company told the government that none of its restaurants was segregated and that restrooms were segregated only where required by law.[6]

Still, the demonstrations against Walgreen continued. Frances Sims brought more protestors to Huntsville. On March 20, 1964, the regional director of the U.S. Post Office in Memphis, Tennessee, cancelled Federal contracts totaling $4,000 with two Huntsville, Alabama, Walgreen Drug Stores.

In previous histories, Plans for Progress has been criticized for never canceling a contract with a company that violated the terms of its agreement with the government. But the contract that was cancelled with Walgreen demonstrates that the apparatus that John Feild created inside the government was in fact working long after he left. John Hope II, assistant executive director for government employment, notified the Plans for Progress Advisory Council about the cancellation in a letter on March 10, 1964.

While Walgreen, Jr., was eager to escape from the bad publicity from the demonstrations, he did not understand the core goals of Plans for Progress. One of the primary objectives was for businesses to treat races equally, not to specify that white customers can sit or black customers can stand while eating their meals. Walgreen, who lived in Chicago, may not have known that the Huntsville stores were doing business this way. But as the head of the company, he should have known.

Walgreen also failed to understand the goals of equal employment opportunity, and the drugstores actually wound up hiring more minorities than they were required to. In 1963, the company employed minorities overall in numbers that were proportional to their representation in the population. The drugstore chain needed not to hire many more minorities, but rather to open up all jobs to them. But by 1969, Walgreen had overhired nonwhites in every category except technicians and craftsmen. (Walgreen representatives explained to the Plans for Progress Advisory Council that they were very frustrated not to be able to find or hire a black pharmacist.) By 1969, 19 percent of Walgreen's employees were minority, while approximately 12 percent of the population was minority.

To its credit, the drugstore chain did reduce the proportion of nonwhites employed in the unskilled jobs of laborer and service worker to 53 percent in 1969 from 71 percent in 1963. Laborer is a nonmanagement job that generally requires good physical condition but no formal training or education. Typical titles would have been mover, warehouseman, or construction laborer. Service workers labored in kitchen, custodial, or security jobs.[7] This marked an improvement from six years earlier and this trend was a goal of Plans for Progress.

Walgreen's EEO-1 (Figure 7.1) illustrates how the company, in an inexact effort to make amends for the past, could be seen as segregating minorities into blue-collar jobs while simultaneously giving preference to them in white-collar jobs. These two allegations were used to criticize affirmative action generally. Some white workers argued that they were the victims of reverse discrimination because minorities were hired ahead of them. Some minorities and women argued that they

Figure 7.1 Walgreen Drug Stores During Plans for Progress

	June 1963			December 1969		
Salaried Jobs	All	Nonwhite	Nonwhite (%)	All	Minority	Minority (%)
Officials and supervisors	2,365	74	3	2,812	137	5
Professional and administrative	215	2	1	658	65	10
Sales	5,241	235	5	9,504	1,584	17
Technicians	34	0	0	50	0	0
Office and clerical	1,895	119	6	1,828	209	11
Total	9,750	430	4	14,852	1,995	13
Hourly Jobs						
Craftsmen	60	1	2	99	1	1
Operatives	121	23	19	269	82	31
Service workers	4,464	1,128	25	7,643	2,348	31
Laborers	30	9	30	125	39	31
Total	4,675	1,161	25	8,136	2,470	30
Total jobs	14,425	1,591	11	22,988	4,465	19

Sources: "Walgreen Company, Summary of Progress Report, 1963," Plans for Progress, Box 77; "Walgreen Drug Stores-Consolidated Report, 1969 EEO-1," Plans for Progress, Box 59, 1969, National Archives II, College Park, MD.

were hired but became stuck in the worst or most limited job categories. These arguments would play themselves out in courts over the next decades as workers of all races and genders competed for jobs. Both arguments were clearly grounded in fact. The highly individual ways that companies applied affirmative action frequently gave it a bad name, laying the groundwork for it to be slowly replaced by the Supreme Court's diversity decision in the late 1970s.

Although Walgreen clearly had plenty of minority employees in the pipeline, 25 years later, by 1995, the company still had no women or minorities in executive officer positions. It usually takes 20 to 25 years for a college-educated employee who starts at the firm to work his or her way up the ladder to the corporate suite. If the employees Walgreen had hired in 1969 would have stayed two decades at the firm, done well, and developed into highly effective managers, presumably they could have proceeded to the executive suite. But by 1995 Walgreen lagged behind the other Plans for Progress companies in the *Fortune 100*; 61 percent had promoted at least one female or minority to executive officer.

In 1995, nearly 35 years after Plans for Progress had begun, there was no acceptable reason for a company, after being involved in such comprehensive emergent and dominant integration strategies, not to have females and minorities as executive officers. In other words, although the companies had the people, whether they had developed the employees enough to assume leadership roles or trusted them in such roles were separate questions.

IBM

If any company would have promoted people of color and women to the highest, most trusted positions in the company by 1995, IBM seemed as though it would have been the one. The company contributed two personnel specialists to the Plans for Progress Advisory Council, James Burg and R. A. Whitehorne. Burg was the recruiter for Federal Systems, the computing work that IBM did for the space and other agencies. He was actively looking for talented job candidates and advertised repeatedly in the scientific and trade magazines.

Thomas Watson, IBM's CEO, anticipated that business would double in the 1970s and that the company would be hiring more scientific and sales employees. One-third of IBM's employees in 1962 had college degrees, and the lowest educational requirement was a high school diploma. Factory jobs at the firm were decreasing.[8]

Donald Green, an African American, was teaching science to white honors students at a junior high school in Washington, D.C., in the early 1960s. Green himself had gone to a segregated school in the District, Dunbar High School, and graduated in 1954, the same year the Supreme Court ordered that public schools had to be desegregated. After he earned a bachelor of science at Georgetown University, he became the first African American to integrate the white school where he taught.

But Green wanted bigger things for his life. He considered applying for medical school and was discussing his plans with a friend who recently had started at IBM and who encouraged him to apply. As part of the job application, Green had to take a data processing aptitude test, which had the reputation of being a very rigorous exam. "I took the exam at IBM and got an A," he said. "There were very few people, not just blacks, but any people doing that, so I was a hot number. Everybody wanted to interview me."[9]

Green hoped to go straight into marketing because he had

studied IBM and found that the Watsons, the family that had come to run the company, had been great marketers. But Green was required to spend the first year as a systems engineer who would assist the marketing representative. The sales rep sold the IBM/360 computers, which had debuted in 1964 and which were smaller and speedier than earlier models, and Green helped install them. Green believes that if he were white, he could have started off as a marketing representative. "They were very, very concerned about how the customer would react seeing a black face. They thought the customer might kick the equipment out," he said.[10]

After a year, Green was made a marketing rep and allowed to go out on his own. To show the government that IBM was hiring minorities, his bosses assigned him and his black colleague to the District area. Green developed business at the Federal Reserve, the Veteran's Administration, the Bureau of Engraving and Printing, and the Federal Bureau of Investigation.

Because he had technical knowledge of the 360 system, which most marketers did not, Green developed a distinctive sales strategy. First he contacted the head of technology at an agency, met him for lunch, and sold him on the system. Then he met with the agency's upper management and made his presentation. Management naturally consulted the head of technology, who then demonstrated technical knowledge of the 360. "These places were all buying," said Green. "It was a real wild time; selling like crazy."[11]

What was going on in the outside world could not be contained or held separate from what went on in the business-world. Four days of riots broke out in Washington after Martin Luther King, Jr., was assassinated in Memphis, Tennessee, on April 4, 1968. A group of young black men in the District began going from business to business asking them to close their doors out of respect for King. As the crowds gathered in the streets, they demanded the stores close. The crowd turned ugly, and things began to spiral out of control. Hours after King had been murdered, hundreds of rioters were smashing store windows and stealing merchandise. In 110 cities across the country, rage over King's death resulted in the looting, rioting, and burning of inner cities.[12]

Black workers at IBM were upset too. They thought the company had not done enough for blacks. A rumor began to spread that the group was plotting to bomb a building at IBM. As the cities burned and the confrontational Black Panthers replaced the nonviolent civil rights movement, white panic filled the air. Green's branch manager asked him to attend a meeting with a top vice president of the District region, who wanted Green to "talk to the brothers" and calm them down. That night, Green met with eight or nine black leaders within the company and tried to reason with them about the direction to take at IBM. "I truly believed that being militant at that point would not pay off for us," said Green. "'You're trying to move ahead and violence will not do it. You need to try to understand the man, and play along with him,'" Green told his black colleagues.[13]

He talked to the men during a long and difficult night. They called him an Uncle Tom right to his face. "It got rough and tough," said Green. "In their mind, I was acting white."[14]

No bombs were found at the company at that time; the scare was more rumor than reality. But IBM had far to go to thoroughly integrate its company because it had started out so far behind. It increased its minority representation to only 6 percent in 1969 from 1.5 percent in 1962. In the process, IBM, like Walgreens, had created a predominantly black job category among laborers. At the same time, it had maintained a job category at the top of the blue-collar jobs—that of craftsman—for whites.

Still, the computer maker had accomplished a significant milestone that the other Plans for Progress companies had not. By 1969, it had hired more minorities for white-collar jobs than for blue-collar jobs. In 1962, 75 percent of minorities at IBM were employed in white-collar occupations. Seven years later, 82 percent of minorities at the company were employed in white-collar jobs, which illustrates that large numbers of well-educated minorities existed; companies simply had to find and hire them. (See Figure 7.2.)

Don Green's leadership and his sales success earned him a big promotion. He became the first African American to be a marketing manager in the Far West, a vast sales region that stretched from Denver all the way to Honolulu. Based in San Francisco, he supplied computers to the Pacific Stock Exchange and almost all of the banks and insurance companies in Northern California.

Green wanted to work in the chairman's office, an elite assignment in which he would learn all about the corporation by assisting the head of IBM. Instead of getting that job, he was transferred to Wall Street, where he became the IBM representative for the brokerage industry and the New York Stock Exchange. Green was moving very fast. But after nine years in sales and just six months on Wall Street, he still wanted to learn the overall organization. He still wanted to go to the chairman's office.

In 1975, Green got his chance. He was assigned for 18 months as one of five executive assistants in Chairman Frank Cary's office. "It was a busy, wonderful job. You got to see all

Figure 7.2 International Business Machines Corporation During Plans for Progress

Salaried Jobs	December 1962			December 1969		
	All	Nonwhite	Nonwhite (%)	All	Minority	Minority (%)
Officials and supervisors	8,062	45	0.6	18,218	309	2
Professionals and administrators	11,882	240	2	39,778	1,847	5
Sales	7,183	29	0.4	8,193	211	3
Technicians	24,093	263	1	40,289	2,351	6
Office and clerical	15,102	348	2.3	28,403	2,962	10
Total	66,322	925	1.4	134,881	7,680	5.7
Hourly Jobs						
Craftsmen	6,950	44	0.6	9,486	295	3
Operatives	7,920	168	2	10,658	1,264	12
Service workers	721	94	13	798	119	15
Laborers	11	5	45	94	63	67
Total	15,602	311	2	21,036	1,741	8.3
Total jobs	81,924	1,236	1.5	155,917	9,421	6

Sources: "IBM Summary of Progress Report, 1962," Plans for Progress, Box 77 and "IBM Corporation-Consolidated Report, 1969 EEO-1," Plans for Progress, Box 58, National Archives II, College Park, MD.

aspects of the corporation," said Green. "The other executive assistants were promoted at least to director."[15]

But Green was not promoted. He was the only black person in the group. Becoming a director was the first step to higher management. The next steps were to vice president, senior vice president, and executive vice president. Green never got onto the first rung of the ladder. "There were zero blacks at the time in the executive offices, no Asians, no people of color at that level, and they had never had any Hispanics," said Green. "Look, it's tough for anybody at those levels. But it was commonplace for us to be treated this way."[16]

Although he was not put into the executive track, Green continued to have a very successful career. He spent the next decade traveling internationally when he was assigned to the Americas and Far East Asia. He covered from Canada all the way down to Argentina and from New Zealand up to Taiwan. He was usually the only African American flying in business or first class, which provoked great curiosity among his fellow travelers, who often would ask him what he did for a living. "I was IBM for these people," said Green, whose high-profile job amplified the company's appearance as a high-minded, cutting-edge company. "IBM was a people company."[17]

At least that is what its advertising said. More distinctively from the other companies, IBM profiled its employees to illustrate how modern it was. In its 1969 annual report, IBM featured a female manager, a Japanese employee, and an Italian worker, in addition to its white male leadership. The company described how IBM personnel had programmed, maintained, and operated the five large IBM/360 computers at the Manned Spacecraft Center in Houston that were used in the moon mission.

Yet other employees put the company in a different light.

Bernard Duse, Jr., an African American who was a program manager for IBM from 1970 to 1984, sued the company, alleging that he was denied a promotion and later fired because he was black. The computer giant settled with Duse for an unspecified amount, without admitting liability.[18]

Louis Gerstner noticed the lack of diversity in IBM's upper reaches when he was hired to turn IBM around in 1993. He described a meeting with all of the country general managers as a "United States congressional hearing" with the nobles seated around an enormous conference table and a double row of younger executives behind them. "All the principals were white males, but the younger support staff was far more diverse," wrote Gerstner.[19]

He had been brought in to save the $65 billion company that had only 90 days of cash left. Sales of its mainframe 390 computers had dropped dramatically due to competition from Amdahl and Hitachi alternatives. The stock had plummeted from a high of $43 per share in 1987 to $12 in 1993.[20] The press was declaring the mainframe dead, and the company a dinosaur.[21] The corporation was in crisis.

Although Gerstner shook up the company's leadership, he did not change the color or gender of the executive officers. Gerstner had previously been CEO of RJR Nabisco for four years and president of American Express before that. He had also spent 12 years at the management consulting firm, McKinsey. When he got to IBM, he replaced six out of the 14-member executive officer team with outsiders. Three he had known at Nabisco, and three were from other industries. All were white men.

Gerstner wanted to get rid of the "I" strategy where IBMers had become more interested in their slice of the pie rather than the success of the whole company. He wanted to *inte-*

grate the company, to make people work together, instead of in pursuit of their own self-interest. He was trying to do with his employees what he wanted them to do with their products: get them to work with other products outside the IBM line. He wanted employees from different departments of IBM to collaborate. He wanted people to move from conformity to a diversity of ideas and opinions, from "value me" to "value us."

"IBM needed a dose of shock therapy," he wrote.[22]

Gerstner had a difficult time getting people to change, but he was not really setting the example. He had brought in his cronies from outside, and, although he thought them to be the most qualified, probably many others were just as qualified. He did not undertake an extensive search to find diverse candidates inside or outside IBM. He did not model the change he sought. Yet, when an organization is in crisis, there is often no time to engage in a more participative process.[23]

When Don Green retired in 1995 after 30 years at IBM, there still were no people of color and no women among the company's executive officers. Although the corporation had been a leader in Plans for Progress and did in fact employ well-educated women, blacks, Hispanics, Asians, and Native Americans, it had not advanced any of these individuals to the highest ranks.

General Electric

On any given day in America back in 1960, it is very possible that every person who lived in the United States used or benefited from something made by General Electric. They may have used the lightbulbs, refrigerators, or stoves the company made, or consumed the electricity it generated to run them. Or they might have ridden to work on a train pulled by an engine made by GE or been protected, as a soldier, by the fire control systems the company designed for weapons. "GE," as the company claimed in its prolific advertising, "brings good things to life." But its products also touched lives in a pervasive manner; the electricity GE supplied, as well as the lamps, the appliances, and the systems it made to use electricity, had a multiplying effect on its business. Ralph Cordiner, the chief executive of General Electric, described it as "the benign circle of electric power."[24]

As one of the largest corporations in America, GE reached deeply into people's financial lives as well. In the mid-1950s, Cordiner expounded on his idea of "people's capitalism," in which he described how nearly everyone in the country participated in the ownership of the corporation. At that time GE had 358,000 shareholders that included individuals (almost half were female), nearly 13,000 institutions, pension funds, schools, and churches. Almost half of its 250,000 employees were also becoming owners through the company's savings and stock bonus plan. Life insurance and other financial instruments enabled everyone to participate in the ownership of industry.[25]

To Cordiner, "people's capitalism" was a whole new form of capitalism that was made possible by the amplification—the multiplication—of wealth through corporations that had become even more involved in people's day-to-day lives than the government. In fact, the companies supplied governments with needed products such as electricity, street lighting for their cities, and public transportation. Corporations had become more important to people than government.

"As the first nation in the world to break through the ancient barriers of scarcity into an economy of abundance, we have a unique experience that we ourselves need fully to understand and to communicate to the rest of the world," Cordiner told a young class of business students at Columbia University.[26]

Given the sweep of his discussions on "people's capitalism," it is strange that General Electric did not offer a more public and more detailed embrace of Plans for Progress. Increasing the employment of people of color would surely lead to a more abundant economy. The company had a profound opportunity to exercise leadership in this area and to amplify the wealth of the country through the embrace of equal opportunity. Yet it fell shorter in its contract and in committing personnel to the project than smaller companies did. GE missed an opportunity for larger leadership. And it failed to expand its notion of people's capitalism even though a 1962 study, circulated by the President's Committee on Equal Employment Opportunity, explicitly stated that the black population was on the move, reaching for and demanding the achievement of physical, material goals.[27]

Fred Borch succeeded Cordiner as CEO in 1963 and remained chief executive until 1972, throughout most of the Plans for Progress era. Borch could have extended Cordiner's people's capitalism to include race, ethnicity, and gender. But he did not. Borch firmly kept to business concerns; he did not sally forth with grand pronouncements about the universe or GE's place in it. He saw part of his task as reviving GE's image, which had become tarnished in a scandal over a price-fixing conspiracy.[28]

Not discussing the internal dynamics of GE was very much part of the company's public relations strategy. At the time, GE was the fourth largest manufacturing company in

America, and it had three distinctive audiences: consumers who bought appliances and electricity; businesses that bought motors, turbines, engines, and electricity; and the government that purchased guidance systems, spacecraft, and electricity. It wanted to keep customers focused on its products.

But beneath General Electric's all-business persona and despite its refusal to sign a detailed Plans for Progress in 1961, the gigantic company eventually became deeply involved in the struggle for equal employment opportunity because of its immense workforce and ongoing need for new employees.

In the late summer of 1964, Elbert Johnson, an African American, saw a newspaper ad for employment at GE's Fort Wayne, Indiana, plant calling for men and women with high school diplomas to enter a company training program. He went to the location and filled out an application. He was called for an interview a couple of days later. A man by the name of Myers asked him if he could take any shift, and Johnson said he could. But Myers did not call him back. Johnson returned to the plant four days later, and Myers told him that he would not be hired because he had a police record. Johnson denied he had a record. Myers warned him not to come back to the plant with the kind of record he had.

Johnson returned home and told his mother what had happened. She went to GE and told Myers that her son did not have a record. Myers told her he did have a record, that he would not hire Johnson, and not to press the matter further. She asked to see Myers's boss, who declined to meet with her.

Faced with no other recourse, Elbert Johnson and his mother filed a charge against GE. "I don't know if you would call it discrimination for race or for color or not," wrote Johnson. "In the office is a sign stating no discrimination."[29]

The Plans for Progress Advisory Council was sent a copy

of the allegation. The Council in turn notified General Electric of the formal complaint and offered the company the choice of resolving it themselves or sending it through government contract compliance. GE's J. Roy Fugal, a personnel consultant to GE at its New York headquarters, said the company would investigate. In December, Fugal responded that the complaint had been resolved to the satisfaction of Elbert Johnson. He had been hired.[30]

GE was often on the front line of the integration struggle. On the 3-to-11 shift on September 9, 1964, at General Electric's lamp production facility in Warren, Ohio, two women exchanged blows. Gloria Jeanne McKinney, a black worker, allegedly hit her white supervisor, Eleanor Blastic, who allegedly hit her back and called McKinney "a dumb black-assed nigger." The foreman, Kenny Hayes, reportedly told McKinney to go home and Blastic to return to work. McKinney, who had worked for the company for only 15 months, was discharged because she had violated the company's rules prohibiting fighting on company property. In a complaint filed with the government, McKinney wrote she did not know about the rule prohibiting fighting and asserted that Blastic had struck the first blow, provoked the argument, and "got off scot free."[31]

The Advisory Council notified GE of the complaint, and the company requested 14 additional days to investigate the incident, which were granted. But then Fugal requested that the appropriate government agency take over the case. The case was turned over to Lieutenant Colonel William J. Tipton, Air Staff Projects Officer for the Equal Employment Opportunity Program.

The McKinney case illustrates how companies had real reasons to fear racial antagonism from workers who were not yet attuned to the necessity of treating one another with dignity and respect. Although many onlookers in the late twentieth century mocked the political correctness that rose out of the civil rights movement as being so polite as to be meaningless and devoid of content, nonoffensive speech was adopted to avoid the very real and incendiary results of using derogatory language. The use of racial slurs and cursing could quickly escalate to clenched fists as a way of resolving disputes. The McKinney case also reveals how companies needed to teach employees about integration in the workplace and to create an internal process for resolving racial issues fairly and effectively.

Virgil Day, a vice president of the firm, described the ongoing difficulty of offering equal opportunity in a giant decentralized organization like GE with dozens of plants all over the nation. "Hiring decisions are made or influenced by literally thousands of General Electric people, ranging from professional personnel specialists to the individual local sales manager who is trying to determine which of several qualified applicants he wants to serve as his secretary," said Day, a GE personnel specialist. "Once the fundamental criteria of qualification have been established, employment decisions may tend to become more subjective than objective. And the factors affecting promotion are so diverse as to be almost infinite."[32]

The company waited until race riots were upending big cities with large minority populations and businesses were burning before it faced the problem head-on. In 1968, GE commissioned a study that concluded the urban minority problem will be "the dominant one on the domestic, social, political and economic scene for the next ten years."[33]

Fred Borch produced a short movie that was distributed internally advertising the company's commitment to equality.

"We can no longer delay action," he said in the film. "We cannot—as a society—bear the cost of chaos in the lives of millions of our citizens."[34]

A GE advisory council was created to educate the company on minority issues inside and outside the plant. Virgil Day was given corporate responsibility for equal employment and minority relations. In 1969, Day assigned responsibility for carrying out GE's hiring and promotion policies to all operating managers, who then informed their managers. If the corporation had signed a real Plans for Progress contract in 1961, the managers would have been given responsibility for affirmative action eight years earlier.

From 1962 to 1969, GE hired 15,927 minority workers, but the same proportion—82 percent of minority employees—still worked in blue-collar positions, while 18 percent still worked in white-collar positions. (See Figure 7.3.)

However, the company definitely increased the representation of minorities where they previously had been underrepresented. Of the new operatives hired from 1962 to 1969, 8,024, or 45 percent, were minority. But the slightly higher position of craftsman was still dominated by whites. From 1962 to 1969, 8,997 new craftsmen were hired, but only 1,448 or 16 percent were minority. Whites held better jobs than minorities, but this may well have been the result of unions using a seniority system; new hires would come in at the bottom as more senior members moved up and into better jobs.

At GE, the smallest percentage increase among minorities was in sales, the public face of the company: 0.3 percent. From 1962 to 1969, the company hired 15,576 new salespeople, but only 73 were people of color. At the same time the company decreased the total number of technicians by 9,463. Yet 531 new minority technicians were hired. Technicians are usually

Figure 7.3 General Electric Company During Plans for Progress

Salaried Jobs	December 1962			December 1969		
	All	Nonwhite	Nonwhite (%)	All	Minority	Minority (%)
Officials and supervisors	17,525	71	0.4	23,024	195	0.9
Professionals and administrators	38,779	307	0.8	53,624	1,068	2.0
Sales	4,270	6	0.1	19,846	79	0.4
Technicians	14,062	195	1.4	4,599	726	15.8
Office and clerical	36,998	461	1.2	40,807	1,844	4.5
Total	111,634	1,040	.93	141,900	3,912	2.8
Hourly Jobs						
Craftsmen	44,805	892	2.0	53,802	2,340	4.3
Operatives	71,227	3,158	4.4	88,910	11,182	12.6
Service workers	4,887	405	8.0	3,689	660	17.9
Laborers	1,813	161	9.0	23,745	3,489	14.7
Total	122,732	4,616	3.8	170,146	17,671	10.4
Total jobs	234,366	5,656	2.4	312,046	21,583	6.9

Sources: Source: "General Electric Summary of Progress Report, 1962." Plans for Progress Report, Box 79; "General Electric Company-Consolidated Report, 1969 EEO-1," Plans for Progress, Box 58, 1969, National Archives II, College Park, MD.

highly skilled in their field as a result of education or specialized training. Their titles would include draftsman, electronic
specialist, nurse, or photographer. Salespeople sold the company's products over the phone, in person, or along a truck
route. It appears that the company preferred whites to be concentrated in sales and minorities to be technicians.[35] Sociologist
Donald Tomaskovic-Devey has explained racial job segregation as social closure: the effort by whites to distance themselves from minorities. The distancing by job description enables whites to preserve a higher status in the workplace, to
maintain their authority, and to exclude minorities from better
jobs.[36]

GE provided a statistically significant share of technician
jobs to minorities; 15.8 percent was higher than the level of
college-educated minorities in the overall population in the
late 1960s. The company's employment of 0.9 percent minorities in the top jobs of official and supervisor was slightly less
than the proportion of minority college graduates in the overall population at the time.

GE's segregation of its minority force into the two lowest-
skilled jobs was better than other Plans for Progress companies. At General Electric, 15 percent of service workers and
laborers were minorities, compared to 20 percent at IBM, 25
percent at Lockheed, and 31 percent at Walgreen Drug Stores.

Racial job segregation, especially in blue-collar jobs, in-
tensifies competition in the working class because the majority
of U.S. workers of all races in the 1960s had a high school
education or less. The hiring of minorities overwhelmingly
into hourly positions created the conditions for claims of reverse discrimination from whites, who felt excluded from
those jobs. Job segregation with minorities at the lowest end

of the ladder and whites concentrated in higher jobs set the stage for future allegations of discrimination.

As one of the largest private employers in the United States, General Electric deeply influenced the lives and livelihoods of its workers. But it rarely discussed its workers in public. GE focused on its products, not its people. The company never mentioned equal employment opportunity or the gains it had made in minority employment in its 1969 annual report. But it featured a full-page photograph of astronaut Alan Bean holding a radioisotope generator, partly developed by GE, which helped power his experiments on the moon. The company was a prime contractor for the moon mission, creating everything from the launch motors at Cape Canaveral, to the silicone on the soles of the astronauts' boots, to the clear Lexan plastic on their helmets. GE clearly took pride in its participation in the national triumph, but it celebrated the products that were created, not the people who created them. The main mention of its people came in the first pages of the report where it discussed a long strike in the last part of the year that cut deeply into the company's earnings.

Behind its public image, however, the company had become deeply enmeshed in the social and racial issues that shaped this country. GE employed a greater proportion of female workers, 25 percent, in 1969 than IBM or PepsiCo did, but far fewer than Walgreen did. As in most of the Plans for Progress firms, the women were overwhelmingly white. More than one-third were concentrated in office and clerical positions. (See Figure 7.4.)

In the 1970s, GE became the epicenter of a conflict that would become a milestone for working mothers. Martha Gilbert was working at a GE manufacturing facility in Salem, Virginia. In 1971, at the age of 28 and as a new mother, she

Figure 7.4 1969 Employment by Race and Gender (%)

Company	Caucasian Male	Caucasian Female	Minority Male	Minority Female
GE	68	25	5	2
IBM	80	14	4	2
PepsiCo	72	12	14	2
Walgreen	34	46	10	10

Sources: "GE Consolidated Report, 1969 EEO-1"; "IBM Consolidated Report, 1969 EEO-1"; "PepsiCo Consolidated Report, 1969 EEO-1"; Plans for Progress, Box 58; "Walgreen Drug Stores Consolidated Report, 1969 EEO-1," Plans for Progress, Box 59, National Archives II, College Park, MD.

filed a grievance through her union that the company's disability plan was unfair to pregnant women. The company advised her to stay home for three months without pay before the birth. The plan paid for the medical costs of the delivery but mandated six weeks of unpaid leave after her daughter was born. The stipulation meant that Gilbert had to give up four and a half months of pay each time she had a child. Her grievance turned into a lawsuit that was joined by six other GE employees who had also experienced the same loss of pay due to motherhood. The custom was standard practice for companies throughout the United States, who thought it was a gender-blind practice.

GE argued that its plan was gender neutral; it gave the same benefits to men and women. In other words, women should not get special benefits such as paid leave for a natural course of events such as giving birth, when men would not receive the same benefits. The women argued that, if men were injured off the job, they would receive disability pay and that pregnant women should receive the same pay.

The lawsuit turned into a class action involving the estimated 100,000 women who worked for GE in the United

States at the time. The suit alleged that the company had violated Title VII of the 1964 Civil Rights Act outlawing sex discrimination in the workplace.

GE fought the lawsuit to the Supreme Court, and it won. In 1976, the Court ruled in the company's favor, saying that removing "one physical condition" from the disability plan did not constitute sex discrimination and agreed that the plan was equal to men and women. Popular opinion, however, did not agree with the Court or with the company. In 1978, a powerful coalition of labor leaders and feminists went to Congress and persuaded legislators to amend the Civil Rights Act to prohibit employers from discriminating against pregnancy.

Within a year after the decision, GE changed its policies and abandoned its forced maternity leave, allowing women and their doctors to determine what was best. It also awarded partial pay to expectant mothers for as early as six weeks before the birth and six weeks postpartum in normal deliveries. Benefits were extended for complicated pregnancies.

"We saw that the mindset of our work force had changed, and certainly we have to change as a company to attract the most talented people," said Ted Meyer, a GE spokesman.[37]

Although General Electric originally tried to avoid affirmative action, it eventually faced some of the most important equal employment issues of the time. The corporation eventually caught up and even surpassed other companies in the proportionality of minority hiring in some job categories. Although only 6.9 percent of its workforce was nonwhite, by 1969 (lower than that of smaller companies) the company had hired nearly 16,000 new minority employees, far more than most other companies. (Figure 7.5 illustrates that the larger the company is, the more difficult it is to integrate.)

In the end, GE outpaced many other Plans for Progress

Figure 7.5 Size Matters

Company	Number of Employees in 1969	Percentage Minority in 1969
General Electric	312,046	6.9
IBM	155,917	6.0
Boeing	131,437	5.9
Lockheed	95,408	10.4
Mobil	38,436	8.2
Walgreen Drug Stores	22,988	19.0
PepsiCo, Inc.	6,444	16.0

Sources: "GE Consolidated Report, 1969 EEO-1"; "IBM Consolidated Report, 1969 EEO-1"; "Boeing Consolidated Report, 1969 EEO-1"; "Lockheed Aircraft Consolidated Report, 1969 EEO-1"; "Mobil Consolidated Report, 1969 EEO-1"; "PepsiCo, Consolidated Report, 1969 EEO-1"; Plans for Progress, Box 58; "Walgreen Drug Stores Consolidated Report, 1969 EEO-1," Plans for Progress, Box 59, National Archives II, College Park, MD.

companies in promoting people of color to the top jobs. By 1995, General Electric had promoted Lloyd Trotter, an African American, to be executive officer after he had worked in several different locations and jobs at the company for 22 years.

In many ways, Trotter epitomized the purpose of the civil rights movement to give people of color equal opportunity. Trotter had grown up in a blue-collar family in Cleveland. His father was a semiskilled worker, and his mother cleaned houses. After Trotter graduated from high school, he went to work at Cleveland Twist Drill in 1963 on a tool-and-die-maker apprenticeship. It was a four-year journeyman program, where he learned to make dies or molds to form specialized drill bits and tools. After he completed the program and became a skilled operator, he was promoted to product design and then to application engineering sales.

He wound up at GE lighting in 1970 at the age of 25 after he helped GE correct some tooling for its lightbulbs. He told the GE manager who offered him a job that he did not want a job, he wanted a career. Trotter already had a job in a family business that had been good to him. The GE manager told him that, after he got a college degree, he would have a career. Trotter had been going to night school and finally received his degree in business administration after nine years from Cleveland State University in 1972. With extensive experience in both manufacturing and sales, Trotter's career took off. He made at least a dozen moves throughout his career in lighting, appliances, and electrical businesses at GE. He returned those efforts by bringing all his energy to each opportunity he received.

As GE's first African American executive officer, Trotter served as vice president of the company's Electrical Distribution & Control (ED&C) division, which generated $6 billion in sales and employed 40,000 people.

8 | Affinity Groups: Plans for Progress for Employees

HOW DID A COMPANY SUCH AS GENERAL ELECTRIC GO from being ahead of other firms—promoting minorities to the position of executive officer in the 1990s—to becoming a white ceiling company in 2009? One reason has to do with its affinity groups.

In 1989, GE's chief executive, Jack Welch, peered down through his glass ceiling when he had no people of color or women among his executive officers. The phenomenon was widespread at the time; studies showed white women and people of color were employed at firms, but usually below the top levels. Welch invited a group of 15 high-potential black employees to meet with him and discuss what was and was not working for African Americans at the company.

At the time, Lloyd Trotter was the highest-ranking African American in the company. He was in the senior executive band, the third highest level from the top tier of executive officers. He got a list of the other African Americans who were going to be at the meeting and invited them to lunch in order to plan for the session with Welch. These people were considered thought-leaders in their businesses.

"The key thing that struck me [was that] I had been in the company almost 20 years, and I only knew three people in the room," he said. "I can't help you if I don't know you, nor can you help me if you don't know me. Because GE is so big, and people are spread over God's little half acre, it's very difficult if you are one of or two of people of color in a business to really network and help each other."[1]

Trotter asked the group to come up with one or two practical things they could ask Welch to do. He warned them, "Let's not make this a moon shot." They decided it was critical for Welch to show leadership on the issue of diversity, as he had with important business efforts such as globalization. They wanted him to express support visibly, in front of the whole corporation.

When Welch received his assignment from Trotter at lunch, the chief executive gave the work back to him. "Lloyd, how many people do you hire in the course of a year?" Welch asked Trotter, who was running a large manufacturing unit.

"A lot," said Trotter.

"You hire more people than I do," said Welch. "I want you to look yourself in the mirror and say, what are you doing for diversity."

The two bantered back and forth about who had more influence on promotions within the organization. "I'm not going to mince words with you, nor am I going to show you the individuals I have mentored," said Trotter. "I'm just going to fall on my sword and say I haven't done enough. But that will be the last time you ask me that question. It won't take you off the hook, however, for showing leadership around this issue."[2]

In the end, both agreed to take responsibility. Yet what they were discussing ran counter to the culture of the company, which had promoted colorblindness, believing itself to be a performance-driven meritocracy. The black executives wanted to enable black employees to connect with one another without disturbing the basic ethos of the company—without being perceived as asking for special treatment. When Welch asked them how they would do that, they did not have an answer.[3]

For the next year, the black leaders studied solutions to the glass ceiling that other corporations had tried. They investigated affinity groups at various companies, including AT&T and Xerox, that were supposedly good at diversity to see how they were being run. African American affinity groups started as early as the late 1960s as a way for black employees to network with one another. A Plans for Progress booklet issued in 1968, "Affirmative Action Guidelines," recommended that companies create a career counseling system to ensure that minorities were not left out of the networks that transmitted information about strategies for advancing within the organization.[4]

Trotter said that some were just feel-good groups that met once a year and did not really accomplish much, while others seemed to be doing real work. He wanted GE's African American Forum (AAF) to help black employees climb the corporate ladder. "It was a self-help group aimed at education, however, the only measure of success was upward mobility and promotions," he said. "It was not a feel-good operation. If we couldn't get more people promoted than were being promoted before we had this then, it's been fun, it was good to know you, but it's not successful."[5]

Trotter himself was promoted to officer in 1990. In 1992, he became the first black executive officer at GE at a time when less than 30 percent of *Fortune 100* companies had any minorities at that level. Trotter had long been on a fast track at the company. But his willingness to assume yet another complex challenge in addition to his business responsibilities clearly added a new dimension to his stature.

The African American Forum (AAF)

When the African American Forum was created, the group got pushback from some employees who wondered whether African Americans were trying to form a black union (they were not). It also encountered resistance from African Americans who thought they could make it on their own, without the Forum. To that, Trotter asked how has that been working for you? The results had not been spectacular. Others worried that if they stood out, they would be hammered down. To that objection, he answered, let's be honest: In this mostly white company, you stand out wherever you go.

The purpose of the group was to network, to get to know one another's strengths, to help each other overcome weaknesses, and to notify one another of job opportunities. Trotter wanted to open his Rolodex to the group, to share information with them, and prepare them with information for job interviews. "Our white counterparts had that, while diverse individuals have a tougher time," he said.[6]

Essentially, the purpose of the African American Forum was to rival the power of the white promotion network. That network itself was segregated, not necessarily by intent but historically, as white men worked through their social and professional networks to find out about opportunities, discuss potential candidates for openings, and make selections.[7] The mere creation of the African American Forum implicitly stated that race as a separate culture within the organization was going to challenge the promotional preferences that white males received. Segregating the black workers into their own network created a lobbying group within the company whose ideas and concerns would have to be included in the organization. They too wished to be counted.

The Forum's ultimate goal was to get more blacks into GE's senior executive band, made up of about 360 people in 1990. From that group, Welch handpicked about 110 officers, and from that smaller group, he selected about 20 executive officers. In 1990, when Trotter became the first black officer out of 110, he brought the accomplishments and concerns of African American employees to the attention of people at the highest levels of the corporation.

In typical GE style, the African American Forum is organized in a hierarchical fashion around geographical hubs where the different businesses are located. Chapters are formed at the sites themselves. Each chapter has an executive board that meets biweekly while the chapter meets quarterly. The officers of the chapter of the African American Forum at GE Aviation in Lynn, Massachusetts, are president, vice president, treasurer, and secretary.

Dane Elliott-Lewis is a board member of the Forum at GE's engine plant in Lynn. He contributes about four hours of personal unpaid time per week to the chapter. Five to six key people run the group on a daily basis. A weekly meeting is likely to be attended by about 15 people, and most have worked for the company for less than 10 years.

Recruitment and Retention

The Forum engages in the emergent practices of recruiting and community engagement just as Plans for Progress did. The African American Forum in Lynn has made presentations to universities and professional societies of black engineers. It has organized tours through the plant to educate interns, new recruits, and the public.

The friendship that results from getting to know other African Americans at the plant and in the region is believed to increase retention. Elliott-Lewis is an engineer who was first hired by GE Aviation in Evendale, Ohio, in 1998. He then transferred to Lynn, where he certifies that GE's products, such as engines, comply with standards set by the Federal Aviation Authority, the Department of Defense, or any foreign agency before they go into the marketplace. He joined the African American Forum at both locations in order to meet people and to make friends after working long days that usually start at 7 A.M. and end at 5 P.M.

"You get out of the workplace and get to go out to dinner together," he said. "There is a chance to unwind and get to know people better."[8]

Mentoring

Members of the Forum who have up to 10 years of experience at the firm mentor interns and summer employees to educate them about how to be successful within the rigid culture of the organization. Elliott-Lewis has advised young black men to tuck in their shirts, shave regularly, and remove their earrings so that they fit into the GE culture. He believes employees need to understand the dress codes of the different businesses and levels of management. He counsels African Americans to dress two levels above the job to which they wish to be promoted. "Two levels above me is an executive. I look at the executives and I don't see them wearing jeans so I don't wear jeans," said Elliott-Lewis. He believes executives are watching to see whether they can "put this person in front of a customer to represent GE or are they going to embarrass us."[9]

He tries to be as candid with younger employees as African American executives have been with him. "To give positive career advice, I found African Americans more comfortable to approach than others, and that is one of the benefits of the AAF. You have that community in which I found people being more frank with me personally," said Elliott-Lewis.[10]

Cultural Education of the Corporation

The Forum tries to positively influence how other employees view African Americans as a group. As part of Black History Month, the group hired a jazz trio and steel drum players to perform during lunch in the cafeteria. It also invited the Tuskegee Airmen, the first black pilots who fought in World War II, to come and speak, attracting a standing-room-only, racially mixed audience.

Career Education and Visibility

The Forum holds an annual symposium in the Washington, D.C., area. A couple of thousand African American employees from around the nation come to hear what is new, what has been accomplished, and what is on the agenda for the coming year. GE's CEO addresses the group, and the senior staff meet with employees to get to know them better and to answer questions. Such a large meeting enables GE's leadership to see minorities in a new light—as a large and multifaceted group. It also enables non–African American executives to experience what it is like to feel like a minority.

Trotter made sure that all the African American interns attended the symposium in order to persuade them to continue working for the company. "Just the dialogue with young folks was exhilarating for me. It's all about talent, and how we get more than our fair share of it at GE," he said.[11]

That kind of large meeting enables a minority group to feel like a majority group. It enables them to see the array of talent that their group provides to the conglomerate's businesses, be it aviation, capital, energy, medical, rail, or water. It expands the psychological barriers that can develop when minorities are unable to see their own kind in leadership positions. It helps remove the sense of isolation and futility that can develop in a limited work environment.

At the symposium and throughout the year, the Forum offers workshops for anyone wishing to advance. One of Elliott-Lewis's favorite sessions was "Best Corporate Secrets Revealed," which refuted the notion that simple hard work would suffice in a complex environment like GE. "Your success is going to be ten percent what you know, your abilities," said Elliott-Lewis, reciting the unwritten rules. "It's going to be thirty percent who sees you and sixty percent is your image. That is one thing that new employees in particular don't get."[12]

The African American Forum gives black employees the visibility that they might not get without it. At the chapter level, the leaders meet with a GE diversity council, comprised of the plant's key managers, to report on activities and request funding. Chapter leaders remain very much in the sight of people who are looking for the next generation of leaders.

Business Development

The executive level of the Forum, comprised of the highest-ranking African Americans at the company, has also reached out to develop business in Africa. They donated $20 million in medical equipment to 20 key hospitals after identifying countries with good governments and solid infrastructure. Although it was a humanitarian gesture, the hope was that the hospitals would become accustomed to using the equipment and buy it from GE in the future. "It's good business for GE because we sell a lot of medical products and generally the products you trained on are the products you buy," said Trotter.[13]

The African American Forum helped raise the number of African American officers from 0 in 1989 to 12 in 2008. The senior executive band—the officers in waiting—grew from one to 34 during the same period. But by the time Trotter retired in 2008, he was still the only African American executive officer. In 2009, there were no African American executive officers at GE.

The Women's Network

In 1997, Jack Welch called a meeting with about 25 of the senior women at GE to the executive dining room and asked them why they did not start a self-help network like the African American employees had. At the time, there were just nine female corporate officers out of 160—less than 7 percent—and no female executive officers. Some of the women felt that Welch was "from a different generation" who underestimated the contributions women could make to business. There was some trepidation as to the type of conversation that would ensue at the meeting. In fact, one of the women said at the meeting that she feared it would turn into a "chick bitch" session.

Welch laughed at that idea, apparently hearing the term for the first time.

Lorrie Norrington, then a vice president, embraced Welch's idea. She felt her career had been good and wanted a critical mass of women to reach down and pull up the next generation in order to ensure that they were highly skilled and could advance quickly.

Four women visited six different companies with women's networks—Procter & Gamble, Deloitte & Touche, and Kraft were among them—to find out about their organization, processes, and goals. They sought advice from the African American Forum and wrote a two-page summary about what worked in the networks and what did not. They came up with a similar structure to the African American Forum, which is organized around geographic hubs. The Women's Network has a hub chairperson, a regional chairperson, and an executive council.

Considerable debate ensued as the senior women discussed what the network should try to accomplish. They argued over how radical a vision of women they should advance. They wondered how much responsibility the group should assume for the hiring, development, and promotion of women. What would the company's position be on child care?

"We made a conscious decision to play within the confines of the culture," said Susan Peters, who was in human resources as vice president of corporate development. "We said it's not going to be a replacement for the efforts that the company should be making on behalf of diversity. We are not going to advocate."[14]

They found themselves in the same bind as the African Americans—wanting to strengthen their own group but unwilling to ask for special treatment fearing it would cause backlash from the rest of the organization. From the beginning, the Women's Network chose evolution, not revolution. Although the group decided to work within the system and not to take on confrontational issues, they still got pushback from some men who feared they were trying to develop an unfair advantage. "Where's the Men's Network?" some men asked.

In response, the women told them they could join the Women's Network, which was open to everyone, or they could form their own network. A few men showed up at early meetings but then stopped attending. They did not form their own formal affinity group.

Despite the women's efforts, in September 2000, an article appeared in *The New York Times* describing Jack Welch's diversity problem; no females reported directly to him.[15] The article featured pictures of all the men, but not one woman. "It kicked people in the butt. It was a black eye, and no one felt proud about it," said Beth Comstock, who worked for NBC and was a founder of the Women's Network. "The company looked terrible, like we were stuck in the Fifties. It was a rallying cry. We said we're not going to continue to have this be the image of our company. It elevated the Women's Network more."[16]

Confronting Bias

Susan Peters, a GE human resources executive, began looking at how women were being evaluated by managers and noticed they tended to be rated either as not tough enough or as too tough if they took a do-it-because-I-say-so approach. Taking command and ordering people around, which was considered a male style of leadership, was deemed "witchy" in women. Her conclusion was consistent with what psychologist Alice Eagly calls role congruity theory, which posits that prejudice develops against women who exercise leadership in a take-charge manner, which is typically thought to be a male style of leadership. Or they are criticized as too passive because women are often stereotyped this way.[17]

Peters found that the women were criticized no matter how

they led. As someone who was responsible for development of corporate leaders, she tried to sensitize other managers to the possibility that women were losing ground because of this perception. She also introduced these ideas to the Women's Network, where they began to explore a more productive way for women to lead in GE's team culture. Consistent with the diversity philosophy of including different perspectives in problem solving, women were encouraged to ask employees to contribute their ideas, to build consensus over which was the best one, and to move forward. They were urged to lead differently so that they would not be penalized for being too weak or too strong, trying to avert some of the penalties of GE's performance measurement system.

By the early 2000s, the women's efforts seemed to be paying off. Jeff Immelt, who replaced Jack Welch as CEO in 2001, promoted three white women to executive offices in 2003. Immelt was widely praised by the Women's Network for these promotions. Many members were convinced that "Jeff gets it."

The Women's Network intensified its efforts at leadership development by pairing high-potential female employees with senior male executives as mentors, so that they could learn from the experts who had the inside track. The Network trained women to develop skills they would need to advance, such as speaking and making presentations before large groups. When openings became available in the corporation, Susan Peters looked through her names in the Women's Network for candidates whom she felt should be considered for promotion. Senior members of the Women's Network advised less experienced women on how to handle tricky situations, such as difficult bosses or stubborn subordinates.

The Women's Network also holds an annual meeting. Like

the African American Forum's symposium, the event offers its members a chance to see themselves in a new light and to be seen as a powerful, accomplished group of thousands of different women who specialize in all aspects of GE's businesses. As they meet, speak with each other, learn about the rest of the businesses, and network, they find themselves—in that room—a majority. As they take leadership roles, they overcome psychological limits and enable others to do the same. In 2006, a GE employee in a video produced for the women's annual meeting spoke of how she had never thought of applying to become a manager before she joined the Network. Like an electric transformer, the Network amplified the power of any one person.

The Network has also experimented with how to engage other employees in the company. When the Women's Network at GE Aviation in Lynn sponsored a speaker, frequently no men would show up. After some trial and error, the women learned that leadership meant providing for everyone, not just their own group. They began sponsoring workshops on how employees should write their EMS. This is an internal resume of educational and job accomplishments that can be accessed through GE's database, in which people describe what they have done and what they would like to do in the company. In a culture filled with competitive types who are always trying to get ahead, the EMS was sort of a puzzle. Everyone had to fill it out, but no one really knew the best way to do it. The purpose of the EMS is to give management a good look at an employee's experience, while positioning the employee to take on new assignments. Once the women started offering seminars, people of every race and gender started attending. It provided a needed solution to a problem with which everyone had struggled.

Professional Education

Because many members of the Women's Network travel frequently, the group sponsors phone events; people dial into a conference call from wherever they are. One guest speaker addressed the importance of communicating across generations and cultures. At GE in Lynn, there are four generations of employees. In addition to communicating with workers of all ages, Terri Graf, an aviation quality manager, speaks to workers in India every morning. Educational seminars help her become more mindful of cultural traditions and sensitivities as she learns to motivate millennials or colleagues of other nationalities.

Cultural Integration

Being a part of the Women's Network has also empowered women to speak up in their own work areas. When Andrea Cox arrived at GE Aviation, she was one of the few female engineers out of hundreds of male engineers. The women were expected to adopt the male culture and were encouraged to learn golf because that's where "the decisions get made." "I was like, 'Do we have to wear pants and use the men's room, too?'" Cox commented.[18] Cox, who competes in triathlons, wanted to have a choice about what activities to engage in during the annual employee meetings, not be forced into one activity. Soon there were more choices: skiing, go-cart racing, mountain biking, and sailing. For people who had no desire or were unable to participate in those activities, there was bingo.

They expanded the culture.

The local chapters of the Women's Network also sponsor work-related activities that give the women a chance to connect and unwind. On one winter night, the Boston area network met at an Ann Taylor store to look at the latest fashions in women's business apparel. When the Women's Network was first founded in the late 1990s, this type of event was denounced by many women who did not want to spend precious time shopping or be associated with a stereotypical female activity. They wanted to network and get ahead in the company. But nine years later, the women engineers at GE Aviation in Lynn were looking forward to the evening as something different from the long days they spent at the office. It was a sign they felt comfortable doing what they wanted without the fear of being harshly judged. "Sometimes you get so wrapped up in your day, but then you go to the event and make the connection with people, and you feel so much better," said Terri Graf.[19]

The Asian Pacific Forum

GE's Asian Pacific Forum began organically in Albany and Schenectady, New York, where Asian employees were highly concentrated. A new hub formed in Connecticut, where GE is headquartered, and then it expanded across the country. In 2002, Jeff Immelt told the senior leaders of the group to take an active role in the organization. He wanted them to focus on the recruitment and retention of Asians. At the time, Yoshiaki Fujimori was already an executive officer of the company. Born in Japan, he had been promoted in 2001 to senior vice president of consumer finance in Asia.

As the Boston hub leader, Rajeshwar Das had 300 people on his distribution list and 100 people who are active members in the Asian Pacific Forum. They formed a mini GE in that almost all of the businesses are represented. Although Asians are the largest minority group at GE, the Forum still engages in recruitment. Representatives from the different GE businesses held a career panel and networking session with an Asian group called ASPIRE that is comprised of ambitious Asian women who are in high school, attending college, or working as young professionals.

To increase cultural awareness within the company, the Asian Pacific Forum sponsored Diwali, a festival of lights that marks the triumph of good over evil. It is celebrated at the end of the fall harvest with sweets and candles in several South Asian countries. More than two dozen employees dressed in native clothing, greeted people at the door, and made a 10-minute presentation about the celebration and the importance of the Goddess Ganesha in the Hindu religion. At the end, they gave recipients a small gift from India.

Das started with GE in 1982 and is one of the most experienced managers in his field of supply chain management. As such, he mentors employees with less experience, putting in an average of 10 unpaid hours of work per week as the hub leader. Yet he also gains more knowledge about the other businesses, which helps him solve issues in his own job. "If something comes up in my work role, where I need to know something about factory automation to help one of our businesses, I now have contacts in many other businesses I can go to and get help right away," said Das. "It has helped me personally."[20]

Das has not experienced any pushback from other groups, but he does not deny that it may exist. When he himself first was invited to attend the national summit of the Asian Pacific Forum, he was not sure what to make of it. "I didn't know if they were trying to put me in a box somehow," he said. "I just went and listened. Just creating a network and teaching people the ways of GE wasn't all that appealing to me."[21]

Yet as he engaged, he reconnected with family traditions he had lost after his father died. Das's father was born in India and worked in human rights at the United Nations. His mother was born in England. Although they lived in the United States, every summer after school let out, while other children would go to camp or play for long summer days, his family spent two months visiting family and friends in rural India. The cultural celebrations and the songs that are part of the Asian Pacific Forum's vitality remind him of the time he spent exploring the vast colorful and spiritual culture of India. The reconnection has encouraged him perhaps to return to India one day to do business on behalf of GE.

The Asian Pacific Forum has asked the members in each of its businesses to propose initiatives for growing businesses around the world and in their own communities. They have explored proposals for developing national electrical grids in India, supplying drinking water in China, and developing auto financing in Korea.

However, despite all the activity by the Asian Pacific American Forum, no other Asians have been raised to executive officer level since Fujimori. In 2009, there were no Asian executive officers at GE. Fujimori is now a corporate officer, the head of GE in Japan.

The Hispanic Forum

Wilhelm Hernandez-Russe joined the Hispanic Forum at GE Aviation immediately after earning his graduate degree in engineering at Cornell University and learned about diversity firsthand. Although he is from Puerto Rico, an unincorporated U.S. territory, other Hispanics were from the United States, from Mexico, or from countries in Latin America. "We are all Hispanic, but many of us have been raised with different values and totally different experiences," he said.[22]

Although all spoke fluent English, many spoke different versions of Spanish at home. And there were conflicting personalities within the group. "The first year, the president did not get along with the community service officer; they were always fighting over the phone when planning an event," he said. "But they were good friends and in the end we found a way to reach consensus. It's a process."[23]

The Boston hub of the Hispanic Forum, which started in 2003, included only about 30 members across all businesses, and 15–20 were in the GE jet engine plant in Lynn. Hernandez-Russe enjoys the Forum because it gives him immediate access to a group of potential friends. It enables him to gain visibility from plant management and an opportunity to demonstrate leadership before he might have been entrusted with it in a job promotion. Still, he wonders why there aren't more Hispanics at the plant and plans to suggest that GE recruit more Hispanics from the University of Florida or from Puerto Rico.

No Hispanic or Latino has served as an executive officer at GE.

The White Ceiling

Despite all of the activity in GE's affinity groups, by 2009, the company had three white female executive officers but no people of color among its executive officers. GE had a white ceiling.[24] White ceiling companies tend to return to having only white executive officers when the number of minorities is kept to a minimal, tokenistic level. GE had promoted only one African American and one Asian to executive officer level. It never achieved a critical mass and kept going. In addition, as the Great Recession unfolded, CEO Jeff Immelt cut the number of executive officers to 10 in 2009 from 28 in 2005 as he reorganized the company and laid off about one-fifth of GE's employees.[25] It is challenging, but not impossible, to keep diversity strong as a company shrinks.

The CEO chooses the executive officers, not the affinity groups. Yet as the affinity groups grew, some became more influential at GE than others. With more than 5,000 members in the United States alone, the Women's Network became the largest and the most powerful affinity group at the company. It was dominated by white women who benefited from sharing the same race as the white male leadership of the company. And perhaps because of its size and the number of senior leaders it had, it was able to question the leadership performance evaluation system.

The solution to the white ceiling is not to penalize white women for doing well, but to consider why they succeed. The Women's Network at GE developed differently than did the African American, Asian, or Hispanic affinity groups. The Women's Network did not reach out to female customers; it was unlikely that individual women would buy turbines, jet engines, water purification systems, or other GE products. Instead, it examined the traditional measurements of women's leadership style at the firm. Then it warned both executives and women to beware of falling into the traps of perceiving female leaders in a stereotypical manner and of women behaving in a stereotypical way. The Women's Network challenged the rules—the internal measurements of performance. It focused on learning leadership and advancing. As a group the women wound up advancing faster than the minorities.

Although companies clearly enjoy having affinity groups develop extra business for the organization, the groups can be just as useful as a vehicle for developing leadership and examining bias in a company. If employees spend their free, unpaid time in these networks and enrich the company in ways that go beyond what their jobs require—by engaging in recruitment, mentoring, cultural education, or business development—the organization should respond by grappling with the question of whether performance measurements of race, gender, or sexuality at a company are equitable or not. (See Figure 8.1.)

Figure 8.1 Causes of White Ceilings in the *Fortune 100*

1. CEO has never promoted a minority to executive officer.
2. The number of minority executive officers has remained at a minimal, tokenistic number. No critical mass is achieved that enables racial representation to continue as executive officers turn over.
3. Women's affinity groups have emerged stronger and more powerful than other affinity groups, and they tend to be dominated by white females.

When a company experiences a white ceiling, Ashleigh Shelby Rosette, who teaches at Fuqua School of Business at Duke University, recommends that managers examine the evaluative process and ask themselves why whites are congregated in leadership positions and minorities are not. She conducted a study showing that whites are perceived to be prototypical business leaders in the United States. "If racial minorities consistently attain objective achievements, but those accomplishments are not reflected by good leadership ratings or positive leadership perceptions, managers should attempt to rectify this disconnect and consider the presence of cognitive biases that may favor Whites over racial minorities," she wrote.[26]

Minority Women

Although women's affinity groups have advanced white women, they have not advanced women of color. One reason is that minority women do not benefit from access to either the living room or the locker room.[27] They are not members of the dominant race, as white women are. They do not share the dominant gender, as black men, Hispanic, and Asian men do with white men. Women's networks tend to be dominated by white women. African American, Hispanic, and Asian networks tend to be dominated by males. In 1995, not one of the companies in the *Fortune 100* had a multicultural women's group. Some companies, such as PepsiCo and IBM, have started special multicultural women's networks to begin to give these women the opportunities that other employees have received from their affinity groups.

In the 1990s, diversity experts complained that businesses were more focused on assimilating women and people of color rather than engaging in serious cultural change within organizations. R. Roosevelt Thomas, in *Redefining Diversity*, wrote "managers continue to talk about facilitating the assimilation of minorities and women."[28] But as they have developed over the years, affinity groups have enabled minorities and women to magnify their voices so that the culture hears them. Through the power of incremental change, by reinforcing positive stereotypes, minorities and women have gained acceptance within the corporation. Chief executives increasingly support

affinity groups to deepen the dominant and emergent processes of diverse employee recruitment, retention, and development, and they often back them with significant company
resources. Hewlett Packard officially spent about $500,000 in
2006 on its employee affinity groups.

The number of affinity groups in the *Fortune 100* doubled
in ten years, from 1995 to 2005. There was a positive correlation between affinity groups and high officer integration; 90
percent of the most integrated companies had them. By increasing the pluralism of the culture, the groups generally have
raised the chances that diverse employees will be judged by a
peer, not necessarily someone from a dominant culture. As
more diverse employees become accepted, they have begun to
question whether companies' performance is really bias free.
But not all of the networks have benefited equally or propelled
one of their own to the highest position.

GLBT Groups

As they have grown and developed, the gay, lesbian, bisexual,
and transgendered (GLBT) groups in some corporations have
worked very effectively to advance workers' rights. At the
computer and printer maker Hewlett Packard, the GLBT
group was one of the first to form. "Their intent really was to
connect and reduce the isolation that they felt," said Cindy
Stanphil, HP's head of diversity. "What most gay people will
tell you is 'I can't be myself if I have to come in and hide who
I am. I spend a lot of time hiding that versus being productive.'"[29]

The GLBT group at HP has invited straight people to help
them understand how to be successful in the system. As the

group has evolved, it has provided feedback to the company to make its processes and systems more inclusive so that they are not measured with "a straight, white male yardstick," said Stanphil.

In addition, the development of affinity groups enabled HP to strengthen its ability to fight discrimination in its workplace. In 2004, the Ninth Circuit Court of Appeals backed the company for asking an employee to remove a poster that HP believed to be discriminatory. In the case, the plaintiff Richard Peterson put up a poster quoting various Biblical passages condemning homosexuality in response to posters the company had put up of African American, Hispanic, Caucasian, elderly, and gay employees, with the caption, "Diversity is Our Strength." Peterson found the poster of a gay man offensive to his religious views. When the company asked him to remove the poster because it discriminated against gays, he sued HP alleging that the company discriminated against his religious views. The court ruled that the company was right to promote an atmosphere of tolerance in the workplace. The court ruled that, although people were entitled to their religious or secular views, no one had the right to persecute other people at work in the name of religion.[30]

By mid-2005, GE had established GLBT groups in only a few locations. Because this population is usually hidden and people are slow to join, the group added an A for "allies" to signal that it was safe for heterosexuals who supported them to join the group.

Richard Friend, a diversity consultant, recommends adding an A for "allies" to every affinity group to decrease the stigma and segregation of the groups and to be more inclusive of people who support the group's aims. Without an A, heterosexuals find it difficult to join a GLBT group without constantly explaining that they are not GLBT. Instead of gathering support, the group loses prospective members.

During the studies for this book, it was not possible to collect enough data to determine how many gay, lesbian, bisexual, or transgendered employees had been promoted to executive officer in the *Fortune 100*. Some corporate personnel said they did not track the information, and others became annoyed by the question. "They ran away before we could tag them," responded an employee of the Walt Disney Company, as if we were tracking a rare breed seldom seen on the corporate landscape. If the personnel we contacted knew of any officers, they did not identify them. Although "don't ask, don't tell" in the U.S. military was repealed by Congress in 2010, it is still alive and well inside corporate America.

9 Importing the Important People

PEPSICO UNDERSTOOD THE BUSINESS CASE FOR RACIAL DI-
versity decades before other companies did. In 1940,
the company hired a black sales representative, Herman
Smith, and two young black business interns, Allen McKellar
and Jeannette Maund, to develop Pepsi in the "Negro market,"
as it was called at the time. To connect with black customers,
they traveled throughout the country under difficult conditions, sleeping on the floors of friends' and relatives' homes
in the South before desegregation when there were few motels
or hotels for blacks. By 1947, black consumer power was estimated to be worth $7–10 billion a year, and PepsiCo, then a
relatively small upstart, wanted to capture the black soft drink
market.[1]

As the black sales force grew steadily to 8, 10, and 12
men, they combed the country putting Pepsi vending machines
on black college campuses, Pepsi-Cola into soda fountains at
black restaurants, and bottles of the cola into stores in black
communities. The company was well ahead of its larger rival
among black consumers. When it became known that Coca-
Cola did not have a single black sales representative, African
Americans boycotted the product in 1950.[2]

One of the early black salesmen, Harvey Russell, opened

the African market for PepsiCo in 1959 when he won three franchises from the Western Nigerian government. Russell was promoted to the head of Negro marketing, and the first thing he did was change the name to Special Markets. He expanded diverse marketing and created a post for a bilingual national coordinator for the Spanish market in 1964. In 1965, Russell became the first black vice president of corporate planning for PepsiCo, Inc. In 1967 he was promoted to vice president of community affairs, becoming the first African American executive officer of the company. This is where the average *Fortune 100* company still was in 2009, with just a little more than one person of color in the executive suite.

Russell was born in 1918 in Louisville, Kentucky, to a "long line of eggheads." He graduated from West Kentucky State College, where his father was president. His mother taught high school, and his grandparents were among the first African Americans to graduate from college. During World War II, he went into officer training with the Coast Guard and was commissioned as an ensign. After the war, he learned marketing and worked part time in the summer steering the yachts of wealthy African Americans from New York to Oak Bluff in Martha's Vineyard. Russell's contacts among the African American intellectual, military, and business elite became part of his vast sales network.[3]

PepsiCo learned early that tapping into multicultural markets would enable it to grow. Its annual report in 1960 was one of the few to depict African Americans. As part of its marketing campaign to position PepsiCo as an integral part of "having fun, thinking young," it showed a young black man playing tennis, and it described sponsoring a tour by Louis Armstrong and the All Stars in West Africa, where the company recently had established franchises. "It not only helped sales, but the resultant good will induced our State Department to sponsor the group for an extension of the tour," according to the report.[4] The cover of PepsiCo's 1969 annual report showed a line of different nationalities in a supermarket—including an Asian woman, a Canadian Mounty, a Mexican Salsa performer, and a black businessman—waiting to buy the company's products. Although some of these figures might be considered stereotypes now, they illustrate how PepsiCo was thinking about not one standard type of consumer, but several.

Yet what is very surprising is how few women PepsiCo employed in 1969. (See Figure 9.1.) Its annual reports and advertising frequently featured happy, smiling women, but just 14 percent of its workforce was female. This was nearly half

Figure 9.1 PepsiCo Employees, December 1969

Salaried Jobs	Caucasian Male	Caucasian Female	Minority Male	Minority Female
Officials, managers	635	11	27	1
Professional	338	40	25	0
Technical	75	2	23	0
Sales	1,000	3	179	1
Office, clerical	117	644	22	117
Total	2,165	700	276	120
Hourly Jobs				
Craftsmen	406	0	26	0
Operatives	1,277	19	252	7
Service workers	154	8	43	2
Laborers	659	28	285	17
Total	2,496	55	606	26
All Jobs Total	4,661	755	882	109
% of Total Jobs	72	12	14	2

Source: From "Consolidated Total—PepsiCo, Inc., 1969 EEO-1," Box 58, Plans for Progress, National Archives II, College Park, MD.

the proportion of females that GE employed, and it was even less than IBM had. As was typical of that period, the women were segregated into office and clerical positions, and very few women of color were employed at all.

By 1995, PepsiCo's management had not continued its exceptional record in promoting minorities; it had not risen above the token level. The company had no white female or male minority executive officers. But it did have an Asian female, Indra Nooyi, who was a senior vice president in charge of strategic planning. Nooyi was born in India; she was one "minority" out of seven executive officers.

When Steve Reinemund became chief executive and chairman of PepsiCo in 2001, a white female executive officer, Margaret Moore, who had worked at the company for more than 25 years, had been promoted to senior vice president of human resources. He kept Moore and Nooyi and promoted two African American men; Lionel Nowell III became senior vice president and treasurer, and Larry Thompson became general counsel. By 2005, there were three white females, one Asian female, and two African American males on Reinemund's 11-person team. He increased the diversity of his executive officers to nearly 55 percent. Not only was it an impressive amount of growth, but it well exceeded the average of nearly 21 percent female and minority executive leadership in the *Fortune 100* in 2005.

Reinemund basically shared the same perspective as Merck's chief executives Gilmartin and Vagelos. He wanted to create an atmosphere where all of PepsiCo's people could rise to meet their abilities. Whenever Reinemund gave an internal talk at PepsiCo, he reiterated his core desire to create an "environment where true greatness can be achieved by valuing people for their differences, strengths, talents and callings that they bring."[5] Reinemund recognized not only the urgent demographic need to include more women and minorities in the company's operations, but the business opportunity that their inclusion presented. "How can you conceive of all the products consumers want, how do you develop those products, market those products and sell those products if you don't have a total team from the front line to the board room that represents the consumers you want to sell to?" asked Reinemund.[6]

PepsiCo, a consumer package goods company, operates under the brands of Pepsi Cola, Lays, Frito-Lay, Tropicana, Quaker, and Gatorade in the United States. At Frito-Lay, for example, the company does everything from producing the seeds for the corn used in Fritos and Doritos to placing the final product on the shelf. They try to ensure that they do business with a variety of races, ethnicities, and genders at every level, from farmers who plant the seeds to people who own the stores. Reinemund believes it is the comprehensiveness of how PepsiCo makes, moves, and sells it products that has enabled it to include race and gender into its overall process from the entry-level position to the CEO.

"That's what makes us strong," said Reinemund. "In 15 out of 17 cities in the United States, the minority is the majority. Take Los Angeles. Walk down any street and walk into the stores and see who shops in there, works there and owns those stores. For the most part, they are not white males. There are very diverse people in those stores."[7]

"If you really want to get the best displays, the best locations, the new products on the shelves, you can go into those stores and speak to those shop owners in their native language," he said. "If you can bring materials that are in their native language that they can put up and communicate with consumers in their native language, you have a much higher likelihood of selling more products. We've proven it. We know it for a fact."[8]

The linkage from the consumer to the PepsiCo employee is strengthened by the affinity groups whose members include sales representatives as well as officers. The groups started in the late 1960s when African American employees began meeting regularly with one another and with management to raise awareness of race issues at the firm. Since then, seven other groups have formed: Women; Women of Color; Asian; Latino; Gay, Lesbian, Bisexual, and Transgendered; Disabled; and even White Male. Over the years, these groups have metamorphosed from employees at the periphery of the business to serving as a club, a support group, a study group, a leadership group, and an entrepreneurial group within the organization. Many groups have reached out into their communities and developed new markets for the company. PepsiCo annually budgeted $500,000 to support the groups, and one insider estimated that the company spent a total of $1 million a year on them before the economic downturn in 2008.

Affinity groups play important and wide-ranging roles in educating and developing employees at the firm. In 2008, employees in the disabled network were investigating how to better serve people with disabilities inside and outside PepsiCo: designing easier ways for customers with arthritis to open juice bottles or improving computer facilities for employees who have vision trouble or who are confined to wheelchairs. Inclusion—learning to value people who look different, move in a different way, or have an accent—is an adaptive process in the workplace. In other words, people have to learn to appreciate others; they cannot just be ordered to do so. At PepsiCo, employees have a built-in incentive. They do not just have a job with the corporation, they have a real ownership in the business. Every employee up and down the organization from the CEO to the person on the line in a manufacturing plant is given stock option grants. One person's success is tied to everyone else's.

"We build an entire dialogue and process around this as people are hired into the organization," said Ron Parker, who is head of PepsiCo's diversity program. "We expect people to act like owners, which breeds an entrepreneurial spirit and brings with it a strong sense of teamwork."[9]

Even though the company is far more advanced than most other companies in cultivating diversity, some problems have still developed over the years. In 1997, some African Americans who had applied to be route salespeople for Frito-Lay at its plant in Harahan, Louisiana, near New Orleans, filed a complaint alleging that the company hired more whites than blacks. An investigation revealed additional problems; the few black salespeople who were hired were assigned to neighborhoods in New Orleans with higher crime rates. In 1999, Frito Lay Inc. agreed with the Equal Employment Opportunity Commission to pay $225,000 in back wages to 233 minority applicants who were victims of discrimination for entry-level positions at the plant.[10]

In response, the company made diversity training of employees mandatory. PepsiCo began to evaluate and measure how well managers were developing and supporting their employees, as well as to weigh these measures evenly with how they were accomplishing their business objectives. People objectives and business objectives were weighted equally, 50–50. Part of managers' compensation was based on whether they were promoting and supporting diversity and inclusion. These items were listed on their professional development review, which occurs every six months. "It was coming at you from all sides," said Gail Quint, head of PepsiCo's internal communications. "It became very persuasive."[11]

To achieve integration, "there have to be some very fundamental things like one, an objective vision, two a set of principles and priorities, goals that you measure, programs that you facilitate, training and feedback," said Reinemund. "I don't believe there is one silver bullet, one thing you can do really well to create a diverse and inclusive culture."[12]

Reinemund routinely solicited feedback to find out how he could be doing better, a practice that occasionally resulted in some very long and painful discussions. Reinemund remembered a notable meeting at the company's headquarters in Purchase, New York. He had invited several black executives to share their thoughts with him on how to attract and promote more African Americans in the company. At the end of the day, everyone was mingling outside on the patio. Reinemund, who is white, stood up on a ledge and addressed the group with some closing remarks. When he got home that evening he found a two-page e-mail from a black female executive who described feeling humiliated by his actions. She said that when he stood above the group and looked down on them, she thought of a white master addressing a group of slaves.

"My first thought was, she was a brave woman," said Reinemund, for having the guts to express such strong feelings to her boss. After reading the e-mail, he said, "I felt embarrassed, ashamed that something I did so naturally would hurt someone's feelings like that." Reinemund wrote back to the woman, invited her to meet with him, and apologized to her during a long conversation in his office. Since then, he tries to speak to all groups while standing on their level. The female employee is now a senior executive at PepsiCo.

Now, a lot of chief executives might have dismissed such a complaint as an irritation that seemed to come from left field. After all, Reinemund had hardly grown up in an elite or privileged atmosphere. His father was a German immigrant who established a brewery after moving to the United States long after slavery had ended. He died when Reinemund was young, and, as a result, the CEO was raised by a widowed mother with few monetary resources. Reinemund hardly deserved to be compared to a slave owner by the young black employee just because he was white. Still, he openly grappled with her psychological projection.

"You can't make progress, move forward, and accept people if there is no license and freedom to talk about the irritations and sensitivities we each feel," Reinemund said. "Any cultural change is hard, but this one, because of the human nature of it, is the hardest single thing I worked on in my business career."

Reinemund's experience illustrates the startling and frank dialogues occurring in corporate America. These days, some of the most serious and in-depth conversations over race and gender occur in the workplace. Although slavery was nationally outlawed by the Thirteenth Amendment in 1865, the memories of it, as told by one generation to the next, can be so powerful as to haunt today's business meetings. Because of the Black Codes, thousands of African Americans continued to experience de facto slavery well into the twentieth century if they broke the laws made only for them. The free, hard labor of the black prisoners and chain gangs benefited the state, businesses, and landowners. Corporations that are the most dedicated to integration today find themselves undoing the slavery legacy, no matter how unconscious by some and forgotten by others the legacy may be.

The government also constrained the rights of Native Americans, Chinese, Japanese Americans, and women. Whether it was the unfair taking of land from native tribes, confining the Chinese to the roles of railroad builder and shopkeeper, interning the Japanese in camps during World War II, or not allowing women to contract, hold their wages, obtain credit, or work during marriage, these and other groups have historically been unable to develop their full potential in the American marketplace. Legally, they are members of a protected class of workers today, because their rights had been curtailed in the past, and as groups, they still lag economically behind white males.

Because Reinemund and Merck's Vagelos and Gilmartin were attuned to inequality, having experienced or witnessed disadvantage in their own lives, they understood that business had the power to transform the thinking, abilities, and prospects of all kinds of workers. They were unafraid to address the racism, sexism, and bigotry in this country that left an uneven playing field for so many groups who historically have been unable to develop their full value in the American marketplace. These chief executives did not offer charity to the workers they hired and promoted; they extended opportunity and demanded performance. They did not limit their reach to the historically disenfranchised, but opened the doors to people of many backgrounds, faiths, and origins. They heightened the ambition of the workplace because they believed integration was just as critical to the basic business goals of their companies as it was to the development of society.

PepsiCo's diversity efforts resulted in the development of new products such as Mountain Dew Code Red, which appeals to African Americans, a wasabi-flavored snack aimed at Asians, and guacamole Doritos and Gatorade Xtreme aimed at Hispanics. The company estimated that in 2004, about one percentage point of PepsiCo's 8 percent revenue growth came from new products inspired by diversity efforts.[13] In December 2005, PepsiCo, which had always been second to its chief competitor Coca-Cola, overtook it in market capitalization for the first time. PepsiCo's stock market value reached $98.4 billion compared with $97.9 billion for Coca-Cola.[14]

An Ominous Trend

However, after Steve Reinemund left in 2006 and Indra Nooyi took over as CEO, the composition of the executive officers began to change. By 2009, the percentage of female and minority executive officers had fallen to 27 percent, slightly above the average integration level for the Fortune 100. Half of the minorities and 44 percent of the Caucasian executive officers were born outside the United States The foreign-born Nooyi chose a diverse international mix for her executive officers. In her competition with Coca-Cola to gain the greatest share of worldwide markets, she has assigned responsibility of overseeing world regions and continents to foreign-born executive officers who came up through the company by working internationally.

Although it projects an all-American image in the United States, only one-third of PepsiCo's workforce is actually located stateside. In 2009, nearly half of its revenues came from outside the country, which nearly aligned with 43 percent of the company's executive officers being born outside the United States In the future, this global company is likely to earn even more profits and employ even more people overseas. If all companies balance their leadership this way, very few native-born Americans will be running the global companies. PepsiCo's composition of international executive officers portends an ominous trend. It undoes the hard-fought work of promoting a homegrown diversity team that people in the United States have struggled for, and it reduces the jobs for native workers.

Nooyi herself followed a route to the executive suite that other foreign-born executive officers have taken; their careers took off after they received graduate degrees in the United States. Nooyi was born in the city of Chennai, formerly known as Madras, which is located on the southeast coast of India. She earned an MBA from the Indian Institute of Management in Calcutta and came to the United States in 1980.[15]

"At 23, I asked my parents if I could apply to American universities. They did not want me to go but said, 'If you get in with a 100 percent scholarship, we can talk about it.' So I applied to Yale, which gave me a very good support package, so I had something to negotiate with my parents," she said.[16]

After she graduated in 1980, she worked in marketing and strategy at the Boston Consulting Group, Motorola, and Asea Brown Boveri. In 1994, she went to work for PepsiCo and rose quickly, becoming the chief financial officer in 2001 and chief executive in 2006.[17]

Nooyi certainly helped make PepsiCo the largest food and beverage company in North America and the second largest in the world, valued in 2010 at $60 billion. But for Nooyi, diversity means the world, not just the United States. Her cohorts, other foreign-born CEOs, behave in a similar manner, promoting a higher percentage of foreign-born employees to executive officers. On average, foreign-born CEOs had nearly four times the level of foreign-born executive officers as the average *Fortune 100* company had in 2009. (See Figure 9.2.)

Figure 9.2 2009 Foreign-Born CEOs Executive Officer Diversity (%)

Foreign-Born CEOs	Female Executive Officers	Foreign-Born Minority Executive Officers	Foreign-Born Caucasian Executive Officers	Total Foreign-Born Executive Officers
Average *Fortune* 100 Company	17	2	7	10
Alcoa, Klaus Kleinfeld	0	0	38	38
CitiGroup, Vikram Pandit	0	100	8	31
Coca-Cola, Mukhtar Kent	14	100	45	57
Dow Chemical, Andrew Liveris	7	100	18	36
Hartford Financial Services, Ramani Ayer	44	50	0	11
Ingram Micro, Gregory M.E. Spierkel	18	100	56	64
News Corp., Rupert Murdoch	0	0	40	40
PepsiCo, Indra Nooyi	17	50	44	45
UTC, Louis R. Chênevert	7	0	33	33

Several foreign-born chief executives displayed total ignorance of the American mandate to break the glass ceiling. In 2009, Australian-born media mogul Rupert Murdoch had a team of white males; 40 percent were born outside the United States. German-born Klaus Kleinfeld, who was head of Alcoa, also had no females or minorities, and 38 percent of his white male team was born in Europe. Sadly, Alcoa, an aluminum producer, had been one of the first companies to join Plans for Progress in the 1960s. Citigroup also had no females on its executive team, and all of its "minority" males came from outside the United States; they were born in India, Peru, and Mexico. The Department of Labor allows companies to count immigrants as minorities depending on their race and ethnicity in their annual census of workers.

When Rosabeth Moss Kanter published her groundbreaking *Men and Women of the Corporation* in 1977, she described *homosocial reproduction* as the tendency for people to hire and promote people who come from a similar background, went to similar schools, and share similar political or religious beliefs. Because white men headed most large American businesses at that time, they received the biggest criticism for pursuing the old boys' network, promoting people like themselves through informal networks. Yet the studies for this book indicate that most of the white male business leaders who were born in the United States have been listening to the message sent repeatedly to them over the past 50 years that women and other races and ethnicities wish to be part of the team. The same message—to be aware of biases in decision making—needs to be driven home to business leaders of all backgrounds who work in the United States

Companies with a high percentage of executive officers who were born outside the United States may argue that their high foreign revenues entitle them to such representation. However, there is no such correlation overall between foreign earnings and foreign-born executive officers. In 2009, United Technologies Corp. earned 59 percent of its revenues from abroad, and 33 percent of its top officers were born overseas. But GE earned nearly the same portion—54 percent of its revenues from outside the United States—but none of its executive officers was born abroad. Alcoa earned 48 percent of its revenues from outside the United States, and 38 percent of its executive officers were born overseas. But during the same period, Boeing earned 42 percent of its revenues from abroad, and none of its executive officers was born overseas. Exxon Mobil took in the highest proportion of revenues from outside the country, 80 percent, and only 6 percent of its executive officers were born abroad.

Promoting a high percentage of foreign nationals may undermine the American bootstrap tradition. Many foreign nationals have been hired by U.S.-based corporations after gaining an advanced degree—a master's degree or doctorate—at an American university. Foreign students often have to pay for graduate school themselves and frequently are ineligible for U.S. grants and fellowships. Being able to afford college in their home country usually meant that they came from a family with resources. The executive officers who were born outside the United States tend to come from elite, high-status groups in their birth countries. They are not the traditional homegrown minorities that affirmative action and diversity were originally intended to recognize. Yet if they wind up working on the U.S. side of a global corporation, drawing local pay and benefits, they are counted as minority group members in the company's annual census of its workers.[18] This trend is especially impacting homegrown U.S. minorities.

In 2009, more than half of the Hispanic/Latino executive officers of the *Fortune 100*, 53 percent, were born outside the United States. They came from eight different countries in Latin America. More than half, 52 percent, of the Asian executive officers hailed from outside the United States, mainly India. Overall, one-third of "minority" executive officers in the *Fortune 100* in 2009 were born beyond the U.S. borders, suggesting that companies have found a way to use the global worker as a diversity asset here in the United States. The microchip maker Ingram Micro employed 7 out of 11 executive officers who were born outside the United States, including 100 percent of its "minorities." One hundred percent of Coca-Cola's "minority" executive officers were born beyond the borders of this country, in Liberia, Colombia, and Mexico.

There is nothing wrong with hiring people with a different national origin; they are protected by the Civil Rights Act of 1964. Immigration is an important narrative in American history. But some companies, in their drive for global profits, have used diversity to trump affirmative action at the highest level of the corporation. The practice of promoting foreign-born workers is also impacting Caucasian executives as globalization expands.

In 2009, executive officers of the *Fortune 100* who were born outside the country were overrepresented. They comprised an average of 10 percent of executive officers when the foreign-born cohort of people who would be educated and experienced enough to hold such a position comprised just 1.5 percent of the total U.S. population.[19] This illustrates how *Fortune 100* companies—the biggest and richest corporations in the country—favored multinational diversity over national diversity.

Little scholarly research explores multinational hiring and promotions. But one study that examined promotion practices at a multinational *Fortune 500* financial services firm found that Hispanics, some of whom were born outside the United States, were rated as higher-potential managers than native-born blacks and Asians.[20] In other words, employers may have assumed that someone who was born outside the United States would have greater knowledge of how to excel in foreign markets.

But that assumption is not necessarily correct. Homegrown U.S. minorities and whites may have just as much or more experience in developing international markets. Hispanic Americans tend to straddle two cultures growing up in this country, speaking Spanish at home and English at school and work. Chinese and Japanese Americans also practice cultural traditions and speak native languages at home. Asian Indians frequently go to India for months during the summer to reconnect with family who speak Urdu and other languages.

All kinds of Americans study abroad, take overseas assignments, or simply vacation in other countries. Howard University, the nation's largest historically black university, offers an academic program in international business that includes finance, marketing, and management in international cultures. Its students study abroad in India and Europe. More than 150,000 members of the U.S. military have operated abroad since 9/11. The experience and perspective of veterans should be valuable in developing emerging markets. The United States is actively participating in the ongoing internationalization of the world. So the assumption that Americans have fewer skills to operate internationally than those born overseas is a generalization that loses its significance when closely examined. In other words, it is a stereotype that may be true in some cases but not in others. Americans are no longer innocents abroad.

Corporate leaders frequently cite the high cost of sending an American overseas as one reason for promoting more foreign nationals. But only one-third of jobs held by foreign-born executive officers in 2009 was geographically specific, such as president of Latin America or vice president of Asia Pacific. (See Figure 9.3.) Far more jobs, 42 percent, involved typical corporate duties such as human resources, finance, or marketing. Just one quarter of the positions required technical or scientific ability. The high cost of an ex-pat does not explain

Figure 9.3 *Fortune 100* Foreign-Born Executive Officer Roles in 2009

Jobs	Percentage of Jobs Held by Foreign-Born Executive Officers
Geographically specific (global, regional, or continental)	32
Typical corporate functions (CEO, marketing, finance, controller, human resources, risk assessment, strategy)	42
Technical or scientific duties (computer science, engineering, chemistry, or biology)	26

why so many foreign-born workers are in the top jobs in this country.

Companies understandably want an international perspective on their executive officer team. A shrewd strategic move for a U.S.-based corporation might be to harness the best brains of all countries in order to stay ahead of the global competition. However, there is no guarantee that such employees will want to stay in the United States. They could return to their home countries and start up sophisticated—even rival—companies with the knowledge and training they have gained.

Nearly one-third of global companies are headquartered in the United States, and it is clearly in the best economic interest of the United States to keep them here. Multinationals have made outsized contributions to overall economic growth in this country, contributing 31 percent of the growth in real gross domestic product (GDP) and 41 percent of U.S. gains in labor productivity since 1990. The productivity gains have resulted in nearly three-quarters of U.S. real GDP growth since 2000 as a result of their deep commitment to research and development. Even as they invest overseas, they continue to enrich the United States, fueling other medium-sized and smaller businesses as they purchase parts, products, and services and fund research.[21]

But it is also in the best interest of this country to staff these firms predominantly with homegrown workers. According to a report produced by the economic research group McKinsey Global Institute, multinationals contributed 11 percent to employment growth since 1990, even though they represented just 1 percent of all U.S. companies. In 2007, they employed 19 percent of the private sector workforce, and the global companies paid better on average than other employers. For managerial, professional, and technical employees, multinationals paid an average of $102,000 in 2007, which was 37 percent higher than the national average. Multinationals generally provide good jobs and better-paying jobs than medium-sized and small companies. They have a positive impact on the U.S. economy.

Having a rounded mix of views and talents from minority men and women, white men and women, plus internationals might be possible. But getting the right mix will take consistent effort and persistent attention.

Sustainability

Without grooming diverse, homegrown workers for leadership positions at company headquarters, the overall health of the community where the company is located will decline. Sustainability is an important component of the growing understanding of a new role for capitalism. Capitalism used to be all about profit, and anything that detracted from the bottom line was eliminated as shareholders came to demand higher and higher returns. However, the pursuit of pure profit in the financial industry, expressed through the mortgages-for-everybody strategy and the amplification of its predatory effects through the sale of mortgage-backed securities and the empty credit default swaps, has raised concern over the pure play strategy. The near collapse of the financial system and its extensive collateral damage to individuals who lost jobs, businesses, and homes reduced the value of firms in communities that have yet to see any revival since the Great Recession.

As businesses embrace sustainability in the use and consumption of energy, water, and packaging, thought leaders are now encouraging them to take the next stop and create shared value in communities where they operate. Harvard Business School's Michael Porter has advanced "The Big Idea" that capitalism, which was under siege after the Great Recession, needs to change from its limited model of engaging in social responsibility as a sideline to creating overall social value for the community. "The opportunity to create economic value through creating societal value will be one of the most powerful forces driving growth in the global economy," he wrote. "This thinking represents a new way of understanding customers, productivity, and the external influences on corporate success. It highlights the immense human needs to be met, the large new markets to serve, and the internal costs of social and community deficits—as well as the competitive advantages available from addressing them."[22]

Given the United States' history of civil rights and women's movements and its record of class mobility, workers here are not likely to accept companies that do business in their communities but do not employ and promote their people. In the pure play of recent years, Porter writes that communities "perceive that profits come at their expense" and that they are increasingly left out of corporations' profitability. To see that Porter's observation is nothing new, one has only to remember TCI's refusal to give the people of Birmingham what they needed to grow and change, causing itself and the city to decline from economic starvation and civil unrest.

Having a group of homegrown female, minority, and white executive officers with a complement of international perspectives has a multiplying effect. It shows diverse employees that they will get an equal chance, it increases productivity, and it strengthens resilience. It can help reduce the external costs of allegations of discrimination, lead to greater affinity with the community, and enable greater access to more talent, while acknowledging the need for social justice.

10 A New Plan for Progress

AN INTEGRATED WORKPLACE DOES NOT HAPPEN BY ACCI-
dent. It does not emerge magically from the invention
of a new program, or simply radiate from the heart of
an enlightened leader, or result from the mere hiring of a diversity consultant. Nor do promotions automatically continue
after the first glass ceiling has been shattered. Like most things
in life, leadership must be cultivated. The biggest American
companies with the most integrated leadership have worked
constantly to get it.

The chief executives of the companies with the highest
proportion of female and minority executive officers exercised
their authority to select a diverse team. Whether they did so
out of a determination to get the best talent, were driven by a
belief that diversity is better for business, or wanted to create
a meritocratic atmosphere, they led by example, which is critical for change.

The leadership of companies that joined Plans for Progress
50 years ago is now more integrated, on average, than the
companies that declined to join or that were started after Plans
for Progress had ended. This demonstrates that the protocol
was effective and that the longer a company practices integration, the better it becomes at it. The blueprint for change came
from two scions of slavery: John G. Feild was the great grandson of a cotton plantation owner in Arkansas; Hobart Taylor,

Jr., was the great grandson of a slave in Texas. In 1961, these men—one white, one black—launched an ambitious operation to eliminate racial bias from employment in America. They spelled out the steps that companies should take to reach out to schools, communities, and organizations to find and develop minority workers. They encouraged businesses to scale up their recruitment successes and to reproduce their integration practices across vast, complex, commercial empires. Aware of the scope and impact of their efforts in reshaping the hiring process in businesses throughout the country, each man independently proclaimed that he alone had invented affirmative action.

Affirmative Action

Although neither Feild nor Taylor, Jr., invented the phrase *affirmative action*, they certainly defined what became known as the process of affirmative action: going out, finding, and recruiting first people of color and, later, women. These men had an early sense of the importance of their work. Affirmative action in the post–civil rights era has been viewed in a negative light—as giving preference to people who did not deserve it. In retrospect, however, it inaugurated a new epoch, a new attitude by business toward using business methods to solve problems initially deemed to be social, but that were fundamentally economic. The companies themselves broke the monopoly that whites, especially white men, had on the best jobs. By undertaking this enormous effort to reform their hiring and promotion practices, corporations accepted their place in society as institutions that were even more important in the everyday lives of citizens than government was. This represented an enormous shift in the power of corporations in the twentieth century.

In the nineteenth century, affirmative action had been used to describe the actions taken by legislatures to resolve pressing public issues. Legislators themselves described affirmative action as a remedy to a problem that was more constructive than a negative action. Affirmative action meant creating a new set of rules or policies. Negative action meant outlawing an activity or levying a fine or punishment. The phrase *affirmative action* was also used by magazine and newspaper reporters back in the mid-1800s to describe the actions that legislators took on bills.[1]

By the turn of the twentieth century, however, the phrase was being used to describe actions taken by the ruling bodies of business concerns. In 1901, the *Washington Post* reported that stockholders of the Union Pacific Railroad had taken "affirmative action" to amend their articles of association and issue $100,000,000 of new stock.[2] As corporations became established and grew after the Civil War, they adopted the administrative practices of legislators, and the phrase *affirmative action* was applied to describe their activities in performing new, needed actions in governing the corporation.

The evolution of the use of the phrase affirmative action illustrates a power struggle between government and business. By the 1930s, legislators used the phrase to wrest control of the economy from business owners. It appears that the first time the phrase was used by the government in ordering industry action occurred in the Wagner Act, which created the National Labor Relations Board in 1935. The law prohibited private employers from discriminating against employees in labor unions. It ordered the offending companies to "cease and desist from such unfair labor practice and to take affirmative action, including reinstatement of employees, with or without back pay, as will effectuate the policies of this Act."[3] The government's use of the phrase illustrates how powerful companies had become in affecting the nation's employment, rivaling and even undermining the government's ability to steer or shape the economy.

In 1942, U.S. Secretary of the Interior Harold Ickes pleaded with a group of coal miners and operators to extend their workweek to increase coal production to fire all the plants needed to produce the armaments and ordnance for World War II. The group, however, refused to extend the work week immediately and instead took "affirmative action" to postpone discussion of the proposition. In using the phrase, the mining group flaunted its power over and independence from government. The miners did not wish to be ordered around by politicians or civil servants and would make a decision in their own time. Ickes left the meeting in a huff, warning that "we shall lose this war if we can't produce enough coal."[4]

Affirmative action was specifically applied to race by the Fair Employment Practices Committee (FEPC), created by President Franklin Delano Roosevelt in 1941. His Executive Order 8802 declared "there shall be no discrimination in the employment of workers in defense industries or government because of race, creed, color or national origin." Another Executive Order 9346, passed in 1943, required that all government contracts contain the clause agreeing not to discriminate. As the FEPC began to try to enforce the order, it used the phrase *affirmative action*. In 1943, the FEPC informed the Capital Transit Company of Washington, D.C., that it "expected affirmative action" that would lead to compliance with the order. The company, however, said it had wanted to employ people of color but could not because of the attitude of its current employees, the inability to get people to train black employees, and the resistance of customers.[5] Capital Transit failed to accept its responsibility as an organization that played a significant role in the local economy.

The concept of affirmative action as a remedial effort ordered of employers by government to correct unfair hiring practices was already more than 25 years old when President Kennedy signed Executive Order 10925, which prohibited government contractors from discriminating against any employee or applicant for employment. The Roosevelt administration was the first to use *affirmative action* in the same sense that Kennedy, Johnson, Feild, and Taylor generally understood it: to assert control over the hiring practices of businesses.

In the wider scope of history, affirmative action really marks the rise in power of the central importance of the corporation to citizens and society separate from the government. Whether the issue was controlling the mining of resources, the production of goods, or the employment of citizens, the power of corporations rivaled the power of government. In fact, at times it undermined the goals of government and the security of the country. President Roosevelt had pushed for an FEPC partly because he was concerned that a labor shortage might occur if defense contractors kept their doors closed to blacks during the war. Some contractors hired blacks for menial jobs such as janitor, but other defense contractors refused to comply, arguing that they would have to desegregate their entire operations. In response, President Roosevelt increased the FEPC's budget to nearly a half a million dollars and hired full-time staff distributed throughout the country to pressure the companies to comply.

The FEPC met huge resistance as employers rejected their responsibilities. White shipbuilders on the West Coast went on strike rather than admit blacks into their union. In addition, the committee did not have the power to cancel contracts, so its enforcement was limited. Despite the intense struggle for integration during that period, however, blacks held 8 percent of defense-industry jobs, up from 3 percent held before the war. The government wound up employing 200,000 black workers, more than triple the number before the war. But most were still concentrated in dirty, menial jobs.[6]

By applying affirmative action to employment practices in the 1960s, corporations finally accepted how important and central their role had become to American society. Through the best practices developed by the Plans for Progress Advisory Council, the support for employee affinity groups, and the growing awareness of the importance of diversity to many aspects of the business, managers have continuously deepened their emergent and dominant employment processes to create a fairer workplace.

Ten Steps Toward More Integrated Leadership

What's heartening is that companies do not have to have participated in Plans for Progress to have produced a highly integrated leadership. Of the top five *Fortune 100* companies with the highest cumulative integration over the 14-year study, Prudential, PepsiCo, and Hartford Financial Services were involved in Plans for Progress. Hartford was involved as a subsidiary of ITT, but was spun off in 1995 and became an independent company. Neither Merck nor TIAA-CREF participated in Plans for Progress. (See Figure 10.1.)

The companies that were the most integrated at the execu-

Figure 10.1 *Fortune 100* Companies with Highest Diversity Index (%)

Company	Female and Minority 1995	Female and Minority 2005	Female and Minority 2009
Average *Fortune 100* Co.	7.98	18.97	23.99
Merck & Co.	27.79	78.57	50
Hartford Financial Services	N/A	40	66
Prudential Financial	26.31	33.33	33.33
PepsiCo	14.29	54.54	27.27
TIAA-CREF	11.11	35.71	35.72

tive officer level share several beliefs, processes, and activities that most had pursued for years. They had strong ethical beliefs that they constantly reiterated. Before retiring from Pepsi-Co, Reinemund, in every internal talk he gave, spoke about valuing the individual. The core of his belief was to create an "environment where true greatness can be achieved by valuing people for their differences, strengths, talents, and callings that they bring." The leaders demonstrated congruence by acting consistently with their stated beliefs.

In companies with the most integrated leadership, the ethical belief in integration is intertwined with the business strategy, not just one of four or five listed objectives that the CEO believes would be nice to achieve. At Merck, the pharmaceutical giant, which ranked first in the *Fortune 100* for having the highest integration among executive officers, Raymond Gilmartin continually stated the company's creed to never place profits above patients.

Companies must figure out the role that diversity and ethics will play in their core business strategy and intertwine the related concepts to create a vision for the company. As obvious as this need seems, most companies have not recognized it. Instead, they have three clunky and separate statements: a diversity policy, an ethics code, and a business strategy. Fusing the three goals keeps managers and employees mindful that how their work gets done is just as important as its completion.

These are the ten steps taken by most of the companies with the most integrated leadership.

1. They developed a core mantra that fused their diversity goals and ethical principals with their business strategy. Leaders articulated this vision in every internal speech and company communication. They demonstrated congruence.

2. They created a secure, reliable feedback system through which employees from all over the world could communicate safely and directly to a company executive, expressing their concerns over how they were being treated by other members of the company.

3. They provided diversity training to employees and fostered a culture of learning.

4. They administered 360-degree performance measurements to managers in which they were evaluated by subordinates, peers, and superiors. Managers' pay was partly determined by how they were rated and how they developed diverse employees.

5. They cultivated and harvested new talent. They offered summer internships and contributed to funds that enabled underprivileged students to go to college. They widened their talent harvest to historically black and women's col-

leges. They recruited in Latino areas of the country, on tribal reservations, and in communities with recent immigrants.

6. They developed, supported, and funded extensive affinity groups. They made it mandatory for managers and officers to be involved in these groups. The groups then educated coworkers about cultural differences, developed wide networks, learned leadership, and developed new business strategies to reach out to untapped domestic and foreign markets.

7. Companies invested in local communities to improve public school education and opportunities.

8. Executives promoted women and people of color, as well as employees with an international perspective, thereby demonstrating their commitment to the core diversity mantra.

9. Chief executives opened themselves to negative feedback about what was not working by holding regular meetings with managers and employees.

10. They never stopped trying new ideas to foster integration because they realized that companies are highly changing environments.

Although taking these steps enabled companies to achieve high levels of integration among their leadership. it will not be enough to get them through the next 50 years. The processes must be deepened again in a new plan for progress to get all workers ready to win in the expanding global market. Corporate survival, in this age of worldwide competition, requires greater diversity than ever before. It requires a higher diversity index.

Competing in the Globally Integrated Economy

After two painful decades of watching manufacturing jobs go overseas and be replaced by lower-paying service jobs, the United States is just waking up to the reality of international trade. As a percentage of the U.S. economy, international trade grew to about 13.5 percent in 2006 from below 6 percent in 1970. But the comparable figure for European countries today is roughly 50 percent.[7] So the United States has considerably more to learn about global competition.

Practically everything can be offshored these days, and global companies have been steadily leaving the United States. In 2000, 36 percent of the *Global Fortune 500* companies had their headquarters in the United States. By 2009, the portion had slipped to 28 percent. In the global company of the future, an American could even be the minority member of the executive officer team. After all, the U.S. population will soon become just a small portion of the developed world as the Brazilian, Russian, Indian, and Chinese (BRIC) economies continue to advance at high speed. Yet it is in American interests to keep the global company on its own ground.

Companies in the United States are competing with businesses all over the world to find the best talent. To stay competitive in the global economy, businesses must take action by working with schools and government to enable students to understand how they can use their education to take advantage of the opportunities available to them. By some measures,

U.S. high school graduation rates peaked in 1969, the same year that Alan Bean set foot on the moon and the year that Plans for Progress ended. After he gained the White House, President Richard Nixon decided not to fund Plans for Progress anymore. High school graduation rates began to decline through the 1970s down to a national rate of 68 percent in 2001.[8] Today, overall high school graduation rates in the U.S. trail behind those of Denmark, Japan, Poland, and Italy. Nationally, graduation rates for blacks, Hispanics, and Native Americans hover at 50 percent. Graduation rates for whites and Asians range from 75 to 77 percent.[9]

Currently, many corporations cultivate relationships with high schools and colleges to find and encourage students who demonstrate talent in sciences and technology. They provide mentoring, scholarships, and internships. However, there are not enough of these students to fill the needs of business. Corporations should not simply cherry-pick from the best schools, but also develop those students who need additional resources and guidance. Corporations should get involved earlier in the process, at the elementary school level, informing school personnel, parents, and children about the world of opportunities available to them. Businesses must take affirmative action again to develop the workforce in the United States. They must do something.

Businesses, whether large, small, or international, must be brought into the debate on how to improve future workers and to amplify the comparative advantage of the United States with its advanced colleges and universities and highly adaptable service workforce. Ultimately, globalization can open up more job opportunities for Americans as they learn to navigate and embrace overseas prospects. Real sustainability begins with helping communities large and small become educated, productive, and able to shift with the needs of a changing economy.

The comparative advantage the United States had over other countries used to be its system of universal public education. In the 1960s, companies became intensively involved in schools and communities to motivate students to study math and science as part of the race to the moon and to acquire the skills to develop technology-based products. As was the case in 1961, the economy in 2011 is going through a profound transformation due to advances in technology and globalization. Just as the corporation was decentralizing in the 1960s, the multinational corporation today is dissolving in favor of the globally integrated corporation. Corporations have been eliminating the smaller replicas of the parent company around the globe and emerging with one set of processes, carried out by a very skilled and capable workforce, according to Joseph Palmisano, IBM's chief executive, who helped pioneer this trend in 2006.[10]

Americans must now compete with workers all over the world as work flows to the places that produce either the best designed and best performing products or the most efficiently made products. The high unemployment rate of recent years— close to 10 percent from 2007 to 2010—illustrates not only the depth of a prolonged and horrendous recession, but the fundamental changes in the economy. The jobs that have been lost are probably not going to come back. Just as automation was decreasing the number of manufacturing jobs in the 1960s, technology today is increasing the average productivity of workers, so that fewer workers are needed. Technology has also increased the collaboration that can be done across borders and time zones. Workers in the United States can easily communicate with and share work with counterparts in Australia or India. Many companies, like Unilever, are divesting themselves of costly real estate, as they say farewell to the cubicle and more employees are able to accomplish their work on the road or at home. Workers in these situations have to be more independent than before and be able to solve more problems on their own because they will not have more experienced colleagues in the next-door office to guide them.[11] Although new jobs will be available, America does not have the number of educated workers it needs to triumph in the globally integrated economy.

"Not having enough talent keeps us awake at night," said Norma Clayton, a vice president of training at Boeing, a large aerospace company. "The U.S. is only producing about 7,000 engineers a year compared to 30,000 engineers in China alone. We are now rethinking our labor. Raytheon, Lockheed and all the other aerospace companies will also be rethinking this."[12] Boeing has dropped 900 relationships it had developed with universities because the graduates Boeing had hired were not advancing. Officials at the aerospace company had difficult conversations with the presidents of these schools and put 100 institutions on a watch list to see whether they could improve their curricula.

There seems to be a mismatch between the skills companies need and the skills the graduates have to offer, even after certification. President Barack Obama, in his 2011 State of the Union Address, described the floundering economy and the lapses in education as a "Sputnik moment," a rallying cry to the American people to outpace the advances made by other countries. But that cannot be done without the help of businesspeople who know how to develop a series of best practices and scale them up so that they can be followed quickly and efficiently by several different types of companies. Corporations need to actively participate in the reformation of the workforce.

The decline in high school graduation rates is now holding back the expansion of college graduation. Forty percent of all students who enter college require remedial courses. Nearly 50 percent of projected job growth will be in occupations that require higher education and skill levels, according to a study done on workforce readiness by The Conference Board, a non-profit research group funded by corporations. The demand for college graduates and for those with advanced degrees is creating a wage gap between workers who can include the letters BA, MS, or PhD next to their names on an employment application and those who cannot even provide a year for a high school graduation date.

Developing Better Students from an Early Age

Fifty years after Plans for Progress started and became a valuable framework for talent development and recruitment, it needs to be revived and expanded to the elementary school level. It is in elementary school where children develop their linguistic, reading, math, and spatial abilities. It is where they learn how to study. It is where they learn to enjoy learning. Children of all races and especially those in the middle and lower classes need to be exposed early to the options they have for the 50 years of work ahead of them. They need choices. They need to know that dropping out of school is not a good choice and that doing their homework will get them ahead in life.

In a study of high school dropouts, nearly half, 45 percent, said they fell behind in middle or elementary school and could not catch up. Sixty-nine percent of the young people surveyed said they were not inspired or motivated to work hard. Two-thirds said they would have worked harder if more was demanded of them. Seventy percent said they thought they could have graduated if they had only tried. Most, 80 percent, admitted to doing one hour or less of homework each day in high school.[13]

The National Science Board performed a two-year examination of how educators could develop students to become the most creative scientists, technologists, engineers, and mathematicians. It too recommended getting involved at the elementary school level. But the board included only two representatives from business on its panel of 26 members; the others were from government and education. Only one international company, Cisco Systems, contributed thoughts about the kind of education needed for its future workers. Businesses—large, small, and international—must be brought into the debate on how to improve future workers and to amplify the comparative advantage of the United States with its advanced colleges and universities and highly adaptable service workforce. Ultimately, globalization can enable more job opportunities for Americans as they learn to navigate and embrace opportunities overseas.[14]

If companies cannot find the quality of workers they need, they will decline. In fact, smaller companies with less ability to actively recruit and attract the best performers will bear the brunt of higher turnover and lower productivity.[15] This outcome will be particularly hard on the country because small companies are the engine of the U.S. economy. Richer companies will move their operations to areas with higher-skilled workers, or they will hire foreign-born workers. All three choices create costs for the U.S. population in lost jobs and lower public revenues from taxes. At the same time, the corporations will have higher relocation expenses and lower revenues from a large nation of customers who are less able to purchase their products.

One of the reasons that companies say they hire foreign-born workers fresh from graduate schools in the United States is that there are not enough homegrown workers in certain fields. According to the Council of Graduate Schools, in the fall of 2009, 50.4 percent of all temporary residents who were first-time graduate students were enrolled in engineering, mathematics, computer sciences, physical sciences, or biological and agricultural sciences. At the same time, only 15.1 percent of U.S. citizens and permanent residents were enrolled in these fields. The United States is not producing enough homegrown scientists, mathematicians, and engineers to continue to design and create the products that were once the life force of its economy.

Plans for Progress encouraged employers to connect with teachers and students at the high school level to make them aware of the need for scientists and mathematicians, but today that intervention has to start much earlier. "The process to produce an engineer with the capabilities we need really starts at kindergarten and goes right through high school. Because if you don't get the kids in sufficient quantity getting the fundamental math and science curricula that they need at that point, you have no chance of producing enough people with the skill sets at the end of the university pipeline," said Ron Glover, IBM's vice president of global workforce diversity.[16]

Diversity and human resource experts from corporations need to organize themselves into a Plans for Progress–style Advisory Board and meet with faculty at graduate schools, colleges, community colleges, high schools, middle schools, and elementary schools to let them know the type of knowledge skills and qualities they need in their workforce. They need to reach out to community organizations to inform parents, students, and families of the need to upgrade their education and skills.

Corporations especially need to pay attention to minority women. In 2009, nearly 80 percent of *Fortune 100* companies had no minority women among their executive officer ranks. This is perplexing because women, on average, are better educated than men. White and black women's high school graduation rates have exceeded their male counterparts' since 1960. Women earned 45 percent of all bachelor degrees in business in 1984–1985 and 50 percent by 2001–2002. They are also earning a larger portion of degrees in engineering and in the physical and life sciences.[17] Whereas white women have been promoted to the highest levels of corporations, generally minority women have not. Corporations have to start actively tracking the recruitment, retention, and promotion of all women according to race and ethnicity. They should encourage multicultural female employees to start their own affinity groups so that they can help corporations identify potential recruits from their own networks.

GE's Lloyd Trotter was embarrassed when a black employee asked him how many African American females he had at the top of his business. "I couldn't answer the question, which is a travesty for me," he said. "The reason I couldn't answer the question was the way I measured diversity: African Americans, Hispanics, Asians, and women. We lumped them all into groups. Females were females. I went back and said we are going to start changing the measurements and we did a lot better. At the end of the day, you get what you measure. If it's important to you, you will measure it and track it."[18]

When seeking workers who have the ability to excel in foreign markets, corporations should recruit in areas where residents already operate in two cultures, speaking English at school and at work and speaking a foreign language at home. According to data collected by the Census Bureau's 2000 household survey, more than 20 million people who spoke Spanish at home also spoke English "well" or "very well." Seventy percent of people who spoke Arabic, Chinese, French, German, Tagalog, Vietnamese, or Arabic at home also spoke English "well" or "very well."[19]

Several cities in the United States have dual Hispanic and American cultures along the Mexican border and inland, such as San Antonio, Texas, and Denver, Colorado. Slavic immigrants are highly concentrated in St. Louis, as Russian immigrants are in Brighton Beach in Brooklyn, New York. The highest density of French speakers in the United States live in Aroostook County in northern Maine. Corporations that seek employees with international knowledge would benefit by developing students from the high ethnic diversity in the United States before filling out all the paperwork for visas to import workers. The second generation of children of immigrants in the United States will account for most of this country's labor growth over the next 30 years.[20] Corporations should reach out and embrace immigrant families, capturing their ability to straddle cultures and communicate in different languages.

The American bootstrap story is in danger of becoming a relic of the past if people in poor, working-class, or middle-class communities are unable to rise. Especially after a prolonged recession, they have to be shown that opportunities exist for them and that their hard work and educational investment will be rewarded. In 2010, black unemployment stood at a staggering 16.3 percent. Twelve percent of Hispanics were jobless, and 8.7 percent of whites were unemployed. Asians experienced the lowest rate of joblessness, 7.1 percent. These rates were higher than unemployment was in the late 1960s when riots broke out in cities across the country as African Americans became frustrated with their limited opportunities.

If people cannot find jobs in the real economy, they will seek opportunities in the alternative economy, in which drugs, illegal weapons, stolen merchandise, and sex are sold and traded. If people believe they cannot rise, they will stop trying. If people of all races, genders, and ethnicities give up on education, they will help pull down the economy. High school dropouts harm both themselves and society. The highest unemployment rates occur among those with the lowest educational achievement.[21] The wages of high school dropouts have declined over 20 years. They experience more layoffs, higher incarceration rates, a greater use of social services, increased divorce rates, and worse health than high school graduates do. They struggle economically, and their lower overall productivity drains scarce social resources that help keep them afloat.[22] The more public support these individuals require, the higher taxes and social insecurity are likely to be. Improving outcomes at the beginning of a child's life is better for everyone—the child, the family, and society.

Corporate executives have already made extensive recommendations to the government about the new direction that education needs to take. In 2006, a committee of representatives from the National Academy of Sciences, the National Academy of Engineering, and the Institutes of Medicine issued a detailed report on steps the government could take to improve education in the United States. The group consisted of industry leaders, scientists, government leaders, academicians, and Nobel Prize winners. Their book, *Rising Above the Gathering Storm: Energizing and Employing America for a Brighter Economic Future*, provided a detailed exploration of how the government could improve the teaching of math and science by raising the skills of educators. The book suggested that government supply expensive solutions such as more scholarships for students and increased funding of research through grants and special projects. It recommended easing the process for foreigners to obtain work visas.

Yet at the end of 2010, U.S. government debt had surpassed $14 trillion. Democrats and Republicans argued endlessly over budget cuts. President Obama had called for a budget freeze for all areas except for education, research, and infrastructure. At the same time, Republicans had called for nondefense-related budget cuts.[23] After the Great Recession, the federal government was not in a strong position to turn around the educational system, and typically states have more control over schools than the federal government does. It is time for corporations to come forward and connect with the schools and communities that first enabled them to expand and improve the workforce 50 years ago. It is time for them to take affirmative action.

Epilogue

J OHN G. FEILD REMAINED DEEPLY ENGAGED IN RACE RELATIONS after he left the President's Committee on Equal Employment Opportunity in 1963. He spent one year working on a study at the Potomac Institute on how to increase the number of minority employees in the Defense Department. For the next decade, he was a member of the U.S. Conference on Mayors, where he advised cities on how to implement their antidiscrimination laws and apply for federal grants to improve race and community relations. During that period, his budget increased from $250,000 to $4 million, and his staff increased from two to 42 professionals. Feild helped create the Mayor's Leadership Institute and the Urban Fellows Program to assist in educating new leaders and young professionals about the complexity of urban problems. In 1987, he joined the policy staff of the former Housing and Urban Development and retired in 1995.

He and Marilyn, his wife of 63 years, raised two sons and a daughter. Feild died after a heart attack in 2006 in Raleigh, North Carolina.

Hobart Taylor, Jr., served as director of the Export-Import Bank from 1965 until 1968 but was never satisfied with the job. He had no staff and felt he had little power. He returned to private practice as a lawyer in Washington but remained deeply connected to some of the businesspeople he had met. He joined

Hobart Taylor, Jr. (right), wishes John Feild (left) well at a going-away party in 1963. Courtesy Marilyn Feild.

the board of directors of U.S. Steel, the parent company of TCI in Birmingham. He also served on the boards of Standard Oil of Ohio, Aetna Insurance, and several other companies, helping them to improve race relations from inside the corporation. With the help of Bill Miller, president of the defense company Textron, Taylor organized more than $1 million in donations from businesses to the NAACP, the organization that had continually disparaged Plans for Progress.

He and Lynette Dobbins had two sons and divorced after 45 years of marriage. Taylor married Carole Angermeir and retired a multimillionaire in the Bahamas, where he died in 1981 of Lou Gehrig's disease.

Notes

Introduction

1. Stanley F. Slater, Robert A. Weigand, and Thomas J. Zwirlein, "The Business Case for Commitment to Diversity," *Business Horizons*, 51 (2008), 205.

2. See Scott E. Page, *The Difference: How the Power of Diversity Creates Better Groups, Firms, Schools, and Societies* (Princeton, NJ: Princeton University Press: 2007).

3. C. Stone Lowery and Mark Lowery, "6 Ways to Limit Lawsuits," *Diversity, Inc.*, Special Issue 2006, 47–48. http://www.diversityinc-digital.com/ diversityincmedia/2006fl?pg = 70#pg1; Jim Suhr, "Judge Approves $24 Million Walgreen Discrimination Settlement," *Associated Press*, March 25, 2008; retrieved from Lexis Nexis Academic Universe.

4. The Securities Act of 1933 requires public corporations to identify the individuals who have been selected to become executive officers and to describe the positions and offices they have held and for how long. This information is usually contained in a company's 10-K form, the annual financial report to shareholders that is filed with the Securities and Exchange Commission (SEC). During the fact-checking process, the majority of corporations confirmed our findings. Some made valuable corrections. Other companies merely referred us to the Web sites and documents from which we had originally collected the data. Several corporations declined to help us fact-check the information on their officers, citing the privacy of their employees.

5. Justice Lewis F. Powell, "Judgment of the Court," *Regents of the University of California v. Bakke*, Supreme Court of the United States, 438 U.S. 265, June 28, 1978, V, A. Retrieved at http://www.law.cornell.edu/supct/html/ historics/USSC_CR_0438_0265_ZO.html.

6. John Feild, Second Oral History, John F. Kennedy Presidential Library, April 6, 1967, 44.

7. In 2006, with a grant from the Alicia Patterson Foundation for journalism, I launched a study of the affinity groups of the 2005 *Fortune 100*. My researchers and I sent out surveys asking corporations to identify their affinity groups, tell us when they started and describe their activities and functions. Twenty-one companies completed and returned their surveys. We called and interviewed employees at the remaining firms to finish the surveys. If employees refused to assist us, we were often able to complete part of the surveys by compiling information about the groups published on corporate Web sites. In the course of both the officer and the affinity group studies, my researchers and I interviewed more than 300 employees of the firms over the telephone, via e-mail, and in person to find out the techniques they used for finding and developing minority and female talent. This is how we discovered that the companies with the most diverse leadership were using nearly the same techniques.

8. In 2010, I filed a Freedom of Information Act (FOIA) request to obtain recent EEO-1 data from Hewlett Packard, GE, Prudential Financial, Merck, MetLife, Lockheed Martin, Exxon Mobil, and Walgreen. All eight companies declined to release the data, so I had to rely on the less detailed, public summaries that many corporations post on their Web sites

Chapter One

1. "Football, Feminism and You," Season 1: Ep. 6 of *Community* (NBC, Airdate: October 22, 2009). Retrieved at http://www.hulu.com/watch/104028/community-football-feminism-and-you.

2. Erika Hayes James, "Race-Related Differences in Promotions and Support: Underlying Effects of Human and Social Capital," *Organization Science*, Vol. 11, No. 5 (September–October 2000), 493.

3. Jacqueline Landau, "The Relationship of Race and Gender to Managers' Ratings of Promotion Potential," *Journal of Organizational Behavior*, Vol. 16, No. 4 (1995), 391–400.

4. Ashleigh Shelby Rosette, Geoffrey J. Leonardelli, and Katherine W. Phillips, "The White Standard: Racial Bias in Leader Categorization," *Journal of Applied Psychology*, 46. Retrieved at http://www.rotman.utoronto.ca/geoffrey.leonardelli/2008JAP.pdf.

5. Many scientists and anthropologists believe that the designation of race is primarily social and political and not a useful tool for understanding the fundamentals of human beings. The classification of race and ethnicity has a long and controversial history in the United States. Anyone who attempts

to measure progress this way immediately becomes aware of the variety of combinations. The popular understanding is that there are three human races: Caucasoid, Mongoloid, and Negroid. For the study, however, I kept the categories consistent with those used by the U.S. government: Caucasian, Asian/Native Hawaiian and Pacific Islander, Hispanic/Latino, African American, and Native American. People of Arab descent were considered Caucasian, as were people of Persian descent. According to the 2000 Census, 82 percent of people born in Iran who reside in the United States identified themselves as white ("Table FBP-1. Profile of Selected Demographic and Social Characteristics: 2000, Population Universe: People Born in Iran," U.S. Census Bureau, 2001. Retrieved at http://www.census.gov/population/cen2000/stp-159/STP-159-iran.pdf).

6. Donald Tomaskovic-Devey, *Gender and Racial Inequality at Work* (Ithaca, NY: Cornell University, 1993), 62–64.

7. James N. Baron, "Organizational Evidence of Ascription in Labor Markets," in Paul Burstein, ed., *Equal Employment Opportunity: Labor Market Discrimination and Public Policy* (Piscataway, NJ: Transaction Publishers, 1994), 73.

8. Robert Bernstein, Public Information Office, U.S. Census Bureau, e-mail to author, December 1, 2010. (In 1980, the foreign-born population was 6.2 percent of the total U.S. population. Of that group, 24.6 percent of the foreign-born population age 25 and older had either completed college or five or more years of postsecondary education.)

9. Jacqueline Landau, 397–398.

10. Chor Huat Lim, DuPont, e-mail to author, October 15, 2010.

11. Mike Volpe, Office of Public Affairs, U.S. Dept. of Labor, e-mail to author, December 1, 2010.

12. Andres T. Tapia, *The Inclusion Paradox: The Obama Era and the Transformation of Global Diversity* (Lincolnshire, IL: Hewitt Associates, 2009), 86.

Chapter Two

1. P. Roy Vagelos and Louis Galambos, *The Moral Corporation* (New York: Cambridge University Press, 2006), 156.

2. Howery Pack, "Memory Banks," *The American Banker*, September 22, 1986, 4.

3. Vagelos and Galambos, 158.

4. Ibid., 157.

5. Heather Collura, "Celia Colbert Sworn In as New Board of Education Member," Summit Patch, November 13, 2009. Retrieved at http://summit.patch.com/articles/celia-colbert-sworn-in-as-new-board-of-education-member.

6. Vagelos and Galambos, 154–155.

7. Ibid., 154.

8. Ibid., 152.

9. P. Roy Vagelos, author interview, December 15, 2010; Vagelos and Galambos, 153.

10. Ibid.

11. Ibid.

12. Vagelos and Galambos, 171.

13. Raymond V. Gilmartin, author interview, February 24, 2008.

14. Ibid.

15. "Mary McDonald: In-House Pro Bono Champion," *Corporate Pro Bono*, 2000. Retrieved at http://www.cpbo.org/resources/displayResource.cfm?resourceID = 1077

16. Gilmartin.

17. Alicia Grey, "Woman Files Sex Bias Suit Against Merck & Co.," April 26, 1996, *The Star-Ledger*, Newark, NJ, Morris Edition.

18. Barbara Reskin, "Unconsciousness Raising," *Regional Review*, Q1 (2005), 33–34.

19. Gilmartin.

20. Gilmartin.

21. "Black Workers at Merck Pharmaceutical Co. Sue Citing Alleged Bias at Pennsylvania Plant," *Jet*, February 22, 1999, 6.

22. "Nun Asks Merck to Document Diversity in the Company," *Associated Press*, April 21, 2001.

23. W. Bruce and J. Kauffman, *Memorandum and Order*, Julius Webb and Ernest Thomas V. Merck & Co., Inc., United States District Court for the Eastern District of Pennsylvania, No. 99-Cv-413, September 11, 2007, 1. Retrieved at https://www.paed.uscourts.gov/documents/opinions/07D1091P.pdf.

24. Joseph A. Slobodzian, "Judge Rejects Class Action for Merck Race-Bias Suit," *The Philadelphia Inquirer*, April 6, 2002.

25. Ann Pomeroy, "A Passion for Diversity: A Merck & Co. Leader Launches 'Constituency Teams' to Value Similarities—and Differences—Worldwide," *HR Magazine*, March 2008. Retrieved at http://findarticles .com/p/articles/mi_m3495/is_3_53/ai_n24962299/.

26. Anonymous, cafépharma.com, April 14, 2004, 9:07 p.m. Retrieved in 2006 at http://www.cafepharma.com/boards/archive/index.php/t-774.html.

27. Anonymous, cafépharma.com, April 14, 2004, 9:54 p.m. Retrieved in 2006 at http://www.cafepharma.com/boards/archive/index.php/t-774.html.

28. The employees' names have been removed.

29. Anonymous, cafépharma.com, May 10, 2004, 9:41 p.m. Retrieved in 2006 at http://www.cafepharma.com/boards/archive/index.php/t-774.html.

30. Anonymous, cafépharma.com, May 10, 2004, 1:10 a.m. Retrieved in 2006 at http://www.cafepharma.com/boards/archive/index.php/t-774.html.

31. Anonymous, #7, cafépharma.com, September 9, 2006, 12:51 p.m. Retrieved in 2006 at http://www.cafepharma.com/boards/showthread.php?t = 109081.

32. Anonymous, cafepharma.com, No date or time. Retrieved in 2006 at http:// www.cafepharma.com/boards/showthread.php?t = 109081.

33. Anonymous, #17, cafépharma.com, September 21, 2006, 8:26 a.m. Retrieved in 2006 at http://www.cafepharma.com/boards/showthread.php?t = 109081.

34. Merck 2010 10-K, 18.

35. Justice Stephen Breyer, "Opinion of the Court," Merck & Co., Inc., et al., Petitioners v. Richard Reynolds et al., No. 08–905 Cite as: 559 U.S., April 27, 2010, 19. Retrieved at http://www.supremecourt.gov/opinions/09pdf/08-905.pdf.

36. Robert Bazell, "CEO Defends Merck," MSNBC, November 12, 2004, 7:25:32 p.m. ET. 2004-11-13T00:25:32. Retrieved at http://www.msnbc .msn.com/id/6472384/ns/nightly_news.

37. As quoted by Amy Barrett, "On the Firing Line at Embattled Merck," *BusinessWeek*, December 13, 2004. Retrieved at http://www.businessweek.com/ magazine/content/04_50/b3912106.htm.

38. Justine Cadet, "Merck Restructures, in Preparation of Schering-Plough Merger Completion," *Cardiovascular Business*, September 1, 2009. Retrieved at http://www.cardiovascularbusiness.com/index.php?option = com _articles&article = 18578.

39. Vagelos and Galambos, 130, 131; Don G. McNeil, Jr., "Parasites: Learning a Worm-Killer's Modus Operandi," *The New York Times*, November 15,

2010. Retrieved at http://www.nytimes.com/2010/11/16/health/16global
.html?_r=1&src=twrhp.

40. Mirian M. Graddick: First Woman to Head AT&T Human Resources," *The New York Beacon*, March 17, 1999.

41. Theresa Howard, "Pepsi Beats Coke with Stock Surge," *USA Today*, December 12, 2005. Retrieved at http://www.usatoday.com/money/industries/food/2005-12-13-coke-pepsi-usat_x.htm.

42. Stanley F. Slater, Robert A. Weigand, and Thomas J. Zwirlein, "The Business Case for Commitment to Diversity," *Business Horizons*, 51 (2008), 205.

43. Henry W. Gadsden to Charles Spahr, February 7, 1966, Plans for Progress Administrative File, 1961–1969, Box 16, National Archives II, College Park, MD.

44. Owen Ullmann, Washington Dateline, *The Associated Press*, June 26, 1979. Retrieved from Lexis Nexis Academic Universe.

45. Carol Agocs, "Institutionalized Resistance to Organizational Change: Denial, Inaction and Repression," *Journal of Business Ethics*, Vol. 16, No. 9 (June 1997), 917–931.

46. I use the term "token" not to disparage any women or minorities, but to tweak the notion that any individual would serve merely a representational purpose.

47. Belle Rose Ragins, "Diversity, Power and Mentorship in Organizations," in Martin M. Chemers, et al., eds., *Diversity in Organizations: New Perspectives for a Changing Workplace* (Thousand Oaks, CA: Sage, 1995), 106.

Chapter Three

1. Eugene Mattison, "Memorandum for File, Subject: Meeting with Negro Attorney Donald L. Hollowell Re: Colored Problem in the Plant, March 27, 1961, p. 1. Lockheed Investigation, Box 83, Plans for Progress, National Archives II, College Park, MD.

2. Mattison.

3. John F. Kennedy, Executive Order 10925, The White House, March 6, 1961. Retrieved at http://www.presidency.ucsb.edu/ws/index.php?pid=58863.

4. Robert Dallek, *Lyndon B. Johnson: Portrait of a President* (New York: Oxford University Press, 2004), 134. Retrieved at http://books.google.com/books

?id = JIGcq0RXspMC&pg = PA135&dq = % 22plans + for + progress%22&
lr = &cd = 3#v = onepage&q = %22plans%20for%20pr ogress%22&f = false.

5. Peter Braestrup, "Lockheed Signs Equal-Jobs Pact: Agrees to a Plan Advancing Negro Opportunities," *The New York Times*, May 26, 1961, 20.

6. Lockheed Annual Report, 1960.

7. Ibid., 2.

8. Mattison, 2.

9. Braestrup, 20.

10. "Bomber Plant Enforces JC: Anti-Discrimination Job Clause Unheeded," *Afro-American*, September 22, 1951, 19.

11. Herbert Hill, *Guide to Action: NAACP Labor Manual* (New York: NAACP, 1968), 29.

12. John G. Feild, Oral History Interview I, by Michael L. Gillette, LBJ Library, May 2, 1984, 15.

13. Feild, May 2, 1984.

14. John G. Feild Oral History Interview II, by Michael L. Gillette, LBJ Library, July 23, 1984, 14.

15. Hugh Gordon, Oral History Interview, Conducted by Stephen Briggs and John Mckay, Kennesaw State University Oral History Project, Cobb NAACP/Civil Rights Series, No. 16, Friday, November 6, 2009.

16. Ibid.

17. Feild, May 2, 1984, 15.

18. Joint Statement, "Plan for Progress," Lockheed Aircraft Corporation and the President's Committee on Equal Employment Opportunity," undated, Harris Wofford Files, Box 8, JFK Library, 2–3.

19. Ibid., 7.

20. A. H. Raskin, "Negro Makes Job Gain in South Under Initial Drive at Lockheed: Negroes Gaining in Lockheed Jobs," *The New York Times*, June 18, 1961, 1.

21. Ibid.

22. Ibid.

23. Charles Ferguson, Oral History, Conducted by Brent L. Ragsdale, Hist 4425 Bell/Lockheed Oral History Series, No. 17, Kennesaw State University, Saturday, November 17, 2007.

24. Raskin, 1.

25. Ferguson.

26. Ibid.

27. Ibid.

28. Ibid.

29. Lester Granger, "Colored Labor, Foot in Door of Industry, Must Still Make Sale: Urban League Head Cites Employment Gains, Says Post-War Jobs Will Depend on Interracial Peace." *Afro-American,* January 1, 1944, 7.

30. Beatrice Murphy, "Fair Hiring at Lockheed: How One Plant Went About Job Integration," *Afro-American*, February 7, 1953, 22E.

31. Feild, May 2, 1984, 14.

32. Arthur A. Chapin, Jr., Oral History #2, recorded interview by John Stewart, March 31, 1967, John F. Kennedy Library, 41. Retrieved at http://www.jfkli brary.org/NR/rdonlyres/2D7C7E3D-2F70-4BB1-B8E6-ABE0F3839CED/ 49424/ChapinArthurA2_oralhistory.pdf.

33. Ewan Clague, Oral History, recorded interview by Larry J. Hackman, August 17, 1967, John F. Kennedy Library Oral History Program, 65–66. Retrieved at http://www.jfklibrary.org/NR/rdonlyres/C8E255B9-C0B1-473F- 8645-3A62247BBE72/46691/ClagueEwan2_oralhistory.pdf.

Chapter Four

1. *Ridley of Southampton: being the descendants of Nathaniel and Elizabeth Day Ridley of Southampton, then Isle of Wight County, Virginia, circa 1700–1992* (Pensacola, FL: B.B. Nichol, Jr., 1992), 269.

2. Robert Troutman, Oral History, February 2, 1965, by David F. Powers, JFK Library, 122.

3. Ibid., 129.

4. According to Feild, Troutman was later reimbursed for $25,000 of his expenses (Feild, May 2, 1984, 24).

5. Associated Press, "43 Negroes, 2 Whites Arrested for Sitdown in North Carolina," *The Washington Post*, April 22, 1960, B8.

6. Claude Sitton, "Sit-In Campaigns Spread in a Year: Protests on Discrimination Assume the Proportions of a National Movement," *The New York Times*, January 29, 1961, 64.

7. As quoted by Kevin Michael Kruse in *White Flight: Atlanta and the Making of Modern Conservatism* (Princeton, NJ: Princeton University Press, 2005), 191.

8. Sitton, 64; Kruse, 189.

9. As quoted by David J. Garrow, *Bearing the Cross: Martin Luther King, Jr., and the Southern Christian Leadership Conference* (New York: HarperCollins, 2004), 152–153.

10. As quoted by Marshall Frady, *Martin Luther King, Jr.: A Life* (New York: Penguin, 2005), 56. Retrieved at http://books.google.com/books?id = dOR4 QpEE0g8C&dq = martin + lut her + king, + jr. + contract&client = firefox-a.

11. John G. Feild, Oral History Interview I, by Michael L. Gillette, LBJ Library, May 2, 1984, 17.

12. Southern Regional Council, Plans for Progress: Atlanta Survey, Atlanta, January 1963, 2.

13. John Feild, Oral History Interview, by John F. Stewart, JFK Library, January 16, 1967, 27.

14. John D. McCully, *News Release, President's Committee on Equal Employment Opportunity*, July 14, 1961, 1. Harris Wofford, Box 8, JFK Library.

15. As quoted by Louis Lautier in "Looking at the Record," *Afro-American*, December 2, 1961, 17.

16. Marilyn Smith Feild, author interview, January 8, 2010.

17. Feild, January 16, 1967, 2.

18. Ibid., 30.

19. Betty Kaplan Gubert, Miriam Sawyer, and Caroline M. Fannin, *Distinguished African Americans in Aviation and Space Science* (Westport, CT: Oryx Press, 2002), 289.

20. "Minutes, PCEEO Committee Meeting," February 15, 1962, From Dept. of Labor file, Pres. Committee on Equal Employment Opportunity, Microfilm 72, JFK Library, 107–108.

21. Feild, May 2, 1984, 22.

22. Smith Feild.

23. John Feild, *Making a Difference; A Civil Rights Memoir* (Seattle, WA: TFCD, 2000), 12–13.

24. Feild, *Making a Difference*, 13–14.

25. Ibid., 14.

26. Ibid.

27. Marilyn Smith Feild, author interview, January 8, 2010.

28. Feild *Making a Difference*, 24–25.

29. Herbert R. Northrup, "Equal Opportunity and Equal Pay," in Herbert R. Northrup and Richard Rowan, eds., *The Negro and Employment Opportunities* (Ann Arbor, MI: Bureau of Industrial Relations, Graduate School of Business Administration, University of Michigan, 1965), 106.

30. Fair Employment Practice Act, Michigan Public Acts 1955, no. 251, SS 423.307, Sec. h, June 29, 1955, 415.

31. Feild, *Making a Difference,* 25–26.

32. Ibid., 26.

33. Ibid., 28.

34. Ibid., 4.

35. National Association of Intergroup Relations Officials, "Executive Responsibility in Intergroup Relations," New York, 1961, 2 (Harris Wofford Civil Rights file, Box 5, JFK Library, Boston).

36. Dan W. Dodson, "Can Intergroup Quotas Be Benign?" *Journal of Intergroup Relations*, Vol. I, No. 4 (Autumn 1960), 12.

37. Ibid., 17.

38. National Association of Intergroup Relations Officials, "Executive Responsibility in Intergroup Relations," New York, April 1961, 14 (Found in the Harris Wofford, civil rights file, Box 5, JFK Library, Boston).

39. John Feild, "The Emerging Intergroup Profession," *Journal of Intergroup Relations*, Vol. I, No. 3 (Summer 1960), 65.

40. John Feild, "Nature and Scope of Intergroup Relations Work," *Journal of Intergroup Relations*, Vol. I, No. 2 (Spring 1960), 10.

41. "D.C. Woman Lawyer Chosen by Sen. Kennedy: Is Named to Aid Demo Candidate," *Afro-American*, August 13, 1960, 5.

42. Peter Braestrup, "U.S. Panel Split over Negro Jobs," *The New York Times*, June 18, 1962, 1.

43. Timothy J. Naftali, Philip Zelikow, and Ernest R. May, *John F. Kennedy: The Great Crises*, Vol. 1 (New York: Norton, 2001), 543.

44. Ibid., 544.

45. Ibid.

46. Associated Press, "Negro Will Head Job Equality Unit: Hobart Taylor, Jr., Is Named by Kennedy to Post, Aide to Vice President, Degrees From 3 Schools," *The New York Times*, September 11, 1962, 20.

47. John G. Feild, Oral History Interview II, July 23, 1984, by Michael L. Gillette, Internet Copy, LBJ Library, 29. Feild said that he had also seen an FBI file on Hobart Taylor, Jr., that contained unsavory workplace allegations and that he refused to sign off on Taylor's hiring when the Committee was formed. I filed a Freedom of Information Act (FOIA) request with the FBI to obtain a copy of the file. The pages I received were from investigations that ended in 1958. They did not contain any information about Taylor's workplace comportment.

48. Hobart Taylor, Jr., Oral History I, by Stephen Goodell, LBJ Library, Record, January 6, 1969, 19.

49. The Committee had been in flux for several months and had already lost much of its top leadership. Secretary of Labor Arthur Goldberg became associate justice of the Supreme Court. Goldberg's assistant, Jerry Holleman, resigned after becoming involved in a fund-raising scandal. Feild said that he resigned because the committee did not need two directors—him and Taylor.

Chapter Five

1. "North American Aviation Plan for Progress," July 12, 1961, Harris Wofford, Box 8, JFK Library, 1.

2. James Hicks, "Mixed Workers Make Martin Jets, Bombers," *Afro-American*, January 12, 1952, 8.

3. Peter Braestrup, "President Spurs Negro Job Rights: Exhorts Industry As 33 New Companies Sign Pledge President Spurs Negro Job Rights," *The New York Times*, June 23, 1962, 1.

4. "RCA Plan for Progress," July 12, 1961, Harris Wofford, Box 8, JFK Library, 1.

5. R. J. Cordiner, Chairman of the Board and President of General Electric in a letter to Vice President Lyndon B. Johnson, July 12, 1961, Plans for Progress file, Harris Wofford, Box 8, JFK Library.

6. Hobart Taylor, Jr., Oral History Interview I, by Stephen Goodell, LBJ Library, January 6, 1969, 17.

7. Lyndon Baines Johnson's letter to the President, President Kennedy's Office Files, Box 93, JFK Library, February 14, 1961, 2 (Emphasis added).

8. Hobart Taylor, Jr, 11.

9. Ibid., 12.

10. Ibid., 13.

11. Ibid., 2–4.

12. Taylor, Sr., Oral History Interview I, by Joe B. Frantz, LBJ Library, January 29, 1972, 31.

13. Taylor, Jr., January 6, 1969, 1.

14. Ibid., 5.

15. Taylor, Sr., January 29, 1972, 1–3.

16. Ibid., 27.

17. Ibid., 7.

18. Ibid., 24.

19. Ibid., 28.

20. Ibid., 26.

21. "Texas Millionaire Businessman-Politician Hobart Taylor, Sr. Dies," *Jet*, December 21, 1972, 7.

22. Ibid., 37.

23. Ibid., 28.

24. Taylor, Jr., January 6, 1969, 6.

25. *Shelley et ux. v. Kraemer et ux. McGhee et ux. v. SIPES et al.*, United States Supreme Court, May 3, 1948, 334 U.S. 1; 92 L.Ed. 1161; 68 S.Ct. 836. Retrieved at http://www.altlaw.org/v1/cases/382520.

26. John G. Feild, Oral History Interview II, July 23, 1984, by Michael L. Gillette, Internet Copy, LBJ Library, 31.

27. John Feild, First Oral History, John F. Kennedy Presidential Library, January 16, 1967, 22.

28. John Feild, Second Oral History, John F. Kennedy Presidential Library, April 6, 1967, 44.

29. Data from Boeing, Summary of Progress Report, 1962, Box 79, Plans for Progress, National Archives, College Park, MD, GE, Box 79, Plans for Progress, National Archives, College Park, MD. Lockheed, Summary of Progress Report, Plans for Progress, 1962, Box 75, National Archives, College Park, MD.

30. General Electric Company's Answers to the "Questions Asked of America's Leading Employers," by the President's Committee on Equal Employment Opportunity, June 13, 1961, Plans for Progress, Box 79, National Archives, College Park, MD, 4.

31. Ibid.

32. Ibid., 3.

33. Ibid.

34. Ibid., 14.

35. GE, President's Committee on Equal Employment Opportunity, 1962 forms, Box 79, Plans for Progress, National Archives, College Park, MD.

36. Mary McGrory, "No Repentance In Birmingham?" *The Boston Globe*, September 21, 1963. 4.

37. As quoted in "Anti-Bias Job Gain: Agreements with Oil Units and Steel Unit Revealed," *Atlanta Daily World*, July 29, 1962, 1.

38. Memo from John Feild to Hobart Taylor, Jr., December 3, 1962, John Feild Papers, Box 3, JFK Library.

39. Douglas A. Blackmon, *Slavery by Another Name: The Re-Enslavement of Black Americans from the Civil War to World War II* (New York: Anchor Books, 2009), 2, 295–296.

40. Robert H. Woodrum, *"Everybody Was Black Down There": Race and Industrial Change in the Alabama Coalfields* (Athens: University of Georgia Press, 2007), 27–28.

41. Ibid., 158–160.

42. Memo from John Feild to Hobart Taylor, Jr., December 3, 1962. John Feild Papers, Box 3, JFK Library, 1.

43. Ibid., 2.

44. Hobart Taylor, Jr., Oral History Interview, January 11, 1967, Washington, DC, by John F. Stewart for the JFK Library, 12.

45. John Rayburn, "Memo to File, Re: TCI, Birmingham, Alabama, January 10, 1963," Feild Papers, Box 3, JFK Library, 2–3.

46. Paul A. Tiffany, *The Decline of American Steel: How Management, Labor, and Government Went Wrong* (New York: Oxford University Press, 1988).

47. John Rayburn, "Memo to File, Re: TCI, Birmingham, Alabama, January 10, 1963," Feild Papers, Box 3, JFK Library, 3.

48. Horace Huntley and John W. McKerley, eds., *Foot Soldiers for Democracy:*

The Men, Women and Children of the Birmingham Civil Rights Movement (Birmingham, AL: The Birmingham Civil Rights Institute, 2009), xxix.

49. Charles E. Connerly, *"The Most Segregated City in America": City Planning and Civil Rights in Birmingham, 1920–1980* (Charlottesville: University of Virginia Press, 2005), 189–192.

50. Ibid., 170.

51. Ibid., 171.

52. Ibid., 172.

53. Woodrum, 184–185.

54. "Minutes: May 23, 1963 PCEEO Meeting," Dept. of Labor file, Pres. Committee on Equal Employment Opportunity, Microfilm 72, JFK Library; Jeff Shesol, *Mutual Contempt: Lyndon Johnson, Robert Kennedy, and the Feud That Defined a Decade* (New York: W.W. Norton & Co., 1998), 85.

55. James W. Hilty, *Robert Kennedy: Brother Protector* (Philadelphia: Temple University Press, 2000), 301.

56. W. Willard Wirtz, "Memorandum to the Attorney General," June 21, 1963, Box 37, Reading File, Immediate Office of the Secretary of Labor, Box 37, Office Files, 1961–1969, JFK Library.

57. W. Willard Wirtz, "Memorandum to Mr. Hobart Taylor, Jr." June 22, 1963. Department of Labor, Willard Wirtz file, NK-6 MF reel 70, JFK Library.

Chapter Six

1. Hobart Taylor, Jr., Oral History Interview, by John F. Stewart, January 11, 1967, JFK Library, 21.

2. John Feild, Oral History 2, by John F. Stewart, JFK Library, April 6, 1967, 52.

3. See NAIRO's "Intergroup Service in the Federal Government," January 1961, and "Executive Responsibility in Intergroup Relations," April 1961 found in Harris L. Wofford (#8.31), White House Staff Files 1960–1962, Series 1, Box 5, John F. Kennedy Library, the National Archives and Records Administration, Boston.

4. John G. Feild, Oral History Interview I, by Michael L. Gillette, LBJ Library, May 2, 1984, 22.

5. "Plan of Organization: Advisory Council on Plans for Progress," from the Lee C. White Files, Civil Rights, White House, 1963, JFK Library.

6. "Plan of Organization," 3.

7. IBM Plan for Progress, Box 8, National Archives II, College Park, MD, 1961–1969.

8. "Civil and/or Human Rights Agencies," IBM Plans for Progress, Box 8, National Archives II, College Park, MD.

9. Hobart Taylor, Jr., Oral History Interview, January 11, 1967, Washington, DC, by John F. Stewart for the JFK Library, 19.

10. "General Electric Company's Answers to the Questions Asked of America's Leading Employers by the President's Committee on Equal Employment Opportunity," June 13, 1961, Plans for Progress, Box 79, National Archives II, College Park, MD, 8.

11. General Electric Company, 8.

12. IBM's Plan for Progress, Box 8, National Archives II, College Park, MD 1961–1969, 4.

13. North American Aviation's Plan for Progress, 1961, Plan for Progress contracts, Harris Wofford Files, Box 8, JFK Library, 1.

14. Luther A. Huston, "High Court Bans School Segregation; 9-to-0 Decision Grants Time to Comply," *The New York Times*, May 14, 1954, 1.

15. Southern Education Reporting Service, "Statistical Summary State by State of School Segregation-Desegregation," 27–30; Gary Orfield, *The Reconstruction of Southern Education*, 46–48, 355, as cited by Davison M. Douglas, *Jim Crow Moves North: The Battle over Northern School Segregation, 1865–1954* (New York: Oxford University Press, 2005), 11.

16. Davison M. Douglas, *Jim Crow Moves North: The Battle over Northern School Segregation, 1865–1954* (New York: Oxford University Press, 2005), 219–273.

17. Ibid., 272.

18. President Lyndon B. Johnson, "Remarks to New Participants in 'Plans for Progress' Equal Opportunity Agreements," The White House, Washington, DC, December 12, 1963.

19. E. G. Mattison, *Implementing Plans for Progress* (Washington, DC: Advisory Council on Plans for Progress, 1963), 28.

20. Ibid., 26.

21. Ibid.

22. Ibid., 29.

23. Roger Lewis, "Plans for Progress: A Summary of the Activities and Accom-

plishments: 1965–1968," February 28, 1969, Plans for Progress, Box 59, 1969, National Archives II, College Park, MD, 4–5.

24. Ibid., 4.

25. Ibid., 5.

26. Ibid.

27. Mattison, 31.

28. Hobart Taylor, Jr., "Untrained Negro Youths Constitute the Wasted Reservoir," From an address to the National Association of Colored Women's Clubs' Lincoln-Douglas Centennial Program, *Negro Digest*, June 1963, 44–48. Retrieved at http://books.google.com/books?id = ZjoDAAAAMBAJ& pg = PA44&lpg = PA44&dq = hobart + taylor + jr.&source = bl&ots = k0pbNts8F5&sig = 0Qkx8a_xig oqYWD1Mo_A-gLKCHs&hl = en&ei = NE8MS_efJonTlAeqopCjBA&sa = X&oi = book_result&ct = result& resnum = 7&ved = 0CCIQ6AEwBg#v = onepage&q = hobart%20 taylor%20jr.&f = false.

29. Louis Martin, Oral History Interview II, by Michael L. Gillette, June 12, 1986, Internet Copy, LBJ Library, 7.

30. *Ebony*, September 1964, cover.

31. E. Fannie Granton, "Mrs. Hobart Taylor, Jr., Has Key," *Jet*, January 21, 1965, 40–42.

32. Mattison, 3.

33. The letters are in Plans for Progress, Box 16, Administrative Files, National Archives II, College Park, MD.

34. Lewis. The number of companies is in his introductory letter. The list of PFP companies is at the back of the report where there are no page numbers.

35. Ibid., 5.

36. The letter is in Plans for Progress, Box 16, Administrative Files, National Archives II, College Park, MD.

37. Louis Martin, Oral History Interview II, by Michael L. Gillette, June 12, 1986, Internet Copy, LBJ Library, 2–5.

38. Ibid., 4–5.

39. Alfred W. Blumrosen, *Black Employment and the Law* (Rutgers University Press, 1971), 76.

40. Blumrosen, 78.

41. Lewis, 45–46.

42. Plans for Progress, "Affirmative Action Guidelines," published in 1968 or 1969, Plans for Progress, Washington, DC, Plans for Progress, Advisory Report, 1969, Box 59, National Archives II, College Park, MD.

Chapter Seven

1. Herman Kogan and Rick Kogan, *Pharmacist to the Nation: A History of Walgreen Co.* (Deerfield, IL: Walgreen Co., 1989), 50, 52, 223

2. Sheryll Cashin, *The Agitator's Daughter: A Memoir of Four Generations of One Extraordinary African American Family* (New York: Public Affairs, 2008), 132.

3. As quoted by Cashin, 141–142.

4. As quoted by Sheryll Cashin, 143.

5. "Walgreen Company Joint Statement on Plans for Progress," Company Files 1962–1969, Participating Companies, Uniroyal, Inc., thru Xerox Corp., Box 15, National Archives II, College Park, MD, 3.

6. "Walgreen Company Self-Analysis Questionnaire," see answer to Question 10, no date or page numbers, Company Files 1962–1969, Participating Companies, Uniroyal, Inc., thru Xerox Corp., Box 15, National Archives II, College Park, MD.

7. "Typical Jobs in the Various Categories Shown on the Employment Inventory Report," 2, Department of Labor, MF, 72, JFK Library, 2.

8. Thomas Watson, "President's Advisory Committee on Labor Management Policy," Meeting No. 23, October 29–39, 1963. Department of Labor, NK-6, MF, 72, JFK Library, 15.

9. Donald C. Green, author interview, November 19, 2010.

10. Ibid.

11. Ibid.

12. Carol Moore, "D.C. Riots of 1968," 2006. Retrieved at http://www.carol-moore.net/sfm/dc-riots1968.html.

13. Green.

14. Ibid.

15. Ibid.

16. Ibid.

17. Ibid.

18. Donna Rosato, "Bias Suit Settled, *USA Today*, July 7, 1992, 1B. Retrieved through Lexis Nexis Academic Universe.

19. Louis V. Gerstner, Jr., *Who Says Elephants Can't Dance? Inside IBM's Historic Turnaround* (New York: HarperCollins, 2002), 30.

20. Gerstner, 34, 39.

21. Paul Sheppard, "Leading the Turnaround: Lou Gerstner of IBM," *Wharton Leadership Digest*, Vol. 7, No. 5 (February 2003). Retrieved at http://leader ship.wharton.upenn.edu/digest/02-03.shtml.

22. Gerstner, 207.

23. Ronald A. Heifetz, *Leadership Without Easy Answers* (Cambridge, MA: Harvard University Press, 1994), 122.

24. Ralph J. Cordiner, *New Frontiers for Professional Managers* (New York: McGraw-Hill Book Company, Inc., 1956), 10–11.

25. Cordiner, 12–13.

26. Ibid., 1.

27. *A Study of the Negro Market* was produced by the Center for Research in Marketing, Inc., New York. It was described by John D. McCully in a memo to Hobart Taylor, Jr., November 20, 1962, John Feild Papers, JFK Presidential Library, Boston.

28. Thomas F. O'Boyle, *At Any Cost: Jack Welch, General Electric and the Pursuit of Profit* (New York: Random House, 1999), 224.

29. Elbert Johnson, "Complaint to the President's Committee on Equal Employment Opportunity, Sept. 26, 1964," GE Plans for Progress, Box 6, 1961–1969, National Archives II, College Park, MD, 1–2.

30. J. Roy Fugal letter to Edward P. Curtis, December 9, 1964, Plans for Progress, 1961–1969, Box 6, National Archives II, College Park, MD.

31. Gloria Jeanne McKinney, "Complaint to the President's Committee on Equal Employment Opportunity, Sept. 21, 1964," GE Plans for Progress, Box 6, 1961–1969, National Archives II, College Park, MD, 1–2.

32. Virgil B. Day, "Progress in Equal Employment Opportunity at General Electric," 1964, eds., Herbert R. Northrup and Richard L. Rowan in *The Negro and Employment Opportunity Problems and Practices* (Ann Arbor: University of Michigan, 1965), 157–158.

33. David J. Dillon, "Statement on Behalf of the General Electric Company, Columbia, Md.," U.S. Commission on Civil Rights, August 19, 1970, 4.

Contained in August Schofer, "Clarification and Rebuttal of Staff Report, the Civil Rights Implications of Suburban Freeway Construction Presented Before the United States Commission on Civil Rights, Regional Federal Highway Administration, Region 2, Baltimore, Maryland," 906–907. Retrieved at http://www.law.umaryland.edu/marshall/usccr/documents/cr12h8112_C.pdf.

34. Ibid., 921.

35. "Typical Jobs in the Various Categories Shown on the Employment Inventory Report," 2, Department of Labor, MF, 72, JFK Library, 1.

36. Donald Tomaskovic-Devey, *Gender and Racial Inequality at Work* (Ithaca, NY: Cornell University, 1993), 62–64.

37. Jeff Sturgeon, "GE Workers' Suit Paved Way for Paid Maternity Leave Breakthrough for American Women," *The Roanoke Times*, October 11, 1998, B1.

Chapter Eight

1. Lloyd Trotter, author interview, January 7, 2011.

2. Ibid.

3. Mary Williams Walsh, "Where General Electric Falls Short: Diversity at the Top," *The New York Times*, September 3, 2000. Retrieved at http://www.mindfully.org/Industry/GE.htm.

4. Plans for Progress, "Affirmative Action Guidelines," published in 1968 or 1969 (no date given), Plans for Progress, Washington, DC, Plans for Progress, Advisory Report, 1969, Box 59, National Archives II, College Park, MD.

5. Trotter.

6. Ibid.

7. For more details of homosocial reproduction in organizations, see Rosabeth Moss Kanter, *Men and Women of the Corporation* (New York: Basic Books, 1977).

8. Susan E. Reed, "White Ceiling: The Alarming Result of 50 Years of Integration in Corporate America," *The Alicia Patterson Foundation*, July 2011, http://aliciapatterson.org/

9. Ibid.

10. Ibid.

11. Trotter.

12. Reed.

13. Trotter.

14. Reed.

15. Walsh.

16. Reed.

17. Eagly, A. H., and Karau, S. J., "Role Congruity Theory of Prejudice Toward Female Leaders," *Psychological Review*, Vol. 109 (2002), 573–598.

18. Reed.

19. Ibid.

20. Ibid.

21. Ibid.

22. Ibid.

23. Ibid.

24. Jeff Immelt failed to respond to requests for an interview.

25. Caterpillar, the large equipment manufacturer, also reverted to having a white ceiling in its leadership as it reduced the number of executive officers in response to dire business conditions during the Great Recession.

26. Ashleigh Shelby Rosette, Geoffrey J. Leonardelli, and Katherine W. Phillips, "The White Standard: Racial Bias in Leader Categorization," *Journal of Applied Psychology*, Vol. 46. Retrieved at http://www.rotman.utoronto.ca/geoffrey.leonardelli/2008JAP.pdf.

27. Hannah Hayes, "Women of Color: Why They Are Finding the Door Instead of the Glass Ceiling," *Perspectives*, Vol. 15, No. 1 (Summer 2006), 6. Retrieved at http://www.abanet.org/women/perspectives/perspectives_womenofcolor2006.pdf.

28. As quoted by Frederick R. Lynch, *The Diversity Machine: The Drive to Change the "White Male Workplace"* (New Brunswick, NJ: Transaction, 2000).

29. Reed.

30. Sheryl F. Colb, "When Types of Discrimination Compete for Legal Recognition Should Anti-Gay Religious Practices Be Accommodated in the Workplace?" Findlaw.com, January 14, 2004.

Chapter Nine

1. Stephanie Capparell, *The Real Pepsi Challenge* (New York: Free Press, 2007), 15, 20, 37.

2. Ibid., 203–205.

3. Ibid., 106–108.

4. PepsiCo, Inc. 1960 Annual Report, 12.

5. Steve Reinemund, author interview, April 8, 2008.

6. Ibid.

7. Ibid.

8. Ibid.

9. Susan E. Reed, "White Ceiling: The Alarming Result of 50 Years of Integration in Corporate America," *The Alicia Patterson Foundation*, July 2011, http://aliciapatterson.org/.

10. "Frito-Lay Inc. Agrees to Pay $225,000 in Back Wages to 233 Minority Applicants for Discrimination Found at Louisiana Plant," Employment Standards Administration Press Release, U.S. Department of Labor, April 21, 1999. Retrieved at http://www.law.ucla.edu/users/crenshaw/racerem/currentnews2.htm.

11. Reed.

12. Reinemund.

13. Carol Hymowitz, "Turning Diversity into Dollars," *The Wall Street Journal*, November 14, 2005. Retrieved at http://michaelmyers.biz/materials/WSJ_Diversity.pdf.

14. Theresa Howard, "Pepsi Beats Coke with Stock Surge," *USA Today*, December 12, 2005. Retrieved at http://www.usatoday.com/money/industries/food/2005-12-13-coke-pepsi-usat_x.htm.

15. ———, "PepsiCo Names Nooyi Its First Female CEO; She's Held Positions of CFO and President Since 2001," *USA Today,* August 15, 2006, 1B.

16. Indra Nooyi, "Career Snapshot," *The Times (London),* October 8, 2008, 5. Retrieved through Lexis Nexis Academic Universe.

17. Sarah Halls, "First Among Equals: The FT's Definitive Ranking of the World's 50 Most Powerful and Successful Female Chief Executives," *FT Magazine*, September 26, 2009, 33. Retrieved through Lexis Nexis Academic Universe; "Introducing a Woman's Touch," *China Daily*, June 21, 2010. Retrieved through Lexis Nexis Academic Universe.

18. Chor Huat Lim, DuPont, e-mail to author, October 15, 2010.

19. Robert Bernstein, Public Information Office, U.S. Census Bureau, e-mail to author, December 1, 2010. (In 1980, the foreign-born population was 6.2 percent of the total U.S. population. Of that group, 24.6 percent of the foreign-born population age 25 and older had either completed college or five or more years of post–secondary education.)

20. Jacqueline Landau, "The Relationship of Race and Gender to Managers' Ratings of Promotion Potential," *Journal of Organizational Behavior*, Vol. 16, No. 4 (1995), 391–400.

21. McKinsey Global Institute, "Growth and Competitiveness in the United States: The Role of its Multinational Companies," McKinsey & Company, June 2010. Retrieved at http://www.mckinsey.com/mgi/publications/role_of_us_multinational_companies/pdfs/MGI_US_MNCs.pdf.

22. Michael E. Porter and Mark R. Kramer, "The Big Idea: Creating Shared Value," *Harvard Business Review*, January–February 2010. Retrieved at http://hbr.org/2011/01/the-big-idea-creating-shared-value/ar/1.

Chapter Ten

1. "By This Morning's Mail: Government Printing Office—Exchequer—Oregon, Correspondence of The Tribune," *New York Daily Tribune*, January 27, 1843, 2.

2. "Union Pacific's Big Plans: To Increase Its Stock to $300,000,000 and Issue $100,000,000 Bonds," *The Washington Post*, March 24, 1901, 6.

3. As cited by Richard F. Tomasson, Faye J. Crosby, and Sharon D. Herzberger, *Affirmative Action: The Pros and Cons of Policy and Practice* (Washington, DC: American University Press, 2001), 125.

4. Louis Stark, "Longer Mine Week Fails of Adoption: Ickes Warns It Is Needed 'to Win This War' and Walks out of Conference He Called / Group Adjourns to October 21 / Lewis Says Production Goal Set by Coordinator Is Possible Within 35-Hour Limit," *The New York Times*, September 30, 1942, 14.

5. "Orders Rehiring of 300 Negroes: President's Fair Employment Committee Alleges Union Discrimination Men Refused to Pay Dues / West Coast Shipbuilders Say AFL Put Them in an 'Auxiliary' Union," *The New York Times*, July 27, 1943, 21.

6. "The Fair Employment Practices Committee," *The Eleanor Roosevelt Pa-*

pers Project. Retrieved at http://www.gwu.edu/~erpapers/teachinger/glossary/fepc.cfm)

7. As cited by Beverly Crawford and Edward A. Forgarty, *Globalization's Impact on American Business and Economics* (Westport, CT: Greenwood, 2008), xi.

8. Christopher B. Swanson, *Who Graduates? Who Doesn't? A Statistical Portrait of Public High School Graduation, Class of 2001* (Washington, DC: The Urban Institute, Education Policy Center, 2004), v. Retrieved at http://www.urban.org/UploadedPDF/410934_WhoGraduates.pdf.

9. Swanson, 20–22.

10. *IBM Annual Report*, 2009, 11.

11. Susan E. Reed, "On the Death of the Cubicle," GlobalPost.com, December 24, 2009. Retrieved at http://www.globalpost.com/dispatch/worldview/091223/cubicles-office-culture-unilever.

12. Norma Clayton, 2009 Senior Human Resources Executives Conference (New York: The Conference Board, presentation on December 9, 2009).

13. John M. Bridgeland, John J. DiIulio, Jr., and Karen B. Morison, "The Silent Epidemic: Perspectives of High School Dropouts" (The Bill and Melinda Gates Foundation, 2006), iii. Retrieved at http://www.civicenterprises.net/pdfs/thesilentepidemic3-06.pdf.

14. Estimates of service jobs that have gone overseas in the past decade range from hundreds of thousands to millions. But they have not been balanced by new jobs that have arisen in the United States. As of 2005, the United States still maintained a positive trade balance in service activities. J. Bradford Jensen and Lori G. Kletzer, "Tradable Services: Understanding the Scope and Impact of Services Outsourcing," Working Paper Series No. 05-9 (Washington, DC: Institute for International Economics, September 2005), 18. Retrieved at http://www.piie.com/publications/wp/wp05-9.pdf.

15. Mary Wright, "Redefining Workforce Readiness" (Chicago: The Conference Board), presentation on June 30, 2010.

16. As quoted by Andres Tapia, *Inclusion Paradox* (Lincolnshire, IL: Hewitt Associates, 2009), 31.

17. Wirt, Choy, Rooney, Sen, and Tobin, 2004, as cited by Claudia Goldin, Lawrence F. Katz, and Ilyana Kuziemko, "The Homecoming of American College Women: The Reversal of the College Gender Gap," *Journal of Economic Perspectives*, Vol., 20, No. 4 (2006), 153. Retrieved at http://www.economics.harvard.edu/faculty/goldin/files/homecoming.pdf.

18. Lloyd Trotter, author interview, January 7, 2011.

19. William Leap, "True Things That Bind Us: Globalization, U.S. Language Pluralism, and Gay Men's English," in Michelle Bertho, ed., *The Impact of Globalization on the United States*, Vol. 1 (Westport, CT: Greenwood Press, 2008), 185.

20. As cited by Beverly Crawford and Edward A. Forgarty, *Globalization's Impact on American Business and Economics* (Westport, CT: Greenwood Press, 2008), xi.

21. Bureau of Labor Statistics, "Employment Situation Summary," September 3, 2010. Data is not seasonally adjusted and was for the month of August 2010. Retrieved at http://www.bls.gov/news.release/empsit.nr0.htm.

22. Bridgeland, DiIulio, and Morison, i.

23. Lori Montgomery, "Analysis: President, GOP Lawmakers Agree on Austerity, but Will It Create Jobs?" *The Washington Post*, January 25, 2011. Retrieved at http://www.washingtonpost.com/wp-dyn/content/article/2011/01/25/AR201101250784 3.html.

Acknowledgments

I T IS DIFFICULT TO PINPOINT EXACTLY WHERE THE JOURNEY OF a book begins, but this one found direction after Bill Kovach offered me a Nieman Fellowship at Harvard. The courses I took became the pathways to my destination.

The research studies were supported by a grant from the Alicia Patterson Foundation for journalism and steady patience from its director, Margaret Engel. Maryann Sadagopan worked very carefully to find the biographies of 1995 and 2005 officers. She and Karah Synakowski contacted companies and interviewed human resources and diversity personnel about their employee groups. Eleanor Byrne and Sarah Hughes worked efficiently to fact-check the 2009 data.

Librarians at Widener Library welcomed me into the independent scholars' room nearly everyday for a year. The librarians at the Cambridge Public Library chased down strange old publications that I could not find elsewhere. Laura Eggert at the Lyndon Baines Johnson Presidential Library in Austin, Texas, sent me electronic files of oral histories that enabled me to gain access to the materials without traveling across the country. Historian Tom Scott at Kennesaw State University in Kennesaw, Georgia, shared a dozen oral histories with me about the development of civil rights in Southern industry.

The John F. Kennedy Presidential Library in Boston enabled me to listen to the oral histories so I could get a sense of the character and temperament of the key figures of Plans for Progress. It also provided a breathtaking location for me to visit over several days as I burrowed into files and microfilms.

The National Archives Records Administration II in College Park, Maryland, supplied a trove of incredibly valuable documents filled with the fascinating history of this country. It is well worth our taxes to support the staff who care for these documents and the cost of preserving them in such a stunning building.

Every weekend my brother, Guy, listened patiently to my developing theories as I sifted through the research. Donna Elizabeth Reed helped me brainstorm the title and commiserated over every computer failure, of which there were many. They never faltered in their support of the project. Mary Conti prayed for success and speedy resolution. Loved ones near and far waited patiently until my editorial commitments freed me to be with them.

Barbara Reskin offered guidance on scholarly work. Bob Giles invited me to talks and seminars at the Nieman Foundation that advanced my work. Andrea Karls provided entre to important figures and necessary research materials. Deborah Fairley, Judy Greenspan, and Ian Johnson supplied valuable feedback on the book proposal and other excerpts. Geneive Abdo, Vineeta Vijayaraghavan, and Kathryn Wolff read early writing and assisted with editorial planning. Carolyn Johnston helped design some charts in the book. Melissa Powar shared her knowledge of employment law. Alexandra Binnenkade provided editorial advice and access to needed materials. Joanne Reynolds furnished room and good humor during field trips. Pat Geisert remained forever a dedicated and supportive friend. Jack Bauer got me through the final stretch.

The entire AMACOM team—Christina Parisi, Barry Richardson, Andy Ambraziejus, Mike Sivilli, Fred Dahl, Kama Timbrell, and Rosemary Carlough—magically transformed my manuscript into a book that could be read far and wide. They enabled me to scale up.

The book could not have been done without the participation of those who have struggled to make the corporation a better, more human place. I am grateful to all who have trusted me with their stories, their hopes and disappointments, in the ongoing quest to improve the places where we all spend so many hours of our lives.

For those whose names I will remember with a start in the middle of the night and regret that I have not thanked here, please know that I am grateful.

Index